Death of a Hero

Death of a Hero

The Quest for World War One Poet
Richard Aldington's Berkshire Retreat

David Wilkinson

In memory of the late Professor Norman Timmins Gates
who altered the course of my life

PEN & SWORD
HISTORY

First published in Great Britain in 2016 by
PEN AND SWORD HISTORY
an imprint of
Pen and Sword Books Ltd
47 Church Street
Barnsley
South Yorkshire S70 2AS

Copyright © David Wilkinson, 2016

ISBN 978 1 47387 110 6

Printed and bound in England
by CPI Group (UK) Ltd, Croydon, CR0 4YY

Typeset in Times New Roman by
CHIC GRAPHICS

Pen & Sword Books Ltd incorporates the imprints of Pen & Sword
Archaeology, Atlas, Aviation, Battleground, Discovery,
Family History, History, Maritime, Military, Naval, Politics, Railways,
Select, Social History, Transport, True Crime, Claymore Press,
Frontline Books, Leo Cooper, Praetorian Press, Remember When,
Seaforth Publishing and Wharncliffe.

For a complete list of Pen and Sword titles please contact
Pen and Sword Books Limited
47 Church Street, Barnsley, South Yorkshire, S70 2AS, England
E-mail: enquiries@pen-and-sword.co.uk
Website: www.pen-and-sword.co.uk

Contents

Illustrations

ILLUSTRATIONS

Acknowledgements

This book could not have been written without the generous and spontaneous help of the following people, all of whom, it is believed, have now passed away. Their recollections shaped my quest but rather than add them to the endnotes, I would rather their names stand here along with the dates when we talked.

Dorothy Adams, October 1981.
Bill Adnams, 1984.
Joan Patricia LeGros Aldington, January 1982.
Mr and Mrs Leslie Austin, August 1981.
William Austin, June 1982.
Ronald Bates, August 1981.
Hilda Cotterell, formerly Brown, and Harry Cotterell, January 1982.
Pamela Gardner, formerly Strange, September 1981.
Mr and Mrs John A.G. Hale, November 1982.
Roberta 'Bobbie' Hards, December 1981.
Hilda Hearn, formerly Hobbs, January and June 1982.
Annie Hissey, formerly Tull, May 1982.
Sir Thomas Digby Legard, 14th Baronet, and Lady Mary Legard, August 1982.
Margery Lyon-Gilbert, formerly Aldington, January 1982.
Brigadier Charles Stuart Mills, November 1980.
Helen Mary Mills, November 1980.
Violet 'Vi-vi' Mills, May 1982.
Sir William Malcolm and Lady Elizabeth Mount, June 1982.
Kathleen North, June 1982.
Albert Edward Pearce and Edith Maskell, May 1983.
Florence Pigg, formerly Roberts, September 1982.
Dr Muriel Radford, November 1981.
Joyce Rouse, formerly Boshier, November and December 1981.
John Rouse, November and December 1981.

ACKNOWLEDGEMENTS

Violet Sambells, formerly Roberts, September 1982 and March 1983.
Florence Emily Smith, formerly Downham, July 1982.
Mary Warwick, formerly Fidler, November 1982.

Particular thanks are due to Mr Douglas A. Lawrence for his constant encouragement and for a number of photographs and illustrations. Thanks also to Mrs Margaret Ridgway for advice and information about her mother, the suffragette Anna Munro. I must also thank the Humanities Research Centre in Austin, Texas, who via the auspices of a researcher made their Aldington archive available. My request was not literary, instead I asked Donna Stewart to pick out references to Padworth and Aldington's life in Malthouse Cottage only. Those letters have subsequently been included in *Imagist Dialogues: Letters between Aldington, Flint and Others* by Michael Copp, appropriate details of which now appear among my endnotes. Thanks are also due to Simon Hewett for access to items in his collection and to Reading Borough Council Reference Library for the drawing of Padworth House by Emma Thoyt. I must also thank Richard Mills for allowing the use of photographs of Brigadier General George Arthur Mills and the Mills family.

Richard Aldington by Man Ray, 1929

Introduction

I have long since moved away but this all started in 1971 when I bought a canal side cottage at Padworth halfway between Reading and Newbury in Berkshire. Within weeks I learnt that the writer Richard Aldington (1892–1962) lived here in the 1920s. His autobiography *Life for Life's Sake* told me that D.H. Lawrence, Herbert Read and T.S. Eliot had all visited him in Padworth. Aldington talked about the village and his neighbours and suggested that the reader, 'if curious, may consult a novel called *The Colonel's Daughter*, in which more appears'. I *was* that curious reader and this book is the result of my curiosity. On face value, *The Colonel's Daughter* explores the fate of one young woman after the loss of so many eligible young men in the First World War. On my first reading of the book, I realised that I may be encountering real people and I began furtively to cast around me for possible parallels. Those thoughts lay dormant until the summer of 1978 when Norman and Gertrude Gates arrived on the doorstep.

Professor Norman Timmins Gates was an authority on Aldington. His introduction to *A Checklist of the Letters of Richard Aldington* was the closest approach to a biography in existence at the time. Gates was the editor of the *New Canterbury Literary Society Newsletter: The Richard Aldington Newsletter* through which he circulated quarterly news of Aldington around the globe. Over the course of an evening meal I tentatively voiced one or two thoughts about the setting of *The Colonel's Daughter*. Gates was enthusiastic and urged me to put together a few notes that he might use. I had never written anything before but, in short, Gates gave purpose to this quest. It took six years to complete during which time I managed to track down most of Aldington's neighbours and became close to his family.

That early draft went off to Gates in 1984 since which time this manuscript had lain dormant. Norman Gates died at the age of ninety-six in early 2010 and Aldington's seventy-two-year-old daughter, Catherine Guillaume-Aldington, passed away unexpectedly only weeks later. These sad losses led me to dust off, re-read and revise my typescript.

In the course of preparing those early notes I began to collect

Aldington's books and manuscripts. Norman Gates spread the word about my work and over the years a number of other researchers made their way to the cottage often returning as friends with their families. Professor Fred Crawford came over from the US and stayed in the cottage for six unruly weeks while he was researching his book *Richard Aldington and Lawrence of Arabia: A Cautionary Tale*. Norman and his wife Gertrude came back a number of times and on one occasion their granddaughter came to see what all the fuss was about.

The nearby University of Reading picked up on Aldington's connection with Padworth and an exhibition based on my archive was mounted to accompany a two-day Richard Aldington symposium on the occasion of the re-issue of *The Colonel's Daughter* in 1986. Aldington would have approved of the celebratory 'end-of-term' meal in what had once been his study. Scholars from all over the world quaffed vast quantities of wine before Mikhail Urnov – a Russian scholar and early champion of Aldington – insisted we all go out into the garden to be engulfed in his national bear hug. This was the very early days of glasnost and the Soviet Union's leader Mikhail Gorbachev had graciously granted Professor Urnov £40 pocket money and a three-day pass to the west. In 1962 Aldington and his daughter Catherine were invited by the Union of Soviet Writers to celebrate Aldington's 70th birthday as their guest of honour in Moscow where, unbelievably, Aldington's popularity ran close on the heels of Shakespeare and Dickens. Professor Urnov was their guide and host. I drove Urnov and Aldington's close friend, the French writer and broadcaster Frédéric-Jacques Temple into Reading town centre. Besides paying tribute to Aldington, their one other wish while they were in England was to pay their respects to Oscar Wilde at the gates of Reading Gaol.

The scholarly clan gathered again for the Richard Aldington Centennial Conference in July 1992 in the balmy climate of Montpellier where Aldington spent a number of post-war years in self-exile. We were there as *Monsieur le Maire* unveiled a civic plaque on what had been Aldington's home and before that, quite coincidentally, the birthplace of Frédéric-Jacques Temple.

My draft manuscript was dated 15 July 1984. There were prudent reasons why it was intended for Norman's eyes only: two suicides, an uncomfortable affair leading to Aldington's messy divorce and the memories of an elderly lady and her family warranted respect. Some of

INTRODUCTION

the people I had interviewed were a little uncomfortable with what they told me and the can of worms I opened up added to my self-imposed guilt. But everyone I met has now passed on allowing this book to be published.

Aldington had left forty-two years before I bought his cottage. It seemed an eternity at the time, but it is only as I re-read my notes that it hit me; the village has moved on again considerably in the further forty-odd years since I moved in and that if I revised my findings to suit the new millennium I would destroy what integrity they possessed. The facts of this narrative are largely as I found them in 1984. I was comparing Aldington's village with my own surroundings in the 1970s and 1980s and that has made me decide to edit my immature ramblings rather than to re-write them. What follows is in effect an oral history firmly linking Aldington and *The Colonel's Daughter* to Padworth in the 1920s. Aldington's neighbours spoke primarily about their village of that time. I hope I have not misinterpreted them.

David Wilkinson
St Ives, Cornwall, January 2016

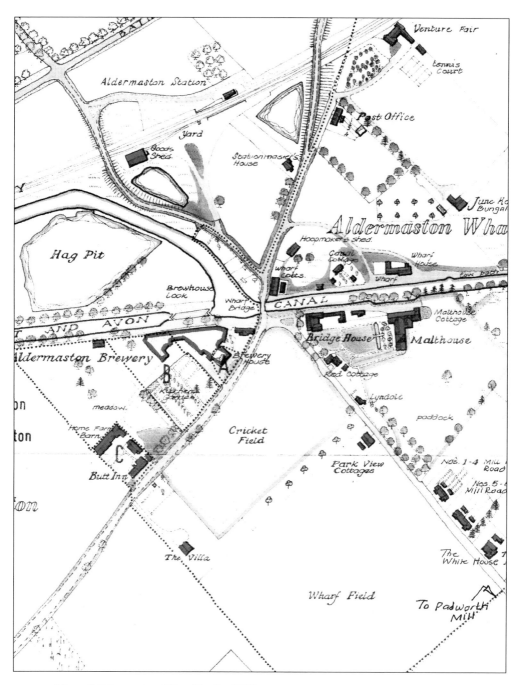

Map of Aldermaston Wharf in the 1920s

Chapter 1

The Quest

Within weeks of buying Malthouse Cottage in 1971, I discovered that copies of D.H. Lawrence's book, *Lady Chatterley's Lover,* had been distributed illicitly from the front room thirty-two years before it was legally available in the UK. More recently I have learnt that the man who was distributing them may bear comparison with Lawrence's fictional creation, Sir Clifford Chatterley. Thirteen years lie between these two discoveries in which time I was involved in a search for both the man and the village in which he lived. The fact that it took that long may well be considered the successful outcome of what was a conspiracy on the part of such eminent people as Robert Graves and Sir Winston Churchill to silence one of the most controversial writers of the twentieth century. For the fact is that not one of the 50-odd books written by Richard Aldington was in print when I set out on this quest because no one was then prepared to republish him.

'Richard who?' I remember asking as, with trepidation, I admitted my ignorance to the woman who had told me about him. Mrs Nin Waghorn had rented Malthouse Cottage in Padworth near Newbury in Berkshire before we had bought it and had made a last pilgrimage to see what we were doing to *her* cottage. She had announced the name of her famous predecessor with pride. She had every reason to be shocked by my response but, as I was only later to discover, Aldington's immense reputation had long since been severely dented so I feel I may be excused a little. 'In that case, I shan't tell you anything more. I shall leave you to find out yourself!' she said. And off she went.

The very next day I went to the library, for I didn't know then whether Aldington was alive or dead or indeed what he had done to impress Mrs Waghorn. The library index recorded only two books by him in their collection. *Lawrence of Arabia: A Biographical Enquiry* was out on loan, but his autobiography, *Life for Life's Sake*, was there on the shelf: 'Memories of a vanished England and a changing world, by one who was

1

bohemian, poet, soldier, novelist and wanderer' was the romantic scene portrayed by the dust jacket. A quick glance showed that a good proportion of the book was based on his time in the cottage. To come across a description of the place as he found it in 1920 was exciting.

> *'It belonged to an impoverished family of gentry and was a tumble-down affair built against the wall of an ancient malthouse. The strategic position of this cottage was superior to its accommodation and perhaps to its appearance. It was 200 yards down a side lane which was a dead end; one flank was guarded by a row of tall unpolled willows and the disused Kennet and Avon canal; otherwise it looked onto a garden, meadows, and osier beds.'* [1]

Those words, 'impoverished gentry' played on my mind. Who could they be? Were they still around, I wondered? In those days before the Internet it was to be a while before I knew the answer. Among an array of names with which I was entirely unfamiliar, there was a gallery of those about whom I had at least some knowledge. I had always been an avid reader but I soon learnt that what I had read had not always sunk in. Here was Ezra Pound alongside D.H. Lawrence, T.S. Eliot, Herbert (later Sir Herbert) Read, Ford Maddox Ford, James Joyce and William Carlos Williams; poets and writers who were all connected in some way with Aldington and the cottage. I felt that I could reach out and touch them. Here, in our dining room in 1929 had been boxfuls of 'Lady Chatts' waiting to be sent out while their author Lawrence, I read, had declared the cottage sinister. I felt indignant.

In his book, Aldington described his writing desk in sufficient detail for me to be able to picture it right in front of the window I had just converted into a new front door. And right outside I had just built a new porch blocking what he described as his 'strategic view' up the driveway. But so much was still recognizable from the book; it took no great detective work to see where his Valet Autostrop razor had been, for example, and even the flowers in the garden bore a strong resemblance to the ones he said he had planted. We subsequently dug up a small flask which just has to be the one from which Harold Monro downed chianti as if it was water. With due respect to Mrs Waghorn there cannot have been that many chianti drinkers in a cottage of this nature.

THE QUEST

There was one particular paragraph in the autobiography which made me want to find out exactly what life in Padworth was like in Aldington's days: to find out who lived in the village and how they reacted to the author in their midst.

'Reluctantly,' Aldington says '...I must give no more space to the local fauna of that district. The reader, if curious, may consult a novel called *The Colonel's Daughter*, in which more appears. There are some fancy and caricature in that book, but on the whole I am prepared to go before a commissioner for oaths and have him say to me of it: "This is your name and handwriting you swear that the contents are true so help you God amen eighteen pence please you must get change I haven't got it", which according to Dickens is the true formula for swearing an affidavit in the United Kingdom.'[2]

It was as if that paragraph had been deliberately written for me to read all these years later. I had nothing to go on other than one book and the challenge. I *was* the 'curious reader' to whom he refers. I managed to find a second-hand copy of *The Colonel's Daughter* and found words rolling out of the page with a sharp ready humour that would be the envy of *Private Eye*. I was hooked. And yet there was nevertheless something about the book that worried me deeply. Even making allowance for the 'fancy and caricature' of which even at a first reading I judged there to be a considerable amount, this book was about real people. The author had said as much. If indeed it was based on his neighbours at Padworth, then they could well have read it and, if so, what on earth would they have thought of it? Were the characters in the novel so real as to be recognizable? And what right had I, if any, to even attempt to open up this can of worms?

Aldington's writing is provocative. It was only as the whole scheme of things progressed that I learned that *The Colonel's Daughter* and his first novel – *Death of a Hero* – were banned by Boots and W.H. Smith's lending libraries. In the context of the times I was not entirely surprised. I had no idea how far his attitudes would bear analysis, but I well remember the initial impression I had after reading only two books. I was fascinated by the power of his convictions. There is a passionate fervour, at times a vehemence, to his writing that I could see might well be frowned upon. He was not the phlegmatic Englishman one might expect. Whether he was right or wrong or whether I agreed with him or not did not matter. I was carried along by his apparent idealism and enthusiasm for life. Despite some severe testing nothing I have subsequently learnt of his period at Padworth has quite wiped out those initial impressions or dulled my enjoyment of his writing. Above all, the power of his conviction is imparted with a most beguiling fluency. As when Mr Purfleet, for example, is talking to Doctor McCall, in *The Colonel's Daughter:*

> *'When you were a sawbones in France, Britannia graciously allowed you fifteen and a kick a day, plus field allowances, to bind up the wounds of Her Gallant Sons fighting on a couple of daily tanners.[3] Don't interrupt me! I know what you are going to say – they fought not for money, but from patriotism; sense of duty, love of country. Two minutes' silence! You and the other millions did "your duty". Result: the extinction of a generation of men, the misery of their women, an utterly senseless "Peace", and the enrichment of noble-hearted men like our old pal Stimms.'[4]*

Later in the same conversation, Purfleet talks about the eponymous heroine. 'Georgie's merely one of the victims of the whole mess. She's an oblation on the diabolical altar of Stimmsdom. In an over-populated country superfluous women have a hell of a life. The involuntary old maid is a piteous spectacle. I'm all in favour of their indulging in non-fertile copulation. They can't all have kids – there are too many anyway. But if Sir Horace gets Georgie's possible husbands killed, or exiled to look after his commercial interests in our far-flung Empire, then I think that Georgie should diddle Sir Horace by having a lover, several if she wants them and can get them. Why have legions of tarts to preserve for Georgie an imaginary virtue she doesn't want?'[5]

These two quotations show one aspect of Aldington that has been badly misinterpreted and may have fired the 'conspiracy'. His depth of feeling, his hatred of injustice, in this instance directed at the plight of 'poor Georgie', was to lead him into some awful scrapes with the literary establishment. The very name Georgie, as was that of George Winterbourne in *Death of a Hero*, is the author's satirical jibe at the era of tree-hugging 'Georgian' poets of those pre-war, Edwardian days.

The recuperative influence of Padworth after the Great War was unequivocal. But only he would have been able to appreciate the bitterness towards him when the village would later read *The Colonel's Daughter.*

While the underlying reason behind his satire was compassion for the plight of his heroine, I felt sure that the woman who inspired the character of Georgie Smithers would never see it that way; no amount of subsequent explanation could ever ease the hurt she would obviously have felt.

Soft Answers, Aldington's book of satirical short stories which, to complete the quote from the Book of Proverbs, 'turneth away wrath' was his way of reeking revenge on those who, in his eyes, had betrayed his trust and confidences. The ordinary folk of Padworth had no such right of reply and yet the memories of those I have met, with one fascinating exception, have healed from the wounds caused by this book. But Aldington did much more than satirical fiction. During the 1920s he was principal correspondent on French literature for the *Times Literary Supplement*. He wrote biographies, poetry and edited Voltaire's *The Republic of Letters* for Routledge & Kegan Paul and other significant out-of-print books that were made available in the UK for the first time in years, in some cases for the first time ever. He translated, he criticized, he edited, he created, he did everything. He was a thoroughly travelled journeymen of letters and yet very few now have heard of him and even fewer know much about him. There is a curious satisfaction in searching out and finding the vast output of Aldington's work. His books, his articles, his poems and his letters have all made their way back to the shelves of his cottage. Along the way I have made contact with a diverse array of people including his family and friends who have visited the cottage in pilgrimage.

To my own surprise I have managed to find someone from practically every one of the neighbouring cottages. But at the start of all this I hadn't the foggiest idea where to start looking and I never imagined that I would ever find much interest. In 1971 when I first read *Life for Life's Sake* and *The Colonel's Daughter* it was only weeks after I bought the cottage. For some years after that I did nothing other than acquire only the occasional snippet of information about him. No one I knew had ever heard of Richard Aldington and so the fact that he had lived in my village was hardly a conversation stopper. I had become content just to know of the connection until one day in June 1978 when a providential knock at the front door was to change everything. Professor Norman Timmins Gates and his wife Gertrude introduced themselves. They were over from the States on an Aldington pilgrimage. Some years before, Professor Gates had studied Aldington for his PhD thesis and had from that day occupied the central role in what is now becoming an Aldington industry. My memories now are of my absolute ignorance and of my total absorption in everything I was told; and yet from the hours of conversation, what did I managed to retain? Perhaps the most significant fact was the reason why Aldington's books were no longer obtainable.

In 1950 Aldington had written a biography of D.H. Lawrence that had not been received well in critical circles. Aldington had dared to show the human face of Lawrence from a position of friendship. The fact that Aldington had long championed Lawrence was of little note. At the time that *Portrait of a Genius But...* was written it seemed nothing short of a eulogy would be tolerated. Aldington found himself damned. Four years later though, he did it again. This time, in *Pinorman*, he used the same position of friendship and wrote what was considered, with some justification, a totally unfair portrait, a combined memoir, of two people he knew well, Pino Orioli – the Florentine bookseller who published the unexpurgated Lady Chatterley that he distributed from the cottage – and the author Norman Douglas.[7]

But what was to destroy Aldington's reputation entirely was advance reaction to his 1955 book *Lawrence of Arabia: A Biographical Enquiry*. The establishment was alerted to the fact that Aldington intended to include less palatable aspects of T.E. Lawrence's life. The fact that it was Aldington of all people, with his hatred of heroes, was totally unacceptable and led to a conspiracy being hatched to prevent its publication.

In *Richard Aldington: Selected Critical Writings 1928-1960* Alister Kershaw, Aldington's devoted friend and literary executor, tells us that the world was led to conclude that Lawrence of Arabia was a compulsive liar and that his reputation was fraudulent.[8] In putting 'forward this view (one which has never been successfully refuted) Aldington was guilty, however, of something worse than insufficient reverence for a "national hero"; his real offence was to have simultaneously exposed the stupefying credulity of all those who had been taken in by Lawrence's self-glorification and who had incautiously recorded their besotted admiration.'[9] Professor Harry T. Moore confirmed the conspiracy theory in his 1970 preface to Kershaw's book:

'... *Aldington wasn't paranoid in imagining such a thing existed; indeed, he was not just imagining. For the Lawrence clique –*

what he called the Lawrence Bureau – had even attempted to stop publication of the book. Kershaw mentions Robert Graves and the late B.H. Liddell Hart. But there were others. The full story was to have been told in the book by Phillip Knightley and Colin Simpson, The Secret Lives of Lawrence of Arabia, but what was originally their twentieth chapter, a detailed account that named names, was withdrawn from their volume because, according to the authors' lawyers, it's quite all right under English law to wage surreptitious war against an author, but all wrong to reveal that this took place!... I have the "suppressed chapter" at hand; it is a most disturbing document, for it shows how Liddell Hart and others tried to influence the publishing house of Collins not to bring out the book. But William Collins, a rather tough old man, refused to be intimidated, and published it. Then the infuriated reviews began, as planned...'[10]

That suppressed chapter later appeared as 'Aldington's enquiry concerning T.E. Lawrence' in the *Texas Quarterly* in the winter of 1973. It tells in detail of the furore surrounding publication of the book, including a bitter row on the BBC Panorama programme on 29 January 1955. 'The anti-Aldington ferocity was overwhelming and, when all was said and done, successful in its intent. The whole country was against him; very few publishers felt they could risk either their money or their reputation by publishing new books or reissuing the old ones which meant that from that date an entire generation has not read Aldington.'[11]

I was fascinated and it felt appropriate that the story was being recounted around the table in Aldington's cottage. My attention was held by hearing of Aldington's contemptuous attitudes towards the First World War, or rather towards the Victorian culture that had led to its outbreak and its attitude towards women and their subsequent role in society. I was intrigued to hear of Aldington's love-hate relationship with England. But most of all though, I was hearing of what is acknowledged to be the pivotal period of his life; the time he spent at Malthouse Cottage. That evening was over all too quickly as may be imagined.

The fact that Aldington himself had implied that *The Colonel's Daughter* was about Padworth had made it all seem so accessible and yet even by the time that Professor Gates and his wife had arrived I knew little that was worth telling. In *Life for Life's Sake* Aldington mentions 'a rude red-faced soldier, a retired Sergeant Major of the Guards' that seemed to fit the required role of the fictitious colonel.[12] I also recognised his 'Gothic fishing lodge' in *Life for Life's Sake*.[13] All I had to do was to prove that the Sergeant Major had lived in the 'bottom' lodge to Padworth House and I was home and dry. Professor Gates was intrigued to know what this local knowledge might reveal. As a result, and rather foolishly I realised afterwards, I offered to send him some 'notes'. It may sound naïve now but it was quite some time before anything constructive occurred to me. I still have the exercise book in which I had made pitifully few jottings the next time I read the *The Colonel's Daughter*. What stopped me from sending it off to Professor Gates there and then was the same curiosity that was roused on my first reading. Some of my notes were firm and positive but far more were speculative observations on the images, the illusions and the thoughts prompted by the book. I held onto the notes determined to check them out if I could.

On his return home Professor Gates sent me copies of his 1977 book, *A Checklist of the Letters of Richard Aldington* along with *Richard Aldington: Selected Critical Writings 1928-1960* edited by Alister Kershaw. *Checklist* records the existence of over 7,000 of Aldington's letters now held in university libraries all over the world. At the time Norman and Gertrude Gates came here I had been in Padworth for seven years; seven years of taking the children to school, of going to the village shop, flower shows, fetes, parish council meetings; seven years of generally joining in. I had long since found that no one I had met had been in the village anywhere near long enough to know Aldington. Had I but known it though, all the clues were there if only I knew the questions to ask. Likewise, odd bits of conversation I later went on to record often meant nothing until months, sometimes years later. It was only as I was completing the form for the electoral register that year did the obvious occur to me. The County Records Office held the registers of voters going back to 1839 and copies of those sheets would give me all the names I wanted. I obtained copies of the years 1918-1930 giving myself a year or two at either end of Aldington's time in Padworth as a margin of latitude. I was convinced that somewhere among those names and addresses I would find the characters from the novel; Henry Benham for example.

I discovered that Lower Lodge was occupied by the Benham family throughout the 1920s. The 'squire' was Christopher William Darby Griffith who, I already knew, had died in 1932; a brass plaque in the church had told me that and Aldington himself confirmed it in *Life for Life's Sake*. Padworth House is now no longer a family home and the estate had long since been broken up. Again, in *Life for Life's Sake* Aldington tells us why. 'The squire was unmarried and the last of his long line'.[14] So it seemed I had already found one avenue closed. The significance of all those names would not register for some time but one or two facts emerged from an immediate reading of this list. I was fascinated to see that with one or two exceptions only, the names of the cottages that I knew had not been changed. Here, not that I needed it though, was positive proof of Aldington's tenancy. He was registered for the years 1921-1929 inclusive which, allowing for the delay between registration and publication, confirmed that he was here from 1920-1928.

Before Professor Gates' visit the only biographical information I had about Aldington had been gleaned from the occasional reference to him in Harry Moore's biography of D.H. Lawrence where I had learned, for example, that the person to whom Aldington refers to as his companion for these eight years was Dorothy (aka Arabella) Yorke, a young American woman.

Arabella had come across with her mother before the war and had been quickly assimilated into the Lawrence-Aldington coterie. But in 1913 Aldington had married another American, the poet Hilda Doolittle known

Fig. 1. Arabella Yorke

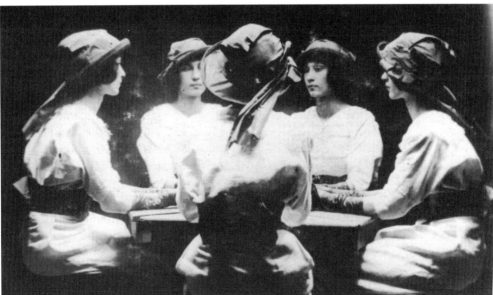

by her initials 'H.D.' and to whom, while he was then separated, he remained legally married until some years after he left Padworth. Professor Moore's biography also revealed the identities of some of the characters in D.H. Lawrence's *Aaron's Rod*. Lawrence himself, obviously, is Rawdon Lilly while Robert Cunningham, who drank wine in 'large throatfuls' is Aldington. Julia Cunningham, 'a tall stag of a thing' is H.D. and Arabella appears as Josephine Ford. This was one of a number of novels that fictionalised this intimate circle of friends during a turbulent period of their relationships.

I began to start up a cardex system, making out a card for every name and address on the electoral register. And there was my first surprise. At a time when Aldington and Arabella were living in the cottage supposedly as 'husband and wife,' H.D.'s name crops up in the registers between 1926 and 1929. To this day the reason remains unresolved. Another very firm image I had recognised in *The Colonel's Daughter* was the situation of the fictional Bess Wrigley's house. It stood 'exactly on the boundary of the three parishes of Cleeve, Maryhampton and Pudthorp ...'[15] for at the point where the lane to Aldington's cottage joins the main road lies the crazy jigsaw pattern at the junction of the Padworth with Aldermaston and Beenham. A circle centred upon the canal bridge at that point would need to have a diameter of no more than fifty feet to take in some small part of those three parishes.

Even making allowance for their newly acquired right to vote, there were a considerable number of women whose names did not appear and of course, I knew nothing of the children of the village. It was with a large amount of trepidation that I set about extending my cardex system to include births, marriages and deaths for the same period.

On one of his regular Sunday morning walks Mr Tom Judd in *The Colonel's Daughter* had been shattered to learn that what his daughter was suffering from was not the indigestion that she had at first suggested:

> *"'What would you say if she was going to 'ave a baby?" Mr Raper had asked him. Mr Judd stopped dead, and removed his pipe. "Goin' to 'ave a baby?" "Yes, goin' to 'ave a baby." "Lizzie?" "Yes, Mr Judd." For about half a minute Mr. Judd contemplated the handsome amber mouthpiece of his pipe with unseeing eyes. This appeared to give him an idea, and he put the pipe in his mouth. He took about a dozen long pulls, and with each*

THE KENNET AT ALDERMASTON,

Fig. 2. Kennet and Avon Canal

pull consternation and surprise seemed to yield to serenity. He walked on in silence for about twenty yards, with the now super-agitated Mr. Raper at his elbow. Finally, Mr Judd delivered his sentence with oracular calm. "Well, 'e'll 'ave to marry 'er, that's all." Mr Raper sweated even more profusely. He blurted out: "But 'e can't marry 'er." "Why not?" "Because 'e's a married man with three children!" Under this new blow Mr. Judd reeled, at any rate mentally. His outward self continued to smoke and walk with a steady dignified tread, but he uttered not a word. Mr Raper walked beside him, with anxious glances. Outside the small wooden gate leading to his own cottage, Mr Raper halted, and his friend stopped mechanically, still sunk in a profound and apparently painful reverie. Mr Raper tried an appeal. "You'll stand by 'er, Mr Judd, won't you? You won't turn 'er out?" Mr Judd ignored this remark. Indeed, he seemed not to have heard it. Suddenly he struck the asphalt with his malacca cane. "What I can't get over is 'ow a daughter of mine could 'a bin so stoopid as not to know what 'ad 'appened to 'er. Indigestion be blowed!" [16]

11

Such severe cases of indigestion were presumably not entirely unknown in the village but if the novel was to be a guide then it must be assumed that such patients would have gained some relief at the workhouse at nearby Bradfield. I was, however, drawn to one such recorded case that may well have proved difficult to pursue. My reticence was later to prove to have been prudent. Already a hazy picture of the village was beginning to emerge. In each of the entries in those registers all the expected occupations were listed; carters, labourers, cowmen, gardeners, wheelwright, dairymen – as well as those of the emerging mechanised age – motor driver, engine driver, gas worker, and those whose occupations gave reason to the name Malthouse Cottage: brewer's labourer; cooper; maltster. White-collar workers were few and far between but included a clerk, a munitions worker, shopkeeper, licensee, brewer. I then went right through the parish council records and the school log books and found that these at last started to give me a variety of anecdotes to be added to the ever increasing number of cards in my system.

Wondrous as it all may seem, my notes for Professor Gates were now in a more speculative state than when I'd started for I found now that I had options and alternatives whereas previously I had no more than an instinctive hunch. And already some of my hopes had to be abandoned. As one of quite a collection of cowmen in the village, Henry Benham's prime good fortune was that he occupied one of the most attractive little cottages in the entire parish. While the Holly Lodge of the story could be nowhere other than the real Lower Lodge I was once again at a loss when it came to its fictional occupant, Colonel Smithers. Indeed it was far worse than I'd ever imagined.

The 1918 electoral register shows a staggering proportion of the village menfolk as 'absent' voters due to active service of one form or another and – time was eventually to show – an almost equally staggering number of officers in Aldington's immediate neighbourhood. 'Memories of a vanished England' has proved to be true. While the countryside around Padworth and the Kennet Valley has the charm of pastoral poetry attributed to it, the immediate vicinity of Aldington's part of the parish was not the huddle of cottages around a village green that may be imagined. It was essentially a tight little working community centred on the brewery (which became Craigie's factory in *The Colonel's Daughter)* overlooked from the top of the hill by the squire's estate and his mansion,

Padworth House. It is no more remarkable than any other similar small community except for one unassailable fact: that in its midst lived one of the most provocative English writers of the 20th century. The fact that he has largely been excommunicated has to be laid to a degree at his own door. He was an outsider and even in the 1980s it was still *de riguer* among many to dismiss him. Professor John Carey in a Sunday Times review 12 July 1981 of *Literary Lifelines: Richard Aldington - Lawrence Durrell Correspondence* (edited by Ian McNiven) still feels that 'Aldington comes across as a man so charged with venom that it would be risky to let him out of doors lest he blight the crops.' Aldington would not be surprised even now to hear what people thought of him. To some extent Mr Purfleet in *The Colonel's Daughter* is Aldington himself; totally harmless but often seen by others as 'a scatter-brain and a dangerous anarchist.'[17]

Chapter 2

The Lads of the Village

'They marched through the empty, muddy streets. It was about midnight. Some one began to sing one of the inevitable marching songs. The officer turned round: "Whistle, but don't sing. People asleep." They began to whistle "Where are the lads of the village to-night?"'
'Where are the lads of the village to-night,
Where are the lads we knew?
In Piccadilly, or Leicester Square?
No, not there; no, not there;
They're taking a trip on the Continong,
With a rifle and a bayonet bright,
They've gone across the water
To meet the Kaiser's daughter,
And that's where they are to-night.'[1]

Every once in a while I used to go back to the library and came away time and again with *Life for Life's Sake*; it was years before I came across a copy I could buy. The more I explored Padworth and the Kennet Valley, the more I wanted to go back to the book. It intrigued me to think that Aldington and T.S. Eliot, for example, had tramped up to the church. There is really only one route between the cottage and the church, past the cottages in Mill Lane and over the 'rushing waters' as the weirs on the Kennet are known locally, past the mill and over the meadows, drawn on by Padworth House and the church on the hill.

My knowledge of the geography of the village was reasonably complete by the time Norman Gates announced himself in the summer of 1978, hence my recklessness in offering him my 'notes'. To learn from the bibliography of Aldington's books in *Intimate Portrait* of the vast array of his work posed a challenge. But in December of that year I came

Fig. 3. Padworth Church

across a book of his short stories called *Roads to Glory,* one of which was particularly pertinent. The bold words 'TO OUR GLORIOUS DEAD' stood out from the page.[2] This was the inscription on the war memorial at Padworth church. It bore investigation I felt and was to lead to a significant insight to the effect that the First World War had on the village, a persistent theme in Aldington's writings. I recognised the well-trodden path that brings you up on the west side of the church where the old iron kissing-gate still exists.

'A man with a rucksack on his shoulders and a pipe in his mouth clicked open the lychgate.'[3] Aldington was a frequent visitor to the churchyard, and he is very thinly disguised in this story. 'Henson crossed the churchyard and went out by the other gate' no doubt casting a wry smile at his 'favourite gravestone' as he passed. He had been this way with T.S. Eliot. It seemed to me that an indication of the date of this story might be judged from what followed, for outside the main lichgate to the church, exactly as it stands to this day, Aldington reports that there 'was a small oblong of flat ground with a new war memorial on it'.[5] The reflective mood that a newly erected war memorial would have induced in Aldington obviously inspired the story. The first edition of the book was published in 1930. If I was correct, then this story could well have lain around in my cottage awaiting publication.

> *'Henson went to have a look. The memorial was a grey granite Celtic cross left intentionally rough with two polished slabs at its base. The slab facing the village was inscribed crisply: "TO OUR EMPIRE'S GLORIOUS DEAD".'*

> *'On the other side were the following names:*
> *Beatson, James*
> *Dodge, John*
> *Ford, Samuel*
> *Judd, William*
> *Naylor, Henry*
> *Templeton, E.J. de F.*
> *Wickham, Thomas*
> *Wickham, William'*[6]

The names on Padworth's war memorial read:

> Clinton, Walter L.
> Harrison, Richard
> Lovelock, Albert
> Pearce, William
> Pearce, Francis
> Pilcher, Thomas
> Preston, James
> Soper, Maurice
> Stevens, Stephen
> Taylor, William.

Ten names instead of the fictional eight. Two thoughts struck me though when I compared the two lists; that both included what would appear to be brothers. On the one there were Thomas and William Wickham while on the other William and Francis Pearce and the fictitious William Judd bore the same surname as the profound Mr Judd of *The Colonel's Daughter*. That this story was set in Padworth I had little reason to doubt.

The fictional village was: 'Obviously, a very small and poor hamlet; in a village of any size the number of names would be doubled. Henson read both inscriptions, and stood contemplating them for some time, leaning on his stick. He even let his pipe go out.'[7] This would be the first official evidence that Aldington would have seen of the names of those from the village who had been less lucky than himself. In *Life for Life's Sake* he tells us that he had made three false starts on what was to be his first novel *Death of a Hero;* his first sighting of the war memorial seems to have prompted one. The words of the song 'The Lads of the Village' are common to both. Aldington would have been deeply moved. What more appropriate under those circumstances than the calming influence of a pint or two in the nearest fictional pub? 'The pub was a little old round thatched affair called The Round Oak.'[8]

Three pubs, no two – well in truth, only one – lie within the convoluted boundaries of Padworth. Aldington makes play of this point. The only one that is truly within Padworth is The Round Oak, up on the common. It isn't round and it isn't thatched – nor was it then – but what images the name would conjure up in the mind of a novelist. Even if the supposed oak tree was still there – which it wasn't – 'a little old round thatched affair' is far more inviting.

Fig. 4. The Round Oak Pub

While the The Butt Inn stands only a few hundred yards from Malthouse Cottage it is, strictly speaking, in the adjoining parish of Aldermaston. The third – or should I say, half of it (for the Padworth-Beenham boundary went right through the middle of the bar) – is the Hare and Hounds, a very old coaching inn on the Bath road, half way between Reading and Newbury and for that reason known locally as 'The Halfway'. However, my cardex proved its worth and showed that the landlord of 'The Halfway' in those days was a Mr William Hood, '…one of the robbin' Oods' his son-in-law Bill Austin was later to tell me. It wouldn't be that often that Aldington would have paid a call at the Round Oak but it is only natural that he would transfer a familiar face to these less familiar surroundings. But Henson wouldn't have known the name of the landlord until another customer came in and made known his presence:

> *'He tapped at the bar, and the landlord came in.*
> *"Mornin', Bert, 'ow's Bert?"*
> *"Middlin', Mr. 'Ood. 'Arf a pint."'*[9]

With only the three of them in the pub it would be inevitable that they would get into conversation and what more appropriate topic than that of the names on the new war memorial. 'If you know'd the stories of all them names y'd 'ave somethin' t' tell about, sir.'[10] It set me thinking when I read that line, but it wasn't until 1982 that I set about a serious search to see what I could find out about the real names on our war memorial. For once, my cardex system failed me. I had no information at all on the families of Richard Harrison, Albert Lovelock, James Preston, Steven Stephens and William Taylor and even now, sadly, I can add very little to their stories.

> *'"An' then there's more as is as good as dead as isn't there at all."'*[11]

Maurice Soper is the only one to be buried in the churchyard. He didn't in fact die until 21 April 1919, five months after the war ended. It is to be assumed that he suffered, but at least his parents would have had the comfort of his body over which to mourn. Most didn't. The rector, for example: Walter L. Clinton was the elder of the two children of Rev W.O. Clinton, rector of Padworth. He was a captain in the Second Battalion of the 6th Rifles. A memorial plate in Padworth Church placed by the 'proud thoughts of his fellow prisoners' records that he died in the Military Hospital, Belgrade, Serbia on 22 November 1918 eleven days after the armistice had been declared '…taken prisoner at Nieuport, Belgium on 10th July 1917 and escaped from Grandenz, West Prussia on 4th October 1918. After many efforts elsewhere, before his death from exhaustion, he just succeeded owing to his great courage and determination in reporting himself to the British Consul in Belgrade.'

To gain any information on the remaining sons of the village though was to prove difficult. Following endless fruitless replies from various agencies, the Commonwealth War Graves Commission accepted the task with a happier heart.

'Harrison, Richard' I learnt was a lance corporal. 9807 Lance Corporal Harrison was born in Padworth before the limits of my cardex system. He enlisted as a member of the 1st Battalion Princess Charlotte of Wales, The Royal Berkshire Regiment. He served in France and Flanders and was killed in action on 14 November 1916. He could well have seen service with Aldington who had met many like him. He had been out there since 13 August 1914 barely a week or so after war was declared. In *Death of a Hero* Aldington asks: 'What were a few million human animals more or less? Why agonise about it? The most he could do was die. "Well, die, then. But O God! Oh God! Is that all? To be born against your will, to feel that life might in its brief passing be so lovely and so divine, and yet to have nothing but opposition and betrayal and hatred and death forced upon you!"'[12]

James Preston, 13199 Private James Preston, was with the 8th Battalion of the Royal Berkshire Regiment. He went out to France on 7 August 1915. At that time there was a desperate push for men. The war was obviously going to last longer than most had imagined. The term 'cannon fodder' was coined. Seven weeks later he was dead – 'killed in action'. He was thirty-one years old. *Death of a Hero* again: 'To be born for the slaughter like a calf or a pig! To be violently cast back into nothing – for what? My God! For what? Is there nothing but despair and death? Is life vain, beauty vain, love vain, hope vain, happiness vain? "The war to end wars!" Is any one so asinine as to believe that? A war to breed wars, rather.'[13]

Thomas Pilcher was another private, No. 37565, this time with 'C' Company 1/4th Battalion of the Royal Berkshire. His regiment had been

1,000 strong when it went out. When it came back it comprised four officers and forty-three men and the other 953 men were dead. Thomas was the son of A.M.J. Pilcher and the late Thomas Pilcher from Binfield, Berkshire and so, presumably, their eldest son. In 1918 his mother lived in Mill Road, Padworth just round the corner from Malthouse Cottage. It seems that there was a second son, John, for he is registered as an 'absent' voter on the 1918 electoral roll. Thomas died on 3 May 1917. John is presumed to have survived but he and his mother must have moved as soon as he came home for their names disappear from the various records. Once more in *Death of a Hero* we see Aldington's sympathies: 'Their enemies – the enemies of German and English alike – were the fools who had sent them to kill each other instead of help each other. Their enemies were the sneaks and the unscrupulous; the false ideals, the unintelligent ideas imposed on them, the humbug, the hypocrisy, the stupidity. If those men were typical, then there was nothing essentially wrong with common humanity, at least so far as the men were concerned. It was the leadership that was wrong – not the war leadership, but the peace leadership.'[14]

Of the others I learnt very little that could be called conclusive. The formal records are of little help. There are evidently four 'Pearces, F.' and six 'Taylors, W.' in the records of the Royal Berkshire Regiment and can only be confirmed or otherwise by their regimental numbers which, were I able to find them, could be checked again. There was no way of telling whether indeed Francis and William Pearce were of that regiment. However, there is a Pearce family grave in Padworth churchyard and something can be gained from that. It would seem I was correct in assuming that they were brothers. Their father William Pearce died in 1902. William was 'killed in action, July 30th 1917 aged 35'. Francis, 'died of wounds August 27th 1918 aged 33', only weeks before Armistice Day. Annie Sarah, their widowed mother must have been heartbroken. She died about six weeks after Francis on 5th October 1918.

Fig. 5. Mrs Ann Sarah Pearce

It had never occurred to me that there would be any problem at all in gaining all this information from official sources and I became very disillusioned. There were so many people whose identities were lost forever in official archives. Aldington took up this theme in 'Lads of The Village': '"Lor' bless yer, no sir. There ain't 'ardly a fam'ly but's lorst some 'un or's got some 'un in a 'orspital or a 'ome f' the blind or a 'sylum.'"[15]

How true that must have been. Though it took me hours to do so I thought an analysis of the cardex system may uncover something significant. I found that in 1918 the population of Padworth, including women and children, was about 200. There were 132 registered as voters, thirty-three of whom were absent through military service. From the evidence of the war memorial we see that nearly a third of those serving gave their lives – in wartime lives are not lost; they are given. The number of families affected was even more than official figures suggest. As far as I can judge there were a further twenty men serving in the forces with families in the village. Practically every family was affected in one way or another. Those who may have escaped immediate suffering would have had distressed neighbours next door, with whom they could share their burden of innocence. One family, I noticed, had three 'absent' sons. William, Albert and Alfred Austin, from one of the first cottages Aldington would have walked past on his journey to the church, had all served in the First World War. I happened to be reading our local paper, the *Newbury Weekly News* of 15 April 1982. A gentleman, it reported, was 'watching with interest as the British Task Force makes its way towards a possible confrontation with the Argentinian fleet. For, nearly 70 years ago, he played his part in an overwhelming victory over the Germans in the first Battle of the Falklands.'[16] That man was William Austin who had lived in Padworth, and fascinating though the article was, I wanted to see what else he could tell me. Amazingly he still lived nearby. For a good three hours he and I talked on a warm June afternoon and all the time he kept apologising for not sticking to what he thought I wanted to know.

I was curious to know what contact Aldington had with those around him. The Berkshire twang and the wisdom of the countryman is strongly evident in his books, put particularly well into the mouth of Mr Judd in *The Colonel's Daughter*. Part of the appeal of his writing is to be gained from the dialogue. That it is witty follows from the author's ready humour. That it is recognisable as coming from Berkshire is due to his powers of observation. Conversely though, it was this same ability to express a soldier's dialogue that had caused problems in the publication of *Death of a Hero* in 1929. That novel could only be published by substituting asterisks for those words and phrases it was felt would be unacceptable to the general reader. That Mr Judd could have been duped by his own daughter's 'indigestion' expresses a reflection of his own naivety as much as the author's appreciation of the literary value of a morsel of village gossip and the propensity to be able to use it to effect. "'An' it's a rum thing," he went on, gloomily pessimistic in manner, " 'ow things can go on under a man's own nose, an' 'im not see nothing." "Yes?" said Mr Judd doubtfully. "I suppose there are fellers like that, no natchral gift of hobservation as you might say.""[17]

If the real Mr Judd was out there, I may get to know the truth of it all. Bill Austin was obviously contemporary to Aldington and was therefore of prime importance in that quest. As they were the only people living down our little lane there is no one with whom Aldington and Arabella would have been in daily contact. Bill Austin was therefore one of their nearest neighbours. They would have a lot in common despite a certain phlegmatic reserve that checked Bill Austin. I wondered whether they knew each other. 'Well 'e knew me… 'e was Alderton wasn't he?… don't suppose 'e's alive now. 'E was older'n me.' In fact Mr Austin was Aldington's senior by a year. 'I read some of 'is books but I've forgotten 'em now. Fairly well-built man. He wasn't puny or anything like that. 'E was interesting in conversation but … we never associated much. I'm not a conversationalist and I was busy on my own life… I liked my own wife sufficiently enough to always be in her company…' which was not surprising when he told me what he'd been through. By the time the family first moved to Padworth – 'a nice place for to bird's nest' – Bill was nine years old and had 'finished with school' but there he had to stay till he was fourteen on his father's insistence. But in 1909, he 'cleared off' from home to join the navy, walking to Southampton to do so, strictly against his father's wishes. But the discipline, while frighteningly recalled, was in the end accepted whereas his father's was rejected. He was a regular in His Majesty's Royal Navy and when war was declared he was a veteran seaman of five years standing. His younger brother, Bert, saw military service too. ''E was in the "Metropolitan Crowd" as a gunner – big guns.' Charlie Austin, youngest of the three brothers who saw active service was with the Berkshire

Yeomanry, the same regiment as their previous employer, the local brewer, Bill told me.

In October 1981 a bookseller's catalogue arrived that set me off on the trail of someone else who lived practically within sight and earshot of Aldington. Even as I write though, this aspect of my search remains open ended. While I have managed to turn up enough to prove the bond of friendship between Aldington and at least one of his then neighbours I have as yet been unable to trace the one surviving member of that family. Item three of that catalogue was in fact a second catalogue. 'A Catalogue of the Collection of Frank G. Harrington Esq' was offered for sale. The asking price was £3. I bought it. Frank G. Harrington had collected Richard Aldington's books. In 1973 he had handed his collection over to Temple University Libraries and this was their catalogue of that collection. Of the hundreds of entries, one in particular caught my eye: '*Remy de Gourmont: Selections from all his books* chosen and translated by Richard Aldington. New York. Covici-Friede Publishers, 1929.' Aldington mentions this book in *Life for Life's Sake*. It was one of many he translated while he was at Malthouse Cottage. My attention was held by what followed: 'two volumes. Presentation inscription "To Jessie and Athol Capper from Richard Aldington, June 1928". Fine photograph of Aldington pasted in Vol 1.'[18] In my cardex an otherwise blank card confirmed the existence of Jessie and Athol in The Bungalow from 1925 onwards. It showed that Athol had previously lived with his mother at The Laurels, a name that had mystified me as much as that of The Bungalow for neither names still existed. Here was the first evidence of a direct link to Aldington.

Fig. 6. Athol Capper

Some time in 1980 I had heard that the owner of a piece of land that was up for sale opposite me was a woman who lived in Ireland. The estate agents were good enough to give me her name and I wrote to her. Her response sent me off on another very interesting tangent but for the moment I learnt that she was brought up in Venture Fair and that before her parents bought it in 1924-25 it had been known as The Laurels. I now had reason to write to her again. The Cappers, she told me, had married following the death of Athol's mother and with the money gained from the sale of The Laurels had a bungalow built in the grounds. That bungalow was what I knew as June Rose Bungalow a timber bungalow in about six acres almost directly opposite Aldington's cottage. As Athol and Jessie had just married, my guess was that they would be of a similar age to Aldington and Arabella. Richard Aldington was thirty-three in 1925 and Arabella was thirty-four.

Athol and Jessie started a chicken farm on their six acres with some degree of success, I imagine, because I was later to learn that Jessie had written books on the subject. But some time during the 1930s they had moved, I was told, to Arborfield about twelve miles or so away. A visit to Berkshire Records Office soon revealed their address. Barely six hours after receiving news of them I was standing on their doorstep. But sadly my optimism was to take another blow. The present owners had no idea what happened to the Cappers but sent me round the corner to the widow of a man who had worked for them. From there I finished up on the doorstep of the woman who had been their housekeeper during their time at Arborfield. Along the way though, I had picked up little bits of news about them that built up a picture of a very loving, gentle, sympathetic couple with one son, John Capper, who was born in 1926.

It was all adding up to a strong bond of friendship between the Cappers and the Aldingtons. Their housekeeper confirmed it all. 'Athol was blinded in the First World War and was registered with St Dunstans.'

Richard Aldington, Bill Austin, Bert Austin and now Athol Capper. I'd heard, too, that Frank Downham, the village postman who lived in Mill Lane, had also been badly wounded. Within a hundred yards or so of each other at the bottom of the village were six men who, each in their various ways suffered acutely as a direct result of their service to king and country. At the top of the village things must have been equally as bad if not worse. I am told that the squire loaned out the family bath chair for the use of those who were disabled.

In the hope of finding out something of the others on the war memorial I put together a letter detailing my findings and in May 1983 wrote to the parish magazine. Almost immediately I had a phone call from a Mrs Pearce who I discovered to my ignorance, lived up on the common a few doors away from The Round Oak. Mrs Pearce is the widow of Albert Edward Pearce who was a member of the East Surreys. He was injured in France in the First World War. He had just turned sixteen when war broke out but he volunteered. He and his brother Tom

Fig. 7. Jessie and John Capper

both survived their experiences though and saw out the rest of their lives with their families. I soon learnt from Mrs Pearce that Maurice Soper had been gassed, and that a Taylor went down with his ship. Between us

Fig. 8. Francis Pearce

*Fig. 9. The memorial cross to
Francis Pearce. Bagneux
British Cemetery, Gaizencourt,
south of Doullens*

though we couldn't work out which Taylor, nor could Mrs. Pearce
remember which ship.

Mrs Pearce's husband, Bert, was indeed the younger brother of
William and Francis whose names appear on the war memorial. At the
time he joined up Francis was 'in service' in East Anglia and joined the
1st Essex Regiment.

Francis Pearce 'died of wounds' on 27 August 1918 and is buried at
Bagneux British Cemetery, Gaizencourt, south of Doullens, in France.
Mrs Pearce showed me a photo taken within days of Frank being buried,
long before the formal war grave was erected.

Mrs Pearce also had a deeply personal memorial card announcing Frank's death. It bears the arms of the Essex Regiment and the following words:

'Somewhere in France in a soldier's grave,
Lies my dear one amongst the brave,
Only those that have lost can tell
The grief for one they loved so well.

May the winds of Heaven blow gently
On that sweet and sacred spot.
Though sleeping in a far off grave,
Dearest one, you are not forgot,
For I often sit and think of you
When I am all alone,
For memory is the only thing
That grief can call its own.'

There is no such grave for William though and hence no memoriam card. There was no body to bury. He was in the Royal Berkshire Mrs Pearce believed and she still remembered seeing the official letter. 'They put "Killed in action" but he was actually missing. What you don't know is that he was probably blown to bits. They didn't ever find him. It's awful. They just put "killed in action…" Mrs Anne Pearce lost two sons and a third was wounded. She had lost her husband four years after Bert was born. She may have never seen Bert and Tom again before she herself died on 5 October 1918. She was only sixty years old. She had always been a cheerful lady but '…she would hear the church bells ringing at Padworth and was in tears.'

Fig. 10. William Pearce

'Somewhere in France in a soldier's grave,
Lies my dear one amongst the brave,
Only those that have lost can tell
The grief for one they loved so well.'

Had he been granted one magical wish I feel sure Aldington would have rewritten history to exclude the reign of Queen Victoria. His hatred of the Victorian 'cant' that failed to keep the peace was paramount. The later authorized edition of Death of a Hero shows that the asterisks in his phrase 'Prehistoric beasts, like the ichthyosaurus and ***** *******' referred pointedly, to Queen Victoria.[19] 'It was the regime of Cant before the War which made the Cant during the War so damnably possible and easy. On our coming of age the Victorians generously handed us a charming little cheque for fifty guineas – fifty-one months of hell, and the results. Charming people, weren't they? Virtuous and far-sighted. But it wasn't their fault? They didn't make the War? It was Prussia and Prussian militarism? Right you are, right ho! Who made Prussia a great power and subsidised Frederick the Second to do it, thereby snatching an empire from France? England. Who backed up Prussia against Austria, and Bismarck against Napoleon III? England. And whose Cant governed England in the nineteenth century? But never mind this domestic squabble of mine – put it that I mean the 'Victorians' of all nations.'[20] The destructive influence of the Victorians on the start of the twentieth century represented everything that Aldington hated. His invective was at its strongest and most vehement when he was faced with the damage done to the world, to England and the English way of life. The effect of the First World War was everywhere. It would have been a constant topic and a discussion on those lines took place in his fictional Round Oak.

> *'"There's young Bill Judd, now, I was a tellin' y' about. Good lad, 'e was, rode a 'orse like a jockey, and the best cricketer we ever 'ad. 'E was young Mr Templeton's servant in the Army. 'Is father and mother lives up the Manor now as caretakers. But they don't seem to take no pride or pleasure in it. Old Bill Judd, 'e usto come in 'ere ev'ry evenin' pretty nigh 'e did, for 'is pint and a bit o' chat and a sing-song. Don't come in twice in a year now, sir. Seems kind o' 'opeless like. See 'im mouchin' along the road, I do, mopin' about like a lame mare what's lost 'er first colt."'[21]*

Different people were affected in their differing ways. After all these years Bill Austin's feelings have matured into a gentle philosophy of his own. 'It was a job that had to be done and you volunteered to see it through.' Aldington took a slightly more hardened view in *Death of a Hero*: 'The extension of the Kiplingesque of a kicked-backside-of-the-Empire principle was something for which George was not prepared. He resented it, resented it bitterly, but the doom was on him as on all the young men. When "we" had determined that they should be killed, it was impious to demur.'[22] Bill Austin's ship, *The Kent*, he recalls 'carried a hundred ratings extra… to take the place of those who would be killed and wounded.' Amid all this gloom, he told me one quite remarkable story about his brother Charlie who was on board ship in the Mediterranean. 'He went to school at Padworth and when his ship was torpedoed… one of the boat's crew which came to pick up the survivors and what could be picked up, was one of his schoolmates from Padworth.' I have no idea who that person was and neither could Bill recall the name. He suggested however that those in the trenches 'suffered more than we did'. Aldington was suffering from shell shock or 'war nerves' as the army preferred to call it. The army at the time refused to acknowledge the existence of it as a mental illness; in their eyes such men were cowards. Many deserters were suffering from shell shock and they ended up being court-martialled and shot. Shell shock reflects the sensitivity of the man. The effect on Aldington was damaging and permanent and he knew it. It was to remain as the bedrock of practically everything he was to write.

Death of a Hero is largely autobiographical. Aldington becomes Winterbourne named after the Berkshire village close to Hermitage where Aldington lived before coming to Padworth. Aldington was in a pioneer battalion and over the Easter weekend of 1917 on his second tour of duty, he was digging trenches and saps, laying signals cables and sitting for long hours in observation posts on the outskirts of Lens while the Battle of Vimy Ridge was in full spate. Later that year he spent one night lying trapped in no man's land under the shadow of Hill 70 while that battle raged on.

'For Winterbourne the battle was a timeless confusion, a chaos of noise, fatigue, anxiety, and horror. He did not know how many days and nights it lasted, lost completely the sequence of events, found great gaps in his conscious memory. He did know that he was profoundly affected by it, that it made a cut in his life and personality. You couldn't say there was anything melodramatically startling, no hair going grey in a night, or never smiling again. He looked unaltered; he behaved in exactly the

same way. But in fact, he was a little mad. We talk of shell-shock, but who wasn't shell-shocked, more or less? The change in him was psychological, and showed itself in two ways. He was left with an anxiety complex, a sense of fear he had never experienced, the necessity to use great and greater efforts to force himself to face artillery, anything explosive. Curiously enough, he scarcely minded machine-gun fire, which was really more deadly, and completely disregarded rifle-fire. And he was also left with a profound and cynical discouragement, a shrinking horror of the human race.'[23]

For his first few years at Padworth, Aldington suffered considerably. His sister Margery told me that: 'Richard was still suffering from the shake-over in the war. He used to have nightmares and wake up lashing about – and shouting. Poor Arabella dealt with that. She was a wonderful girl.' But even in Padworth, far removed from the scenes of war there were still reminders of that shared experience of the horror that accompanied the whine of artillery fire. Immediately beyond the Capper's bungalow and right alongside Venture Fair was the main railway line to the west country and the acoustic effect created by the houses on that side of the canal was akin to that of a railway cutting into which the noise of the trains would disappear only to emerge again with an urgent ferocity, an attribute that Aldington transferred to his third novel, *All Men Are Enemies*. It was the same on board ship where Bill Austin was often at sea for periods of up to a year. Life on board must have been atrocious. 'Some of them died through mental trouble. Some people couldn't put up with it. But not me.' But Bill Austin recalls the torment he went through on his return home. 'I had a nervous breakdown when I came out of it… The doctors at Aldermaston didn't seem to be doing any good. No use at all. It lasted about three or four months, a bit longer perhaps. Lots of servicemen suffered. I had a good wife to comfort me and I expect that's what happened to the majority of 'em. I had to go to a London psychiatrist. I didn't have nightmares but I had insomnia. I shook it off in about a year. You can't go through all those things without it having some physical effect.'

Like Aldington, Bill Austin used to go for long walks to help shake it off. Everyone who has shared their memories of him, recalls that Aldington 'was a great walker.'[24] By many standards Aldington and Bill

Austin were the lucky ones. Given time they were able to recover but Aldington never forgave those responsible for the predicament to which they all returned. He had a vendetta of the 'dead against the living'. He admits as much in *Death of a Hero*. 'Yes, it is true, I have a vendetta, an unappeased longing for vengeance. Yes, a vendetta. Not a personal vendetta. What am I? O God, nothing, less than nothing, a husk, a leaving, a half-chewed morsel on the plate, a reject. But an impersonal vendetta, an unappeased conscience crying in the wilderness, a river of tears in the desert. What right have I to live?'[25] What right indeed, I have heard it said.

Aldington's strength lay in the fact that his writings gave voice to an entire generation of men. Yes there were other novelists writing on a similar theme. *Death of a Hero* was published late in 1929, the year that Aldington left Padworth. It came out in a flurry of war novels all of whose authors had apparently, and coincidentally, needed an entire decade over which to muse. *All Quiet on the Western Front* by Erich Maria Remarque; Ernest Hemingway's *Farewell To Arms*; Robert Graves' *Goodbye to All That*; Henry Williamson's *Patriots' Progress* and Frederick Manning's *Her Privates We* all came out within a month or so of *Death of a Hero* to create a new era of anti-war novels. Despite the fact that Aldington's book was banned by the popular lending libraries at Boots and W.H. Smith, it became an immediate best-seller. But that was yet to come.

As I have said, he was one of the lucky ones. Ten men killed and say, half a dozen permanently disabled from the thirty-three Padworth men were a big loss for a tiny hamlet. Athol Capper was one of those 'permanently disabled' and presumably had no argument with what Aldington had to say. Aldington's photograph in Athol Capper's book gives credence to that. And Athol had more reason than anyone to be bitter; he was a Quaker and Quakerism equates with non-violence and yet he obeyed the call to duty and was severely injured as a result. I began to get confirmation from those who knew him at Padworth. Athol '…was invalided out of the army, he was so crippled up… He had a silver plate in his head as a result of his injuries… Athol was injured in the Great War… He had terrible injuries and TB when he came out of the army. They had that place built with a little veranda so he could sleep out there.' Presumably, Athol suffered claustrophobia too, but whereas Aldington could sometimes walk it off, Athol Capper hadn't the same degree of freedom. From what little I have been able to ascertain, his blindness was a worsening ailment. 'He was blind up to a point... He could still see a certain amount but could still manage... Nice fellow, he was.' But in later life he was totally blind 1 am told and while St Dunstan's (the blind veterans organisation founded in 1915) can find no trace of him in their records, I am assured by two people who knew him well that Athol Capper was registered with them.

Aldington settled in Padworth just before Christmas 1920 at a time when war memorials were springing up in all the neighbouring towns and villages. Aldermaston was one of the first. They unveiled theirs in July of 1920; in November of that year Thatcham, Kingsclere, Woolton Hill and Hungerford followed. Brimpton, Burghclere and Yattendon saw theirs for the first time in the following January. So fast indeed were they being built that they were becoming a traffic hazard. *The Newbury Weekly News* of 10 February 1921 discusses the need either to provide a warning light or to mount a guard on 'many of the War Memorials which are dotted about at cross roads and other places all over the Rural District.'[26] A nasty accident had occurred at Chaddleworth where a car crashed into their memorial. Two people were hurt and in its edition of 18 November the previous year a minor admonition was handed out to Newbury Town Council for lagging behind the villages. But that was as nothing compared with Padworth. It didn't get a war memorial until 1926. The parish council minute book for 8 March 1926 has the following entry:

'A special meeting of the parishioners was called at Padworth House by Major Darby Griffith among those present at the well attended meeting were Mrs Sykes, Mrs Mills, Mrs Draper Strange, Mrs Kersley, Mrs Kent and many other ladies, Messrs E. Gyles and W. Austin, Parish Councillors, J.H. Benyon Esq representing the B.C. Council, Brig General Mills and other Gentlemen.' After other matters were dealt with 'An open discussion concerning the Padworth War Memorial then took place.'[27]

In view of Aldington's feelings, I should like to think he was at that meeting but he may well have been away at that time. In fact, it may well be that we see here a record of the political manoeuvres of village life for the same records show that the annual parish meeting – a totally different meeting – was to take place a fortnight after the special meeting and that the minutes of the annual parish meeting record the fact that they too discussed the matter and that Major Darby Griffith was in the chair at both meetings. Present at the second meeting were parish councillors Hearn, Gyles, Kersley and William Austin Sr, the father of William, Albert and Charles. 'Also present' were Messrs C.W. Strange, Major Crook, G. Tull and the clerk, George Earley. The one person whose name is not mentioned as being present at either meeting is that of the then rector. Rev Henry George Lancaster wanted the memorial inside the churchyard and Major Darby was determined it should stand just outside the gate. And of course Rev Lancaster had only been around since August 1924 and the squire's family had been in Padworth for hundreds of years. John Hale (whom I was to meet much later) recalled his mother's recollections of that first meeting. John's parents knew Padworth church well. His father was a bell ringer and both he and John's grandfather are buried in the churchyard. 'The vicar wanted the war memorial put in the church and Darby Griffith didn't… So he had a public meeting… and entertained (the parishioners)… and got them all on his side. Obviously they all had a good evening out at the squire's home and at his expense too.

Fig. 11. Grenadier Guards at Padworth House

[Afterwards] they had a sort of soup and wine party… and he said to my mother "You come and sit with me" (presumably she was on his side)… and they had those soup cups with two handles and it was hot.' But resulting from what he must have judged to have been a well fought and deservedly won campaign Darby Griffith was by now in a more cheerful mood. He relaxed over his hot soup. "Well I don't know about you," he said to Mrs Hale "but I'm going to saucer mine!"'

That the squire did win the day with the rector is evident. The war memorial stands outside the church. It was unveiled amid all the pomp and circumstance that the squire could organize. The presence of the band of The Grenadier Guards was solely due to his past history with that regiment.

The boy scouts, the girl guides and half the village turned out in response to the squire's rallying call. The last post was played as the unveiling ceremony was performed by the defeated rector – six years later than all the neighbouring village memorials.

"'If you was to take a look at our new memorial sir," said the landlord to Henson, "You'd see the names of all our glorious dead."

"I saw it as I came along."

"You did? And what did y' think of it?"

"Very handsome and very tasteful,"…

"Cost a lot o' money, too, didn't it, Bert?"

"Ah."'[28]

Chapter 3

The Berkshire Kennet

After six years of research I can only guess why Aldington actually chose to come and live at Padworth. That he spent a year at nearby Hermitage beforehand is well documented in his autobiography. He says his cottage in Padworth was tumbledown but it obviously suited his purpose. Its strategic position is even now unchanged. Although the adjoining building now houses our neighbours, in those days it was a working malthouse. At the time I began these notes Norman Gates' introduction to his *Checklist* was all that was available as a biography of Aldington.[1] Neither is what follows a biography but it does show the immediate and fascinating influence that his surroundings had on Aldington.[2]

In *Life for Life's Sake*, Aldington admits that by virtue of his own actions his life was in a hell of a mess when he was demobbed. He and Arabella had become lovers during a 'Blighty break' but circumstances were not quite so cut and dried. Biographers writing of the interwoven lives of Aldington, Arabella, D.H. Lawrence, Frieda Lawrence, John Cournos, Brigit Patmore and others have taken up acres of competing print. Lawrence, Cournos, Brigit Patmore and H.D. all fictionalized these events and the early part of *Death of a Hero* is Aldington's version. Despite the obvious but frequently misguided respect he shows towards the colonel's daughter, there is a curious ambivalence in Aldington's attitude towards women. The truth is that he couldn't resist them but he chose to kiss and not tell.

> *'Yeats used to say of George Moore: "Other men kiss and don't tell; George Moore tells and doesn't kiss." I would give a great deal to write as well as George Moore, but in this respect I prefer to be like other men.' In the light of what I have subsequently learnt I judge his motives to be not so much based on prudence as on strategy. 'I have burned a good many boats in my time, but only after considerable resistance to the impulse.'* [3]

During his second tour of duty, Aldington was well aware that his impulsive affair with Arabella would contribute towards the destruction of his marriage. At the end of the short break from war he certainly found himself in a sorry predicament which he wrote out of his system in *Death of a Hero*. At times he must have wondered precisely what he was fighting for. He had little reason to look forward to at the end of hostilities other than the relief that the fighting would be over. These thoughts together with his self-conscious, sensitive nature would collectively put him in the front line for shell shock. He came home a broken desolate man. There was little purpose to his life. To live in London to follow his literary aspirations was out of the question. 'I had almost resigned myself to a dreary existence of rented rooms in London when unexpectedly Lawrence turned up on his way to Italy and offered to hand over his cottage. It was at a place romantically called Hermitage, in Berkshire. In my then state of mind you could have offered me nothing more attractive than a hermitage, and I accepted the offer without seeing the place.'[4] There was only one person to whom he could turn at this time – Arabella. So it was that in February 1919 they moved to Chapel Farm Cottage at Hermitage, a few miles north of Newbury and then, after the expiry of a year's lease, to Malthouse Cottage. It was just over two years after Armistice Day but Aldington was still in a mental torment. He could not rid his mind of the images of war.

> *'I do not need the ticking of my watch*
> *To tell me I am mortal;*
> *I have lived with, fed upon death*
> *As happier generations feed on life;*
> *My very mind seems gangrened.'*[6]

Were it not for his poet's sensibility to the horrors of war he may have accepted his lot with a little of the philosophy adopted by Bill Austin. But the war had put Aldington firmly into the category of war poet. His *Images of War* was published in 1919 in London and 1921 in Boston, a matter of months after he came to Padworth. *Images of Desire* was published in tandem and offsets the horrors of war with the sensuality of love. Aldington was a man of contrasts and these contrasts can be seen in practically everything he writes. His choice of titles was significant. As a young man he cut a central role in the imagist movement, a school of poetry that laid the foundations for the modernist poetry of the twentieth century. *Exile and Other Poems* (published in 1923) is significant in that it shows those contrasts. The fact that it was published two years after he came here contrasts the tranquillity in Padworth with his state of mind when he arrived. The initial appeal of Hermitage was purely the peace of the place compared with active service; he must have longed, yearned for, some respite in the ceaseless bombardment.

'Let there be silence sometimes
A space of starless night –
A silence, a space of forgetfulness
Away from seething of lives,
The rage of struggle.'[6]

Aldington's enemy was never the German soldier. It was always the elder generation, the politicians on both sides who had failed to keep the peace. He never forgave them. He was not just to suffer mentally from the memories of war; his physical condition was poor, too. In a letter to Amy Lowell, American poet and proponent of imagism, he talks of the benefits of the countryside at that time. It was impossible though to shake off the effects of the war in a matter of months. Shell shock was with him for years in its most severe form. Padworth provided a tranquil backdrop to his work. He came to the village with a reputation as a poet and that tag still remains among those who still remember him. Many of his neighbours at the time may have known nothing of him other than that fact; 'Oh, yes, the poet'. The change that was to come inside him though was a slow process indeed. At the beginning he found it extremely difficult to relax and to sleep. He must have dreaded that moment when he knew he ought to be sleeping.

'It is at night one thinks,
At night, staring with sleepless eyes
At the narrow moonlit room.
Outside the owls hoot briefly,
And there are stars
Whose immortal order makes one shudder.'[7]

During the time he had lived here he became known as a great walker.

Already he was getting to know the beautiful valley of the River Kennet. Like Bill Austin 'Have I not striven and striven for health? Lived calmly (as it seemed) these many months, Walked daily among neat hedged fields'[8] and yet real peace eluded him.

> *'I have done all this,*
> *And yet there are always nights*
> *I lie awake staring with sleepless eyes,*
> *And what is my mind's sickness,*
> *What the agony I struggle with,*
> *I can hardly tell.'*

> *'As I sit here alone in the calm lamplight,*
> *Watching the red embers*
> *Slowly fade and crumble into grey dust,*
> *With that impenetrable silence*
> *Of long night about me*
> *And the companionship of the immemorial dead*
> *At hand upon my shelves'[9]*

To some extent though, it must have seemed to him an inward-turning spiral the centre of which – like a black hole – would have been frightening. There are passages in *Death of a Hero* that give credence to his belief that at times he was near to insanity during his time at the front and that suicide must have presented itself as one of two options; that or to be killed. It never crossed his mind that he would survive. That he did and that he was not wounded would have isolated him from official sympathy. As Bill Austin speaks of *his* wife, Arabella was the only person to whom Aldington could turn. She must take credit for just being there with him. But he was in the countryside and solace was at hand in the form of the nightingale. The descendants of his nightingale still sing on a May or June night and it is always, without fail, in the same oak tree that he would also have known. If walking can be added to the sinful occupation of overwork then he found himself guilty on both counts. The one was to compliment the other. Writing was his means of earning a living. He is justifiably proud that he never needed to earn money in any other way.

'I also might have worn starched cuffs,
Have gulped my morning meal in haste,
Have clothed myself in dismal stuffs
Which prove a sober City taste;
I also might have rocked and craned
In undergrounds for daily news,
And watched my soul grow slowly stained
To middle-class unsightly hues ...
I might have earned ten pounds a week!'[10]

But he didn't. During his time at Padworth he became a most prolific translator, reviewer, editor and biographer. But throughout his solitary period here, he took in imperceptibly but surely everything that went on around him, from the opening of a single flower to the most intense village politics. Among the prolific and diverse titles listed in the brief bibliography at the back of Norman Gates' *Richard Aldington: An Intimate Portrait* one title drew my attention. The seventh of a total of nineteen books of poems listed was *The Berkshire Kennet*. I had seen a reference to it in *Life for Life's Sake* without knowing what poem it was. 'I suppose I must admit that the valley of the Kennet is tame and domestic, but it has the charm of pastoral poetry. If I didn't think it offensive for a man to quote his own verses, I should be tempted to cite some octosyllabic verses I wrote on this theme.'[11] Only fifty copies of the first edition (Curwen Press, 1923) were printed, one of which sits comfortably in the reference section of Reading Library. One small passage in it confirmed my belief that Aldington's slow recovery was largely due to his surroundings at Padworth.

The 'solitude,' the 'peace' and the 'silence!' he says: 'Have cleansed the wounds of war away/and brought to my long troubled mind/the health that I despaired to find.'[12] It was from a small note in the back of the first edition that I learnt that the poem had first been published in September 1923 by which time it was reasonable to assume he had walked in Padworth and knew it well.

As a walker the 'strategic' position of his cottage was better placed than perhaps he first imagined. Standing on the bridge at the head of the lane leading to his cottage Aldington could have set off in any of six directions leading to all points of the compass. Any one of these would provide a stimulating walk according to his mood. But time and time again he would be drawn south eastwards down Mill Lane, towards the church. There is something about that walk that would have drawn him, tugging him over the Kennet towards the centre of the parish, the church and the squire's house. All his visitors were escorted in that direction. But there is more to it than that. To a man with his sense of the past it is a walk back in time. It would take him from the industrial bustle of the brewery at the bottom of the village past the nineteenth century cottages in the lane to the eighteenth century Padworth House and park and further back in time to the eleventh century Norman church, all in the space of a mile or so. We know for a fact that T.S. Eliot and Harold Monro took this walk and it follows that when they visited, F.S. Flint and D.H. Lawrence would have joined him, too.

That Eliot enjoyed his visits here is evident. Shortly following what I believe to be that first visit in the summer of 1921 Aldington planned a walking tour that would take him and Arabella away from Padworth and he offered the cottage to Tom and Viv Eliot. In his reply of 6 July, Eliot says that had circumstances been favourable he should certainly have accepted as he recalled it as a paradise. Aldington tells us that: 'Among the people who came to see me, Eliot was most responsive to the history, Lawrence to the natural beauty and the flowers. Eliot was far from being insensitive to such things. For instance, he was interested in wild birds and knew a lot about them, which one mightn't suspect from his writings.'[13] On either subject, history or nature, Aldington would be the perfect companion. His translations, articles and certain biographies reflect the work he was involved in at the cottage and the novels and poems have recognisable passages that relate to his surroundings at Padworth. In *Life for Life's Sake* he tells us of walking to Sherborne St John about eight miles south of Padworth with T.S. Eliot. On the way they would pass through Pamber that crops up as a supposedly fictional village in *Death of a Hero*. In *All Men are Enemies* we see Anthony Clarendon setting out on this same walk.

> *'On Saturday morning he dressed in his oldest clothes, with a sense of satisfaction as if making a gesture of defiance, and set off for a long walk. The nominal objective of the walk, which went nearly the whole way by footpaths and abandoned lanes half choked with undergrowth, was a hamlet about eight miles to the southeast. The few houses and farmsteads almost hidden among*

huge elms and beeches made the village look like a ship of greenery stranded in a little bay of the bare chalk down, with the church trying to tug it off. In the church were several fourteenth-century tombs, crude, vigorous work, lacking both the grace and intellectual subtlety of contemporary Italian and French sculpture, but authentic.'[14]

The walk up to Padworth Church is at the heart of *The Colonel's Daughter*. Practically every step he took is recorded in his writing and to follow in his footsteps is as much a journey through his writing as through the village. In the intervening years a spindly coppice of willows has grown up around the field adjoining his cottage but I am assured that the moment he stepped out of his cottage door he would have had a full view of Padworth House on the scarp of the hill to the south east. The canal was to his right as he set out. The 'ancient' malthouse against which his cottage 'butted up' was largely ignored. 'Old' Dave Wickens the working maltster would no doubt tip his cap towards his neighbour. Leslie Austin, Bill's younger half brother from his father's second family would come round for his holiday job 'putting lables on bottles' or 'clearing the ventilation holes' in the upper floors of the malthouse. Fifty yards up the lane were the old empty stables at the back of Bridge House, the home of

Fig. 12. Bridge House, Padworth

the 'impoverished gentry' to whom Aldington paid his weekly rent. He would pass the back door and the kitchen windows before turning left into Mill Lane.

Two of the girls who were in service at Bridge House remember Aldington and Arabella very well. 'They'd be continually up and down [the lane]. We'd see them at the back door. They were marvellous. They were always out walking together. We'd see them constantly. No one else had reason to go down that lane. It's lovely and quiet down there.' It was that fact as much as any that appealed to Aldington; the cottage was strategically secure against all invaders. 'No wealthy fool, no titled whore/Passes this quiet cottage door.'[15]

Although now lacking its arm, the black and white painted post that directed visitors 'To the Mill' now stands purposelessly on duty at the junction with the main road. Aldington would follow its direction, passing the cricket field on the right that passed the front of Red Cottage, whose front gate is always associated in my mind with Purfleet's gate.[16]

Chris Strange lived there. Major Christopher William Draper Strange, to give him his full name, was a cousin to the brewery family and a school governor and was 'one of the sweetest rogues you could possibly meet' a near neighbour of his was to tell me. He was a renowned artist in

Fig. 13. Red Cottage, Mill Lane, Padworth

Mill Lane, Lower Padworth, Berks.

Fig. 14. Lyndale, Mill Lane, Padworth

Aldington's day and lived there with his widowed mother. With no justifiable reason whatsoever this brings to mind a picture of Purfleet and Doctor McCall in *The Colonel's Daughter* where, one 'clear frosty night... they had walked out to the garden gate, where McCall's car stood by the roadside.'[17] Perhaps 'Red Cott' is no more than a Purfleet-type of house.

Lyndale was next, a pretty little cottage where the girls from Bridge House came to live with their mother.

Over from them was a pair of semi-detached houses erected, as the plaque proudly announces, by the brewer John Thomas Strange in 1901. In the first one lived the Brown family who later moved 'up the top' and indeed took over The Round Oak pub. Next door at number two were the Austins. William Austin senior was the chief clerk to the brewery and therefore, if I read Aldington quite literally, the model for Mr Raper in *The Colonel's Daughter*. The then young Leslie Austin remembered the Aldingtons 'very well. I can see him walking down Mill Lane now. He was a thinnish chappie. He had a sort of limp... very thin in those days... and he always walked with a stick... He was always walking. And his wife was a small, petite sort of woman' whom Leslie Austin had always imagined to be French as he found her so attractive.[18]

A bit further down Mill Lane on the left still stands that 'infamous block of cottages' in which dwelt that entirely fictitious and notorious family the Wrigleys of *The Colonel's Daughter*. 'Although their cottage was at the far end of one of the rows in which Craigie stabled his hands, the bull's hide of land on which it stood was exactly on the boundary of the three parishes of Cleeve, Maryhampton and Pudthorp.'[19]

In fact there are two rows each of four cottages here, the first being built, again by the brewery in 1864. The second row as its plaque shows, followed on in 1876. Dave Wickens and his wife lived in number three, number seven was the home of Frank Downham the local postman who delivered Aldington's mail. If we take Aldington literally in his description of Bess Wrigley's cottage as being situated at the far end of one of the rows then it can only have been either number four or eight Mill Lane; the former occupied by a family of which nothing is now known in Padworth and the latter by the Stacey family that I know from experience couldn't *possibly* be the Wrigleys. Nevertheless, we are forced to accept that if ever an item of gossip was to be found abroad in the fictional Cleeve then its origins may well be traced to one of these cottages. 'Mr Raper tattled it to Mrs Raper; Mrs Raper tattled it to Mrs Attwood (who had to do washing because Mr Attwood was frequently, in both senses of the phrase, prone to the bottle); Mrs Attwood tattled it to the Postmaster's wife, who confided it under the seal of secrecy to the Postmaster, who at once ran out to tell the Postman, who delivered it everywhere along with the letters.'[20] The injustice that these cottages represented was to Aldington, in the guise of Purfleet, unacceptable. 'Have you observed that at least twenty-five people have to live in an area about one-half the size of Craigie's own house, so huddled together that when a man coughs at one end of the row Granny Burton drops her false teeth with fright at the other end?'[21] The occupants of all of these cottages would be quite accustomed to Aldington and his friends walking up and down the lane particularly with Harold Monro, the proprietor of the Poetry Bookshop in London who, on one occasion when he was staying at Malthouse Cottage made his presence known in an all too evident fashion by hugging every tree he came across.

The next house, the White House, marked the boundary of the squire's estate, the closest it came to Aldington's cottage at Lower Padworth. The

White House is a high gabled Victorian house shielded from the lane only by a few feet and an intervening hedge, and in the same way that I believe Red Cott to be the fictional home of Purfleet, so the White House, I feel, must be the home of the entirely fictitious bigot, Mrs Eastcourt who was 'one hundred and eighty pounds of monogamous and matriarchal flab, possessed of an unknown but apparently limitless reserve of oleaginous spite'.[22] By virtue of its Victorian proportions The White House is the most dominant house in the lane. Aldington says that 'Mrs Eastcourt's bow-window occupied a position which gave the maximum of observation with the maximum of cover. Unkind people, who exist everywhere, even among folk so neighbourly as the philanthropic Eastcourts, remarked that as Mrs Eastcourt sat knitting in the window with saintly resignation to her infirmities, the window blind was so disposed that she had a first-rate observation post over the whole village.'[23]

The White House seems to have become a lodging house for those of the squire's friends and acquaintances who had fallen on hard times. Major Crook lived here for a period. Moreover, it seemed incumbent upon those who took up residence here to pass on the wisdom of their years and the benefits gained in the far-flung empire on the hapless children at the village school. The school log books, for example, record that Marion Scollick went up there from the White House on 24 May 1923. 'Empire Day was celebrated by special lessons and the singing of patriotic songs. Ms Scollick kindly brought her gramophone and allowed the children to hear their Majesties message to the children of the Empire. C.W. Strange and several visitors were also present.' It seemed the school couldn't get rid of Mrs Scollick. She was back again on 3 August playing her gramophone and on 23 November she and the squire inspected the children's work and she was there again in December the next year 'and entertained the children and parents for an hour.'[24] Mrs Scollick had been preceded at the White House by the widow of Sir James Inglis, at one time the general manager of the Great Western Railway, so well was the squire connected.

Despite there now being an avenue of mature chestnut trees beyond The White House, in Aldington's day the area would have been open to the fields. *'By some unwritten and unspoken convention Mr Judd almost invariably met Mr Raper on these Sunday morning parades, and they would walk together in grave converse… [Mr Raper] walked with his pale freckled hands clasped nervously behind him, an anxious Napoleon of rural industry. Mr Judd, on the contrary, was clad like Solomon in his glory… For a while they walked in silence, Mr Judd admiring the splendour and the beauties of spring … and gazed apprehensively across the placid fields with their rich spring grass and grazing cattle and criss-cross lines of elms, poplars and willows.'*[25]

A few hundred yards further on stands the mill that at one time would have been the industrial heart of the village, for here lies the mill stream, a tributary of the River Kennet. Vivid recollections of the Kennet between here and the water meadows on the other side of the river caused Aldington some years later to set part of his novel *Women Must Work* here. He would have come here, time and time again, it is so peaceful, or was until recently when a fish farm was set up nearby. Had it been in his power Aldington might well have set himself down here for life. By another coincidence the mill itself is now occupied by the son of a friend and contemporary of Aldington to whom Aldington inscribed a number of the books that once more sit on the shelves of Malthouse Cottage. In *Women Must Work* his leading lady takes on Aldington's own aspirations. She knows this area well. On her first visit 'Etta bathed before breakfast, and afterwards explored the tributary in a canoe, going further than she had ever been, until she was halted by a weir and mill-race, near an abandoned mill.'[26] It is alongside the mill that Mill Lane comes to an end. From this point it becomes a footpath over the weirs to the water meadows beyond.

In those days the footpath turned right immediately beyond the mill and ran for about fifty yards past Mill House to the first of the present weirs on the Kennet. It was here that Mr Judd and Mr Raper used to come on the Sunday morning walks. 'The end of these morning excursions had been immutably fixed by Mr Judd at a bridge over a small stream about fifty yards beyond a sharp turn in the road.'[27] The course of the River Kennet beyond the mill has been altered slightly since the 1920s so Mr Judd's bridge may well have been moved slightly. Not so the Mill House though and the Bates family who lived there knew Aldington well. Ron Bates' father used to keep a small herd of cattle on the island nearby and Ron himself used to deliver Aldington's milk. He still remembers him. 'He was an author and used to do a fair bit of walking. He was a customer of ours. I wasn't really old enough to know much but I've read one or two of his books, mind you.' As you go over the first set of weirs there still stands the old generator house that used to provide the power to Padworth House up on the hill. One of the tasks of Ron's father was to 'run the electric light for the big house.' Ironically when I first came to Padworth the owner of the Mill House as distinct from the now converted mill itself was the Hon. Pleydell-Bouverie, the son of Earl of Radnor and a Pleydell-Bouverie, I learnt later, was literary executor to Brigit Patmore, herself a central figure of the Aldington-Lawrence circle and who became another one of those 'contributing factors' that finally made Aldington decide to leave Padworth.

Almost alongside the generator straddling the next weir there is a building that looks more like a boathouse than anything else. Alongside it on the balustrade to a slatted footbridge must be one of the earliest and most incongruous street lights in the country fed presumably by the squire's generator. While long since defunct it would have provided essential light to what would have been a fairly busy thoroughfare in its time. The inscription on the ironwork reads 'Plenty & Son, Engineers' who were based in nearby Newbury.[28] The footpath then drops away to rise again over the main weirs at the point where the Kennet divides on its journey eastwards towards the Thames at Reading. At this point stands the main footbridge over Aldington's Kennet. 'In Mr Judd's childhood this bridge was a sixteenth century stone affair resting in the middle on a large diamond-shaped pile. On each side there had been a triangular recess in the upper wall, where it was pleasant to sit on summer evenings when the old mossy and lichened stones were still warm from the sun.'[29] I could go on – Aldington does – but it's all too much to hope for. There is nothing like it in Padworth, nor, I imagine, was there ever. Nevertheless, this passage demands our attention as it reminds us of Aldington's fascination with the spot.

The Kennet nowadays divides at this point and joins itself again a few hundred yards downstream. Ron Bates recalls that his father leased about thirty acres from the squire, seven acres of which was the island between the two branches of the river. 'My father used to mow that with a scythe. We used to graze cows out there too. We used to take them over a footbridge.' Old postcards remind us of the old mill house as it was before the present replacement was built. It was an old house – one room wide with an L-shaped piece coming down towards the river. Aldington and Arabella would often visit it as on the far side of the island there were 'leafy screens of willows, aspens, and Lombardy poplars, so that we found nooks where, without scandal to the neighbours, we could taste the luxury of bathing without suits.' They were lucky not to be seen though for the use of that pool was not exclusively theirs. Leslie Austin used to go there with his friends when he was a small boy. 'We used to use the swimming pool. Of course it's been altered a bit since then. It used to wind its way round and we had quite a little bathing pool there. It was looked down upon by Padworth House.'

A couple of miles away across the fields to the east lies the village of Ufton Nervet which Aldington tells us in *Life for Life's Sake* 'possessed a fine (E-shaped) Elizabethan mansion, an Italian formal garden, and the remains of fish ponds, dating from the middle ages… [It was the home of Arabella Fermour] to whom Pope dedicated the "Rape of the Lock"… Whether the rape of the lock really happened at Ufton is not known, but I used to tell my visitors the story when I took them to see the house.'[30] Images of Ufton House spring to life in Aldington's 1934 novel, *Woman Must Work*. Dymcott is firmly based on images of Ufton Court but in the novel it is transferred to this one magical spot on the River Kennet at Padworth.

'Gradually and then quite rapidly Etta grew accustomed to Dymcott, then liked it, and at last came to love it deeply, so that her dream of felicity was to live at Dymcott, with Ralph "for ever"'. …and indeed it was a pleasant place. Ada had searched for months before she found it, then waited a year to get possession, and had spent more money than the old house was worth to make it what she wanted. The E-formed Elizabethan manor had degenerated into an insanitary farmhouse; Ada restored it, and modernised the upper floor. Etta particularly liked the old hall, which had been re-panelled and turned into a combined library and music room. The windows looked over the sloping lawns and flower-beds to the river and the wooded water-meadows beyond, with their lines of poplars and aspens, elms and sycamores. The low hilly bank on which the house was built sheltered it from the east wind, and except for the orchard and one small field was covered with beech copses among which stood tall individual trees.

'A passion for solitude sprang up in Etta. Where the high ground suddenly sloped to the north of the house a small tributary ran into the river. Here was a covered boat-house, and a little higher up a small wooded island connected with the land by a Venetian-

arched foot-bridge with a locked gate. On the far side of the islet was a bathing pool. Etta had keys to the boat-house and bridge, and spent the days bathing and on the river or lying under the trees, sometimes reading but more often lost in reverie. The swift lapse of quiet water was very healing, and she loved to watch the aspen leaves quivering over her head and the white clouds moving over the sky beyond them. The river banks were lacey with meadow-sweet, and she gathered the scented water mint, loose-strife, both gold and purple, and the tall rose-bay. The scent of hay drifted over from the shorn water-meadows, and the summer air was moist with sweet river breath. In that charmed interlude of peace Etta forgot shames and cares, past, present and future, called a truce to the mortal strife in herself and with the world. '[31]

Towards the end of the novel the author finally gifts Etta the money to buy the place. '*After dinner on Saturday Etta went out alone into the garden, and walked slowly up and down the lower terrace lawn. The house was hidden from sight by the rock-garden wall of the upper lawn, but occasionally she heard the faint tinkle of a piano. Etta liked this lawn, with the scent of invisible roses in the darkness and the river gently swirling below. At one end was a thick row of tall rhododendrons, and from the other end she could look down on the dark tree-tops of the islet. It was her favourite place in the warm dusky evenings.* '[32]

Aldington wrote this six years after he left Padworth but the memory remained strong for him as well as for his heroine. 'With this recognition came an utterly unexpected flood of memories, sweeping away her mood of exultant possessiveness. For the first time she realised that she had bought something more than Dymcott itself – the obligation to confront the ghost of her own youth and to render an account of what she had done with it.'[33] The final link in this chain of images comes right at the end of the book where we can almost see Mr Bates's cows going over the old bridge to the island. 'Etta opened her eyes and looked about her. If she looked to the right she saw the ghosts of a girl and a young man walking up and down the terrace and then standing in passionate debate in the heavy shadows of the tall rhododendrons. If she looked to the left she saw the trees on the islet, a glimpse of the curved bridge, and knew that from the bathing pool the white ghost of a naked girl was holding out her arms entreatingly and despairingly to the house.'[34]

If anything, Etta might well have been spotted by two gentlemen in the earlier novel. Mr Judd and Mr Raper were leaning on the nearby fictitious bridge. The old stone bridge had long since been replaced by a hideous metal affair much to Judd's chagrin;

> 'Mr Judd regretted the loss of his bridge, but he bowed to the onward march of science and transport. He still had one consolation left in four magnificent elms, which in thirty years seemed scarcely to have changed, except to grow more majestic and spreading, more solidly indifferent to the tearing winter gales. Mr Judd loved his elms. On setting out that morning Mr Judd had reckoned that the first leaves would be on the elms, and looked forward to a pipe and chat with Mr Raper under their green-gold flickerings. Absorbed in his public-spirited reflections on the lamentable spread of crime, Mr Judd had forgotten the elms. Suddenly he halted.
>
> '"What's happened to the elms? Where are they?" There was anguish in his voice. Mr Raper, who was totally indifferent to the spectacle of Nature, replied phlegmatically. "Cut down by order of the Council. There's been trouble with the bridge agen, and Mr Gould 'e told the council the roots was disturbin' the concrete foundations, and the drip was ruinin' the road."
>
> '...Mr Judd gazed at the ruin now revealed to his eyes. Four tremendous stumps, each large enough to make a table, were rawly visible at ground level. The great trees had crashed to earth, splintering twigs and branches with the force of their fall, and the young leaves were already withering. Mr Judd felt confusedly as if part of his life had been massacred.'[35]

To Aldington, elm trees were as essential as the well-being of 'Chaucer's England'. Throughout his writing they were to symbolise everything he valued in the England. In this singularly destructive act his England was shattered. Halfway across this meadow, Aldington might urge Eliot to pause.

> 'Stand here a moment, friend,
> And look across the silent garnered fields;
> See how they turn like huge-limbed country gods,
> Their labour ended, to a solemn rest –

50

A rest so like to death that if they think
Their thoughts are those that are befitting death.
With them is peace,
Peace of bland misty skies and hushed winds
Steadily whispering comfort above them,
Peace of the slowly-rising tranquil moon,
Peace of the sombre woods whose leaves,
Heavily drooping, pine but fall not yet;
Peace that the fruit is plucked, the wheatstalks shorn,
And entered all the increase of the year,
Peace, humble but august.

'Would you not joy to share in such a mood,
The long task fitly ended, peace at heart,
Under such skies, at such an hour as this?

'O friend, why is it that the fields have peace
And we have none? I press my hands
Softly against my aching eyes and feel
How hot they are with scanning many books;
My brain is dry with thoughts of many men,
My heart is faint with deaths of many gods.
I know I live only because I suffer.
I know of truth only because I seek,
Only because I need it know I love... '[36]

Ahead of them lay Padworth House. 'From a distance Padworth House looked like a coloured engraving, illustrating an early 19th-century novel – the kind of place where Mr and Mrs Bennett might have lived. In fact, for all I know, they did live there, for the place is within Jane Austen's limited area.'[37] In late Victorian times Emma Thoyt had placed a small archive about the surrounding villages in the care of Reading Reference Library. Accompanying these were a number of beautifully executed pencil drawings by her mother, I believe, all dated around 1827 just a little after Jane Austen but there is one that would have inspired Aldington. As he says, 'Parts of the estate had that wantonly rustic look of George Morland's pictures – one always expected to see a blushing cottage maid in 18th-century costume emerge from the trees.'[38]

51

Fig. 15. The main approach to Padworth House. Drawing by Emma Thoyt.

The whole of the Kennet Valley has inspired poets and painters alike. A second drawing from the Thoyt manuscripts shows the Kennet almost as George Morland might have drawn it with a distant view of Padworth House between the trees. Chris Strange was frequently spotted walking these fields in his plus fours with an umbrella or sunshade under one arm and his easel and paints under the other. Mrs Hissey remembers him. 'He'd hardly speak to anyone. More like one on his own. He spent hours in his studio… but walked miles to paint.' It was here that Mr Judd and Mr Raper would turn towards Cleeve. Aldington would follow on, slowing slightly, as he began the slope up to Padworth House. 'Beyond the water meadows the land rose on either side, with woods and coppices, which were full of primroses and violets in early spring, and a little later everywhere lay pools and sheets of lovely blue wild hyacinths.'[39]

Aldington's sister, Margery Lyon-Gilbert, has fond memories of the numerous walks they took together as children. 'To walk in the countryside with Richard' she assured me, 'was one of the most wonderful experiences because he knew his English countryside as very few did. He knew the names of all the flowers; he knew the names of all the birds. He knew their habits and their habitat and everything about them. And so it was a lovely experience to go for a walk with him in the country.'

The fields open up again as Aldington and Eliot approached Padworth House. The rutted tracks echo still to the rattle of Major Darby's coach as it headed down to the once gracious 'Gothick fishing Lodge' that lay below them in the valley.

The public footpath claims rights alongside the squire's walled garden and passes through Home Farm. Aldington imagined poetically that the 'park and particularly the grounds near the house had been redesigned by a landscape gardener of the early Romantick epoch. There was an enormous copper beech in just the right place, weeping willows, and a small pond surrounded with dark conifers where one could go and be romantically dismal, or even commit a romantic suicide in the sure and certain hope of being seen from the servants' hall and rescued in time by the butler.'[40]

Even on first encountering Padworth House, Eliot would see the rundown nature of the estate. Aldington tells us that the '...*fences of his estate were rotten and broken, the sure sign of a negligent landowner. His*

Fig. 16. Lower Lodge, Padworth

vast unkempt shrubberies harboured thousands of starlings, and his rookery was the biggest I have ever seen – the nests extended over nearly two miles of trees, and the cawing in March was prodigious.' An air of semi-dereliction that Aldington witnessed still prevails in Home Farm. A barn built in emblematic, Berkshire brickwork still survives but it has long since lost its roof. The Squire *'was always lamenting that he lost money on the Home Farm, and claiming that he only kept it up as a patriotic duty. Instead of having the turf of his park grazed by fallow deer, he rented the land to a sheep farmer. Although his coverts were crowded with pheasants, at Christmas he bestowed on each family in the parish exactly one rabbit apiece… It's a fact that Stimms last year lost five hundred pounds on the Home Farm – about which, by the way, he made a confoundedly indecent bobbery and tried to pose as a universal benefactor to humanity.'[41]*

It was during the early part of 1921 that T.S. Eliot struggled up to Padworth church with Aldington. That summer was an absolute scorcher. The fields were parched and dry. Little imagination is needed to see the lasting effects of that struggle. Eliot's fundamental poem *The Waste Land* was first published in *The Criterion* in October 1922. At the time they walked together in Padworth, Aldington had intense admiration for Eliot's work. Eliot, until recently a clerk in the Bank of England, was largely unknown as a poet but in as much as it lay within his powers Aldington would have moved mountains for his friend. However, theirs was a short-lived friendship. In 1931 Aldington satirised Eliot in a merciless story, *Stepping Heavenward*. But as Eliot himself says, 'with good intentions and clumsy lack of imagination, I hurt his feelings once or twice very deeply indeed. I was the first to give offence, although unintentionally, which made the breach between us.'[42] But Eliot had every reason to be grateful to Aldington at the time and readily accepted the invitations to Padworth.

Ironically, the parkland surrounding Aldermaston Court, the then home of one of Major Darby's neighbours, was bought by the government just before World War Two and became an airfield. These days it houses the government's Atomic Weapons Research Establishment and is no more than five miles from Greenham Common, the home of the American cruise missiles. Part of what was then the Padworth estate now houses what must be one of the most complex collection, storage and distribution points for aviation fuel in the country. Pipes lead directly from here to practically every American and British airbase in southern England. But as Eliot recorded in 1965 Padworth then 'was still very rural and had not acquired its recent associations.'[43] Indeed during those visits there can have been hardly a cloud on the horizon as they walked the last few yards into the twelfth century churchyard. Like Henson they went in through the side gate, and into the cool interior of this historical little Norman church.[44] Padworth church is no different from any other church in that around the walls are the various monuments and memorabilia of the past squires. One, in particular, is interesting for it informs us that below it lie the remains of Catherine Griffith (who died in 1801) who came to Padworth from Scampston Hall in Yorkshire to marry Christopher Griffith (who died in 1776) Major Darby's ancestor. As Aldington points out in *Life for Life's Sake*: 'At the Restoration the heir of the family recovered his lands and married a wealthy heiress.'[45]

One of the rewards of volunteering to advise in the eradication of dry rot from the church in 1982 was that of being present when – following the removal of the entire floor of the church – the tomb below was opened up for treatment. The wealth of the family was immediately evident. The coffins of Catherine and Christopher Griffith lay before us. Each was interred in a wooden box surrounded by a sealed lead coffin only to be clad again in an outer elm coffin and the whole faced with crimson (now faded to chocolate brown) velvet, studded and plated in brass. While some deterioration had taken place, the outer velvet was by and large intact. Not a shred of evidence of dry rot was to be seen within the brick vault. The Brightwell monument at the west end of the church though, was saturated with dry rot spores and has had to be totally dismantled and taken away for treatment. However, as I write (April 1984) it has just been put back. No one would guess the problems it has faced since that day in 1921 when Aldington and T.S. Eliot stood before it: 'Within the church Eliot read with becoming gravity a long and turgid Latin inscription on a tablet surmounted by weeping and nymph like angels of the 18th century, which tablet recorded the marriage of one of the squire's ancestors to a "co-heiress", who had brought him I don't know how many messuages, hereditaments, and cash securities.'[46]

In the churchyard to the west of the Norman tower Aldington would have shown Eliot his '…favourite rural gravestone of the loving couple. Under the name of the wife, who died first, was inscribed: "Rock of ages cleft for me"; and under the subsequent death of her husband was; "Let me hide myself in thee"… Sacred to the memory of Eliza Hawkins who died Nov. 16th 1875 aged 45 years... also of Thomas Hawkins, Husband of the above who died Nov. 15th 1915 aged 81 years.'[47] The spirit of Aldington's 'place' still lingers at this spot often on the most unexpected occasions; in his poem 'Having Seen Men Killed' for example:

'When by chance
As I turn up the brow of the hill,
At a glance
I perceive there's a new grave to fill,
And I see all the poor apparatus of death –

'The straight hole
And the planks and the lowering rope;
And the toll
Of the bell and the mirage of hope
In the words
Duly mumbled for those that remain –

'Then I smile
"Fine morning," nod to the sexton's nod,
For a while
Wonder if Einstein proves or disproves God,
But how soon
Find myself cheerfully humming a tune.'[48]

The Berkshire Kennet
by Richard Aldington[49]

"Amongst the hills and holts, as on his way he makes,
At Reading once arrived, clear Kennet overtakes
His Lord, the stately Thames... [Drayton's Polyalbion]

Turn from the city's poisoned air
And dwell with me a little, where
The Kennet, gently flowing, speeds
His scent of green and bruised reeds
And water-mints that root in mud,

THE BERKSHIRE KENNET

Cordial and faint; or where his flood
Breaks in a low perpetual roar
Beneath the weir, abrupt and hoar
With ragged foam and trembling spray
Whose perfume damps the hottest day
With cool invisible sweet breath.

Old willows, stout, but near their death,
In winter wave their naked boughs
Beside the stream that roughly ploughs
The loose earth from their roots; in spring
Winds lighter than the swallow's wing
Touch their pale fluttering leaves which throw
A green light on the stream below.
The water-meadows, cool and lush,
Fringed with the ragged hawthorn bush,
Bear lonely elms with shaggy stems –
Green petticoats with ruffled hems –
And oaks in distant clumps, as round
As Latin domes, and poplars sound
And tall as Lombard bell-towers, and
Long aspen-screens on either hand.
And all the river's way is lined
With broad reeds rustling in the wind,
And flowers that bend as if they gave
Farewells to every passing wave –
Tall meadow-sweet spreads out as stiff
As Queen Anne's pocket handkerchief;
And amid willow-herb the sprays
Of loosestrife gold or purple blaze;
And August sees the guelder-rose
Hung with her clustered fruit that glows
Robust and crimson, where in June
Gleamed whiter than the ashen moon
The cold and delicate flowers that shine
Upon the thorny eglantine.
And far across the fields and marsh
The peewit clamours shrill and harsh,

Or – out of sight he wings so high –
The snipe falls drumming from the sky,
Or wary redshanks flit and flute
Clear notes to hush their young brood mute.

O solitude, O innocent peace,
Silence, more precious than the Fleece
That Jason and his fellows sought,
Our greatest riches though unbought,
And hard to find and ill to praise
In noisy and mechanic days!
Yet in these humble meadows they
Have cleansed the wounds of war away,
And brought to my long troubled, mind
The health that I despaired to find,
And, while their touch erased the pain,
Breathed the old raptures back again
And in their kindness gave to me
Almost that vanished purity.

Here where the osiers barely sigh
Hour upon hour still let me lie,
Where neither cannon roar nor noise
Of heavy wheels my ear annoys,
And there is none my face to scan
Save some incurious countryman;
And in my cool and hushed nook
I read some old and gentle book
Until in thought I lift my eyes
To rest on dappled English skies,
And hear the stream go murmuring by
And watch the bubbling eddies fly
As Kennet's waters glide for ever
To wed the elder, nobler river . . .

As on the verge of sleep I nod
I see the ancient river god
Lean on his smooth and polished urn;

THE BERKSHIRE KENNET

His hair is twined with rush and fern,
And in his beard are waving reeds
And in his hand are lilly seeds.
Ever the marble urn expels
Cool water, pure as that which wells
From some untainted northern hill;
Ever his languid hands do spill
The flowers that nod and dip and smile
Along his banks mile upon mile,
Nor ever do his green eyes shun
The glances of his grateful son.

And if I now invoke him here
What supercilious lip dare sneer,
What heart that never loved the earth
Dare turn my piety to mirth,
And what vile truckler to the crowd
Scorn me, who lives remote and proud?
Then, noble river, take my praise
And grant me more such happy days,
Each evening bring untroubled sleep
As your own waters still and deep,
If grief come with revolving years
Grant me the saving gift of tears,
Yet as you sparkle on the morrow
Teach me to joy in spite of sorrow,
Send peace as only wise gods can
To the inner and the outer man,
And let my wealth be more or less
So it suffice for happiness,
And keep in my untroubled life
The kindness of a comely wife,
And let the years I have been lent
Bring me not fame but sweet content,
And when my days run out and I
Must go, then teach me how to die,
To leave my well-loved solitude
For an enduring quietude.

Chapter 4

Malthouse Cottage

Aldington's tenancy of Chapel Farm Cottage at Hermitage was not satisfactory for it was sublet from the Radford family and they at times forgot to hand on his rent to the owner of the cottage. 'In fact I should have been evicted if I hadn't gone to a more energetic lawyer than my father.' Neither was his tenancy permanent. He had a year's lease that was due to expire at the end of December 1920. Searching through the archives of *The Newbury Weekly News* one day I was struck by the apparent aptness of a small ad placed with them and appearing on 14th October: '4–6 roomed cottage wanted in any village of Newbury District; within two miles of station: permanent tenant: good rental paid. Box 312.' Various reasons cause me to believe, albeit without any proof whatsoever, that this may well be Aldington's advert. First it is the only one of many which suit his circumstances both in its timing and in the stated requirements. A modest cottage seems to be indicated as the number of rooms was not intended to be the number of bedrooms as might be supposed nowadays. Four rooms would be his minimum and six rooms would cater for his intended library. There is evidence in his autobiography of the appeal to Aldington of the Newbury district and in the context of the times, a two-mile walk to the station was not beyond even the average person let alone a walker. 'Permanent tenant: good rental paid.' It all seems to add up, for in giving his new address to Eliot on 26 November 1920 he puts the word 'permanently' in brackets. While it is only conjecture, it is easy to imagine that the 'impoverished gentry' to whom Malthouse Cottage belonged would have had reason to respond to such an advert. The electoral register indicated that the cottage had been empty for a year. The added income even from a small cottage would have presumably been welcomed in their circumstances.

Aldington needed to travel to London fairly regularly and the fact that this cottage is no more than a few hundred yards from the station would have been fundamental to his decision to come here. On the strength of that alone he may well have come to that decision without seeing the cottage in which case even despite its 'tumbledown' nature the surroundings would have been a bonus. The lethargic flow of the Kennet and Avon Canal past the front of the cottage is even now soporific. Aldington tells us that it was really beautiful in the late spring and summer. It still is. As we step out of our front door of an evening, the sun is setting over the cottages across the canal and our greatest pleasure is to sit on the bank and watch the world go by. 'On summer evenings we [Aldington and Arabella] had dinner out of doors, and watched the light fade and the stars come out as we sipped yellow Puglian wine from tall tulip glasses. I doubt if the gay twenties with their hip flasks and hangovers enjoyed life as much.'[1]

The cottage even at the time I bought it in July 1971 was very basic. It is as Aldington describes it 'built against the end wall' of what was the 'ancient malthouse'. It must always have been a staff cottage for the brewery and was no more than a two-up two-down with the dubious advantage of a second staircase and two further rooms in the attic. In Aldington's time it looked onto a garden, meadows and osier beds that in the intervening years have all been deposed by a rough, copse-like, woodland surrounding 1940s gravel pits. Presumably a lease was quickly negotiated for, on 11 November 1920 Aldington, in writing to F.S. Flint from Hermitage told him: 'Just at the moment I'm busy arranging to transfer my goods to another cottage I've rented…' and on 26 November to T.S. Eliot [from Hermitage]: 'In a few days I leave here. I shall be in town on Dec. 3rd…' For whatever reason though Aldington seems to have opted to forego the stress of the actual move and left poor Arabella to 'fix' the cottage while he chose to 'take a short trip to Devon… Moving is a cheap form of hell.' He stayed at Woodlands Cottage, Hunters Inn close to his friends John Mills-Witham and his wife June, who he had made friends with on his first visit there in 1916. It had been during his stay there, with his wife HD and John Cournos, that Aldington and another one of those living there, Carl Fallas, had received their call-up papers. But by Christmas 1920 Aldington was 'permanently' at Malthouse Cottage. At the age of twenty-eight, he finally had a place of his own. Obviously Arabella had accepted the role readily and he had relaxed a little for in a letter to T.S. Eliot Aldington says he was settled in a sort of indolence which greatly pleased him.

Like HD, Dorothy Yorke was American, and very, very beautiful. In assuming the name 'Arabella' she was doing no more nor less than what was fashionable at that time. Ethel Elizabeth Patmore, who was to succeed her in Aldington's affections, was known as Brigit. Arabella had come over to London on the grand tour with her mother Selina Yorke and had fallen in again with her American friend John Cournos who, Mrs Yorke decided, was a lost cause if ever there was one. Of all those involved in these turbulent passions of pre-war London, Arabella's story is the one that remains to be told. Had Arabella been a writer, or had she kept a diary, her side of the story would make an interesting read, but she wasn't a writer, she was an illustrator. Around the time of their move she had made the drawings for and hand coloured one of Cyril Beaumont's books

Fig. 17 - Arabella Yorke: Drawing of Lydia Lokopova

from the Beaumont Press, *The Art of Lydia Lopokova* was Beaumont's tribute to the Russian ballerina who was to become the wife of Bloomsbury economist John Maynard Keynes. Nine of Arabella's drawings of Lopokova, as well as a portrait by Picasso, accompanied the five pages of Beaumont's 'appreciation' of her performances that had stunned London in 1913. Arabella had also designed the cover for this slender book and would have spent many an evening colour washing her illustrations, presumably to order, in the weeks perhaps before and after her move here with Aldington.

The Newbury Weekly News records that the weather for the first fortnight of 1921 was unusually warm and sunny. Obviously, the mild weather, the new cottage and his evolving relationship with Arabella, all contributed to a peace of mind that he had thought would forever be denied to him and as the year progressed, the weather continued to improve. To Lawrence, spring came to symbolise the end of the harsh winter that was the First World War. Aldington's memories of the trenches, where a single blade of grass would have provoked comment, is significant to an understanding of his new found optimism and the delight he found in his surroundings. As in this extract from a letter of 7 April 1921 to Amy Lowell:

*'There is a hill close to my cottage which is the most marvellous
wild flower garden you can imagine. Think of a slope of about six
to ten acres, facing the sun, with a few largish trees and some
scrub, all of whose area is a mosaic of white anemones, blue wild
hyacinths... large dog violets of several shades of light blue to
dark blue and clump upon clump of the richest yellow primroses
with little clusters of wild thyme. It is simply the most flowery
place imaginable it would delight you with its freshness and
extreme richness.'*

The same sentiments can be seen in a letter of 13th March 1921 to Harold
Monro of the Poetry Bookshop in London. 'I am temporarily sheltered
from misfortune and I have enjoyed this spring more than any since I was
a boy... I like this little cottage.' It is evident from *Life For Life's Sake*
that others did too; when fine weather returned, and particularly if there
was a hot spell, Aldington was astonished to find how many friends felt
so affectionately towards him that they simply had to come and spend the
next weekend with him. But his letters to Harold Monro, for example,
suggest that it was Aldington himself who was anxious to share his
cottage with his friends. At times he cajoles and pleads with him to come
down. He seems to think that the countryside would benefit his friend
equally as much. He takes a sly dig at Monro's problems in his letter of
20 March 1921.

I think my cheerfulness comes from
1. *An active liver*
2. *No alcohol or tobacco*
3. *Daily cold baths and walks*
4. *Discreet use of venery*
5. *Plenty of BOOKS*
6. *No newspapers*
7. *£7 a week.*

Despite the enjoyment of Arabella's company, Aldington yearns to see
his old friends and to be able to share the experience of exploring his new
village. Again, in the same letter, he urges Monro to join him: he could
show his friend some pleasant walks, Elizabethan houses and some empty
cottages. This letter carries a suggestion that Monro should abandon

London entirely and move to the countryside. Whether or not Monro ever had any intention to do so, I cannot say, but Aldington had first raised the matter a week before in his letter of 13 March 1921: 'If you want a cottage I have seen five empty ones within a few miles of here.' Although he never took up Aldington's more permanent suggestions Monro did come down on a number of occasions and from Aldington's report of one particular visit seems to have enjoyed himself well enough. It is possible to build up a picture, an ever changing picture, of the nature of the cottage during Aldington's time here. As Aldington was a smoker and enjoyed a drink, number two on his list of virtues is difficult to accept. His sister Margery told me that 'Richard was so poor he allowed himself one packet of ten cigarettes a week and one pint of beer.'

At the time he went on active service Aldington was twenty-four years old and had been married for three years during which time he and H.D. had done no more than form a base camp for whatever the future held for them. With a bitterness that came from hindsight, Arabella blamed his parents for his chauvinistic attitude to women. She remembered his father as studious and weak and likened his mother to an egotistical and sometimes maternal barmaid[2]. As a result he would not find it easy to take on a responsible role in society and would instinctively shy away from the demands that it would make on him. What he wanted from life was to be left entirely alone, to be exempted from any responsibility whatsoever, let alone that of fighting a war that was none of his making. It was the futility and destruction of war that most exasperated him, particularly as it applied to his own personal circumstances. For following his demobilisation, he had to rebuild his entire life. When he and Arabella came to Padworth she can have had very little to 'fix'. His sister Margery recalls from her visits to the cottage that he or Arabella had made 'most of the furniture upstairs (from) packing cases.' Living conditions at the start were obviously rough, she recalls. 'I think there was an outdoor privy somewhere.' For disastrous reasons during the Second World War the lean-to at the back of the cottage was apparently totally rebuilt in the brick form in which it exists today but in the 1920s things were different. In those days it was 'a long low kitchen' I am told by his sister. 'I believe that they used to cook on a Primus stove in that outhouse…That was all they had, I'm almost certain.' There was no gas and they used lamps and candles. 'I always associate that with the smell of paraffin because they had a paraffin stove.' Margery also has strong recollections of Arabella, or 'Dolkins' as she was known, in the kitchen. 'I used to see Dolkins behind the door stirring something on the stove.' One of Aldington's prime pleasures though was gardening which was just as well for its produce would be essential under their penurious circumstances. His sister, again: 'Richard used to tickle around growing vegetables which of course they were very glad of.' But of course he had work to do and inevitably there would be conflicting priorities. He told Harold Monro that at one moment he was putting up a scarecrow in the garden and still had about a quarter of an acre to dig before the end of the month, added to which he hadn't begun an article for *The Times* which had to be in by Monday morning.

That was a Friday, so he obviously had a busy weekend. To be stuck indoors that spring would have been a tedious necessity. Or perhaps he took his work out into the garden; the weather would be warm enough. He did not to know it then but 1921 was to be famous for its heat and lack of rain. No doubt the garden would have suffered. In November 1982 the original private water supply from the long-disused brewery was finally disconnected from the cottage. Subsequent owners had offered a large contribution to the water board as an inducement to bring mains water to the south side of the canal. It is to be assumed that Aldington's supply would have been equally erratic and that alone would have prevented excessive plant watering.

In early April, Aldington's leisurely outlook on life was to be disrupted once again. His escapist nature was quietly cocooning him in the cottage and he was free of all demands on him except those imposed on him to make at least a modest living from his writing. Already he had established a bridgehead for what was to become a lifeline to success in later years. He was writing regularly as a reviewer of French literature for the *Times Literary Supplement* and among a variety of other duties and projects had taken on the role of assistant editor for T.S. Eliot's *Criterion*. For the first time since before the war his reputation was beginning once more to grow.

He was totally unprepared therefore for the death of his father. Not only would he be deeply moved but he had to attend the inquest and that brought back the horrors of the Artois and the Somme. But the death of his father did more than deprive Aldington of his closest parent; it was to impose on him a burden of responsibility that he could well have done without. He was obliged to take on a father figure role for his younger brother Tony and the elder of two sisters, Margery – a role for which he was entirely unsuited. He also had a younger sister, Patricia, who was little more than a toddler. Despite the miles that separated them he would also, no doubt, have increasing demands from his mother. Somehow though he seemed on the surface to be coping better than might be expected for five months later he told Amy Lowell that life was at last what he wished; quiet and laborious among books in the country. He was forming the nucleus of a little library and his only anxieties were about the extreme difficulties of house tenure and the education of his brother and sister. Whether he found the means to help his mother financially is not known but by that time Jessie May Aldington had firmly established herself as a successful hotelier.

Fig. 18 - Jessie May Aldington

T.S. Eliot was the first of his visitors that summer. Despite Aldington's admiration of Eliot's poetry, he recognised his pious side (which he was to explore ten years later in a satirical characterisation of Eliot in *Stepping Heavenward).* In a letter to fellow poet F.S. Flint we hear that: 'one, Master Thomas Eliot, (my singular good friend) hath honoured me with his presence this Pentecost.'[3] He even puts Eliot into a passing role in *The Colonel's Daughter* as the Reverend Thomas Stearns and again as a critic, Mr T.S. Pym. There is in each of the above snippets a suggestion of the *Portrait of a Genius... But* attitude with which he was later to discuss his relationship with D.H. Lawrence. Furthermore, and it may only be a small point but, there is a strong local indication of the different attitudes he had to his various visitors. With the likes of Harold Monro, the Lawrences and F.S. Flint he is quite happy to have them stay at his house. We read, for example, in a letter to Flint of 1 March 1921: ' ...come down, my dear old lad, by all means; I shall be happy to see you... just as soon as I can, I am going to get a larger bed, so that you and your wife can run down from Sat to Mon...'[4] and a week later came the suggestion 'that if our room by chance is occupied, we can get you one nearby...' or 'you can get put up near (about 200 yards away) provided you are not too middle class in your ideas to object to a pub.'[5]

Flint, he knew well enough would be happy in The Butt Inn. Not so T. S. Eliot or later, Herbert Read or Henry Slonimsky. There was never a suggestion that they would be prepared to slum it at the cottage or even at the Butt and they stayed at the superior, yet still modest, Hare and Hounds. He knew from experience the standard of accommodation to which D.H. Lawrence and Frieda would be accustomed and at the time they visited the cottage in 1926 there is no mention at all of alternative accommodation. It is to be assumed that by then he had got his larger bed and knew that the Lawrences would be quite happy with it.

In the summer of 1921 Aldington was well enough settled to be able to take a short break from work. I would be glad of the rest, he told Holbrook Jackson in a letter of 7 July. For despite all the signs of improvement that can be gained from his letters he was still suffering from the effects of the war. Most of July was spent on the first of his long walking tours, through the West Country and Wales, the pleasures of which were given to his fictional heroine in *Women Must Work*. While he was away the annual temperance fete was held in the grounds of Padworth House. Despite the connotations of the name this was a grand occasion. As far back as 1907 special trains had been laid on from all the nearby towns to bring the hundreds of visitors to Aldermaston Station. From there they would follow in the footsteps of Aldington and Eliot along Mill Lane across the meadows and up the hill. Those from the surrounding villages arrived in some style on whatever farm carts could be

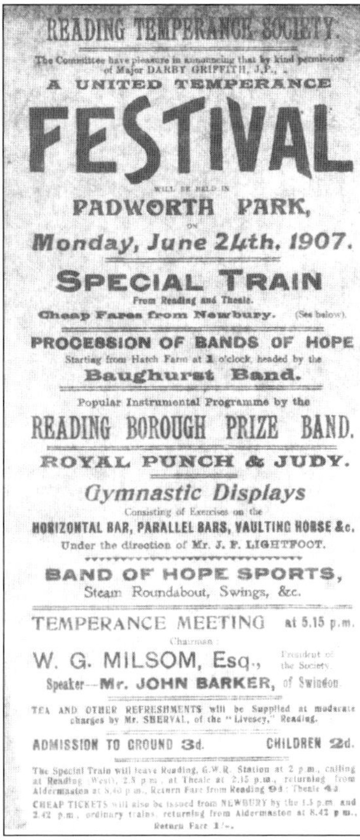

Fig. 19 - Reading Temperance Society Poster. 1907

mustered to carry them. Had T.S. Eliot in fact taken up the offer of Aldington's cottage he could have had a most stimulating time here. On the day before, the school log book records that Sidney Stacey, the son of Aldington's near neighbours, has been unwell from eating green fruit. He would have missed out too.

Despite these visits of friends and Aldington's now weekly visits to London to see his editors, there can have been very few people among those he had known before the war with whom he could talk of shared experiences. It is no surprise therefore to find that, refreshed from his fortnight's holiday, he dropped everything to visit his ailing friend the writer Frederic Manning. Manning, like Aldington in later years, suffered badly from bronchial attacks which were often accompanied by severe asthma. At that time, Aldington was finding it difficult to concentrate. He had been suffering eye strain and took time out to play with the cat, Mrs Todgers who was one of two or three half-wild cats who lived on the plentiful mice in the old malthouse next door. As part of Aldington's tenancy he was bound to look after the cats, a duty he readily accepted.

The remaining walls of that part of the malthouse now form the boundary walls of our neighbour's garden at Number 2. The floor has long since been removed and dug over to form the substance of her vegetable plot and lawn.

Leslie Austin remembers the malthouse as a 'big tower-like thing... two or three floors high ... with a vent on top.' The servant girls from Bridge House used to call in at odd times: 'That was in use when we were there. They were malting there then. We used to go down there and watch them turning the malt over. There was a lovely smell from it. Oh, it was great!'

Mrs Florence Emily Smith was the only person living in Padworth when I set out on my search that I knew may well have been around in the 1920s. She and her little dachshund had practically worn their own little path from Number 4 Mill Lane to the shop by the bridge. She was born in 1892, the same year as Aldington. I was therefore disappointed to learn from her that she had no recollections at all of him although this probably because they both had reclusive natures. After her marriage in April 1926 Mrs Smith moved only three doors away from her family. Her brother Frank Downham was the postman who delivered Aldington's letters. Mrs Smith does have memories of village life. One is of the local celebrations of the Relief Of Mafeking (the end of a famous Boer war siege). 'I was about eight then. I remember the postmen getting on top of the railway bridge and waving their caps.' Another is of the malthouse before the time that Aldington lived there, before the time even when 'old' Dave Wickens, her next door neighbour at Number 3, worked there. She has reason to remember Mr Strudely, 'old' Dave's predecessor as maltster. 'He's my godfather. He used to come out from Reading and do the brewing... He'd stay six weeks. As his godchildren we used to take potatoes down there because he used to have this big furnace to heat the floors to dry the malt and the barley and we'd cook our potatoes in the ashes.' Obviously, though, things cannot have been very much different by the time Aldington arrived in 1920 for he says that Mrs Todgers was attracted by the anthracite fire.

In the context of our times the word 'servant' is severely frowned upon and yet all those years ago the employment of a local lass would be the norm for anyone whose background was situated at least a couple of rungs up the ladder. Early on in my searches I was unaware of quite how penurious was Aldington's situation at the cottage and I remember asking Margery whether he had help in the house. With fiery Aldington pride she told me quite categorically 'No, no! After all a man who only treats himself to ten cigarettes and… a pint of beer a week didn't employ labour in a little place like *that!*' It was said with such strength that it completely dispelled further speculation on the subject. In June 1983, though, I had the unexpected pleasure of seeing before me a name with which I was more than familiar. Towards the end of 1981 I realised the time had come to make a search through Aldington's letters to see what – if anything – they might tell me about his Padworth. Norman Gates' *Checklist* records the existence of more than 7,000 of Aldington's letters now in university libraries all over the world. It took me the best part of a year to collect copies of practically all those available that were written at this cottage and to bring them all back again.

The Humanities Research Centre in Texas is rather like a Fort Knox of literature. Among the thousands of letters in their archives I was given a list of the hundreds either to or from or about Padworth. It proved far cheaper in the end to take up their suggestion and to pay a researcher to go through them all for me. My brief to Donna Stewart was a slightly odd one; all I wanted was the 'Padworth bits.' Among the notes I subsequently received was an extract from a letter from Aldington to his friend Glenn Hughes the American writer. Hughes and his wife were to stay at the cottage in autumn 1928 while Aldington was in Italy. Aldington's list of instructions and advice to them brought my search right back into my own life. The key, he told them, was with Mrs Stacey, 8 Mill Road who would help with arrangements for milk and bread, and will lend them bread on their arrival. I have to confess here that I had known of the Stacey family years before I had even become aware of Padworth for the granddaughter of Mrs Stacey had remained a close friend since we first met in the days of our impressionable youth. Furthermore, her then friend – I discovered to my amazement – is the granddaughter of the 'robbin' 'Oods' at the Hare and Hounds. Obviously towards the end of his stay here Aldington's circumstances had improved sufficiently to allow Arabella some help around the house and garden.

Virtue number 7 on his list to Harold Monro in March 1921 was the precarious '£7 a week'. In a letter of 19 May 1927 to Crosby Gaige, we learn that his annual income had only risen to £400 a year and yet a year or so later, with the patronage of Gaige, he earned £1000. Things had improved rapidly. His rent when he arrived at Malthouse Cottage was 11/6 a week which by the time he offered the house to Harold Monro in a letter of 3 September 1923, had gone up to twelve shillings (either that or he was hoping to make sixpence a week profit). Just before he finally left Padworth he made arrangements to pay Mrs Stacey an extra five shillings for all the trouble she had taken in sorting out his correspondence. At this later period Aldington was also getting help in the garden for in a later letter he tells Hughes to use the vegetables and, if the garden is very untidy, to ask Mrs Stacey to send her little boy round to do some gardening. Two phone calls later and I knew which one of Mrs. Stacey's little boys used to do the garden. To think that I had been so close to him for years was really quite amusing. I had already taken quite a liking to him when I had recorded a note from the school logbook of 20 July 1925. 'Edwin Stacey climbed the roof of the shed and interfered with a wasp's nest after direct prohibition. He was punished with two stripes on the hands.' He obviously had more respect for Aldington than he did for the headmistress for the entry continues: 'He afterwards left the school premises on his own notion. His mark is cancelled.'

As a child, Aldington's life-long interest in books and literature had been stimulated by occasional forays into his father's library. Eventually, some of those books were to find their way to the cottage and Aldington was making contingent arrangements to cope with them. Years later when writing his autobiography in America the strongest memory of the cottage was of his books. On his final journey away from England he couldn't help thinking fondly 'of my cottage under the tall willows by the canal and wondering who now lived in it, and how it looked without my solid walls of books.'[6]

For his sisters Margery and Patricia, the memory of his books remains firm among many others they have of the times they stayed at the cottage. Margery gave me her memories. 'As you approach the cottage the canal is on the left. You came up the drive past the buildings of the malthouse and the cottage was at the far end.' What is now our back door being then where the 'original door faced onto the garden looking towards the fields.

It was just a wooden door. I think it had a funny wooden porch to it. Along the continuing bank of the canal, beyond the point where the lane stops, were 'conifer trees, tall conifer trees' the existence of which is confirmed by the old ordnance maps and by the photo that Mrs Smith gave me of her and her cousin on the opposite bank. The cottage still had essentially the same accommodation when I bought it as Aldington had when he was there. We took out the bookshelves that Mrs Waghorn would have inherited and built the bay window to Aldington's study at the front – the parlour that is now the sitting room. Behind that we converted his living room into our kitchen. These notes are being written alongside my collection of Aldington's books in what was Arabella's lean-to kitchen at the back but in its original state there were only the two rooms on the ground floor of the cottage. Patricia Aldington recalls it though as it was in the 1920s when she visited as a young girl. 'There were three rooms on the ground floor. The [front] door was sort of centre on to what I call the centre room.' So does Margery. That was the room 'with the table where they had their meals'. The confusion of memories continue: Patricia remembers 'Richard's study... with books all over the place.' Margery told me: 'There was a wood fire in that room... I remember that... This was the only fire in the house.'

One whole section of the Aldington correspondence that Donna Stewart sent back from Texas concerned the relationship between Aldington and another of the original imagist poets, his close friend F.S. Flint. The impression gained is that, in the company of Flint, Aldington felt truly at ease. He became the man he would wish the world to remember and there seemed to be a spontaneity in him that was not often seen at Padworth. Frank Flint and his family were fairly frequent visitors to the cottage and following one visit in July 1922 another piece of furniture arrived at the cottage. 'We enjoyed having you here so much and hope you'll come again. Encouraged by your musical aspirations and achievements we bought for a few pounds an old harpsichord that we are having repaired and tuned. So the house will resound to the music of Czerny, until we learn how to play simple songs. Later you must tell me how to get Elizabethan and Jacobean music.'[8] By the time that Lawrence visited the cottage in 1926 the 'piano' as Aldington refers to it in *Life for Life's Sake* was then decorated with a bust of Voltaire, an emulation of whose life Aldington was often thought to be struggling to achieve. It was only later though that I was to discover that Margery Aldington and her friend may well have been as influential as Flint in her brother's decision to buy the instrument. Margery remembers the front room was 'where he had got his spinet and his books'.

Patricia, his younger sister was only seven when she first came to visit her brother. 'I was put on the train and I think Richard met me. I think he had to go to London – if I remember – and he took me down to the Malthouse. I stayed there two or three days. I played the piano. Richard made me practise.' At the time he bought it, however, Aldington couldn't play it. Margery who shared his love of 18th century culture remembers his attempts 'trying to teach himself to play 18th century music. He used to sit there tinkling at it.' It was not that Aldington had very high aspirations to produce music though and in another letter of 4 March 1923 to Flint he indicated where the musical talent was to be found. 'Now won't you try to arrange a weekend in the spring. Bring your Elizabethan music and Ruth shall play to us. We will allow you to sing in rationed periods.'[8] Whether Arabella had talents in this direction we may never know but in a later letter to John Cournos she does have something to say on the matter of Aldington's pretensions.

Sadly, I have been unable to gain any insight into Arabella's true contribution to life at Padworth. Twenty years earlier though and I might have been able to bring back a portrait of her to hang in the cottage for in the Cournos correspondence Arabella asks quite casually whether he knew of anyone who might like to buy a portrait of her by Lawrence. That portrait now forms part of the Norman Holmes Pearson archive at Yale. As time passed Aldington and Arabella were beginning to accumulate the trappings of a more established home. As well as the books from his father's library, the front room, Margery told me, gained 'a certain amount of furniture my mother gave him. He got a few fine pieces.' And if his letters are anything to go by, it would appear that he treated himself to a typewriter for Christmas 1922 for in January we see the last of his handwritten letters, bar the occasional exception.

Whether he ever succumbed to the receipt of a daily paper must remain a mystery but he told Flint in a letter of 5 February 1925 that he would be desperate for news were he not able to tune in to the BBC. Aldington ended his army career as a captain in the 9th Royal Sussex Regiment. His job was to relay signals between units in his jurisdiction. As he would have been proficient in morse code a note to Flint comes as no surprise. 'You will be greatly amused to know that my mother insisted on giving me a wireless crystal set, to my great distress. Fortunately it works so badly that I can neglect it.'[9]

By the time he left the cottage though, he had reached his original expectations as far as the number of books goes. According to his autobiography he eventually had five or six thousand permanently at the cottage. In addition, he would take out fifteen at a time from the London Library, particularly to coincide with Lawrence's stay here in August 1926. He describes his hearth on a variety of occasions, the intimate geography of which he would be well familiar having spent so many sleepless nights studying it. His father's deed box was in the cupboard under the stairs which contained all his junk and periodicals, for similar copies of which I am now having to pay anything between £5 and £20 in an effort to reconstitute something of an archive. Vast numbers of his books can be individually identified from his letters to Glenn Hughes. There was a May Sinclair article here, one by Alec Waugh there and upstairs in the bedroom bookcase – third section from window, shelves three and four from the floor – could be found his own translated *50 Romance Lyric Poems* and *The Love of Myrrhine and Konallis: and other prose poems*.   An article by Ludmila Savitzky was gummed into *Simplicimus* and was amid the junk under the stairs. And on a half empty shelf midway under the Roman classics lay the typescript of his long poem *A Dream in the Luxembourg*. The fact that it was in such a position seems to suggest that it could easily be seen. I only hope that Arabella was unaware of its contents as it was written for Brigit Patmore. A good number of his books were well within reach of the disdainful Mrs Todgers: Bayle's Dictionary lost the labels and most of the gold tooling from its four vast folios and a precious Liddell and Scott had to be moved to another shelf to save them from her claws.

At the time Aldington took over Chapel Farm Cottage at Hermitage, Lawrence had left England for good. With the exception of a few short visits he never lived in England again and he had been away for a year when Aldington came to Padworth. Aldington first met Lawrence, who was five years his senior, in 1913 and from the beginning was stimulated by his charisma. Lawrence's apparent indifference to what society might expect from him obviously appealed to Aldington. Lawrence was impulsive; Aldington was not. And yet Aldington's was not a devotional admiration. They recognised each other's weaknesses and said so.

Aldington recognised the 'genius' in Lawrence as a writer and took every possible opportunity to defend the man against the prevailing criticism and played some part in Lawrence's general acceptance after his death. But when public acclaim began to turn from objective admiration into hero worship it was Aldington who was to remind people of Lawrence's human side. The fact is that between 1919 and the summer of 1926, they had not seen each other. The thought that they might now do so now pleased Aldington enormously: 'for me the greatest event of that year was the return of the Lawrences from America to the European scene. I had not seen them since 1919 and our correspondence had been extremely irregular.'[10]

Aldington's instinctive reaction was to shrink away from anyone who he sensed did not welcome him with completely open arms. He would be well aware that Lawrence couldn't do with his hypersensitive nature and that he did not wholly reciprocate Aldington's admiration. Aldington says: 'And now most surprisingly [Lawrence] wrote from London suggesting a meeting. I promptly wrote and invited the [them] for a long week-end, and in accepting Lawrence sent me some of his recent books which I had not read.'[11] Aldington must have described the primitive conditions of the cottage and made self-effacing comparisons with Chapel Farm Cottage. That Lawrence was equally pleased, though, to have re-established contact with the chance that it offered of a weekend in Berkshire may be judged from his warm, generous response: 'Your letter this morning. Sounds nice, your little cottage (no, don't mention poor Margaret Radford, God's sake!) Don't talk nonsense to me about primitive conditions, do you imagine I've suddenly turned up my nose at the brass tacks of life: I wash dishes and cook soup same as ever – a little better, I hope.' There was even a suggestion that Aldington and Arabella go for 'a stroll round Tuscany and Umbria' with him and another suggestion that Aldington had at least run through events of his life since they had last met. 'Seems to me you need a bit of fresh ground' was Lawrence's judgment. 'I should very much like to come down and see you when I am in England – whenever that will be! So would Frieda (Arabella, we are expecting your letter full of feminine information) – perhaps in July or August. I thought Padworth was somewhere else – in Sussex or somewhere.'[12]

In fact, within little more than a week of their arrival back in England, Lawrence and Frieda arrived at Malthouse Cottage. They came down from London on Friday, 6 August and returned on Sunday. 'The visit began a little inauspiciously, as Lawrence declared the cottage was "sinister". I can't imagine why, as it was sunny and full of books, with bright window curtains and a smiling head of Voltaire over the piano and the garden was brilliant with late summer flowers. And then I had forgotten that in the Midlands you show your respect to a guest by loading the high-tea table with enough provisions to stuff a dozen policemen; so Lawrence was greatly offended by my modest and wineless meal. All this was happily settled by a bottle of whisky for him to have a hot toddy at bedtime, a habit of his which was new to me and had apparently been acquired in America. After that he was in the best of spirits and good humour for the remainder of his stay.'[13] That Aldington was very proud if not deferential to have had Lawrence and Frieda as his guests is plain. He discusses the visit at such length that one might imagine their stay was a fortnight long at the very least. He shows all the classic symptoms of anxiety in his efforts to make them welcome. He had already made arrangements to contrive a meeting between Lawrence and a 'neighbour of ours' and had organised a ready supply of books at hand on a topic which he knew Lawrence was particular interested:

'As I knew he was contemplating a book on the Etruscans, I had a dozen standard works on the subject sent down from the London Library; and we spent a good deal of time turning them over and discussing Etruria, which was very important at that time in Lawrence's private mythology.' He talks of their walks as if they had tramped the country-side for days on end and gives the impression that he had sat, dog-like, night after night allowing Lawrence to hold court. 'Best of all perhaps were the evenings when we sang old English and German folk songs, according to the Laurentian custom, and Lorenzo and Frieda talked of their wanderings and adventures.'[14] Practically every topic of conversation between them is recorded. It is known that the Lawrences were back in London on the Sunday so all this took place in barely forty-eight hours, two evenings at most. Even fifteen years later when Aldington wrote his autobiography he tells of the weekend with an immediacy that suggests that he kept a diary or at least a note of what was said: 'The upshot of this was that I wrote a pamphlet about Lawrence and some of his books, in which I abandoned the hocus-pocus of 'objective' criticism and the desiccated style it imposes, and wrote entirely from my own feelings and allowed my words to flow spontaneously… It seemed to me the most lively piece of prose I had written… To my surprise, Lawrence was not displeased with this pamphlet, but in his letter he said: "It's more about you, my dear Richard, than about me." And I dare say he was right.'[15]

Lawrence's response of 24 May 1927 is interesting. *'Many thanks for your Indiscretion. No need to be in any trepidation on my account – you hand me out plenty of bouquets as you say: I shall save up the ribbons. But caro, you are so funny. Why do you write on the one hand as if you were my grandmother – about sixty years older than me, and forced rather to apologise for the enfant terrible in the family? Why will you be so old and responsible Sei un qiovanotto un piu crudo, sail! And on the other hand, why do you write as if you were on hot bricks? Is the game worth the candle, or isn't it? Make up your mind. I mean the whole game of life and literature - not merely my worthy self. You don't believe it's worth it, anyhow. Well then, don't worry any more, be good and commercial. But don't, don't feel yourself one of the pillars of society. My dear chap, where did you get all this conscience of yours? You haven't got it, really…What ails thee lad?… Tha's got nowt amiss as much as a' that.*'[16]

It appeared to those who knew him well that Aldington had been so badly affected by the war that it was as if he was permanently disabled; his actions had been paralysed by his experiences. It has long since been proven that Lawrence's writing follows directly upon his experiences. Within a very short time Lawrence transfers life to fiction with an immediacy the merits of which have often been questioned. My findings suggest that this was a major influence on those of his friend.

It is believed that Lawrence's close scrutiny of Aldington may well have suggested the disabilities with which Sir Clifford Chatterley was to suffer in *The First Lady Chatterley* and that the inspiration for the book itself may well be traced to Lawrence's weekend at Padworth. It is known that Lawrence started writing that first draft version within a matter of weeks of leaving the cottage, indeed as soon as he would have been in a position to be able to do so and there are indeed certain passages that conjure up a firm picture of Aldington in the character of Sir Clifford Chatterley. Sir Clifford loved a beautiful landscape and flowers and took an aesthetic pleasure from art, pictures and books. The only thing that troubled him, however, was that he was awake a great deal during the night. It was on one such night that Aldington found himself in the coal shed at the back of the cottage where Mrs Todgers demanded his presence while she gave birth to a litter of kittens.

Chapter 5

The Search for Mr Brown

'Down 'ere we gives that there stuff to the pigs.' Of course! This was the clue that had been there all the time and yet I had failed to appreciate its true significance. As time passed I began to realise that there was very little in *The Colonel's Daughter* that wasn't based on real people, real places and, on occasion, even actual events. And yet the inspiration for his prime character, Mr Judd, remained elusive. I had searched in vain for someone in Padworth who would fit the characteristics of Mr Judd. Admittedly, I could see that he could be based on any of two or three people. After all, Aldington tells us in *The Colonel's Daughter* that the secret of Mr Judd's consequence is easily explained. 'He was chief foreman and rather more than half the brains of the small factory at Cleeve.'[1] Translated into real terms, and even making allowance for the 'fancy and caricature' he mentions in his autobiography, this meant that Mr Judd must have worked at Strange's Brewery and that immediately narrowed my search. Everyone that fitted those particular circumstances had passed on but I had, in most instances, managed to trace their relatives and had learnt enough to convince me that while the circumstances of Mr Judd's employment were real enough, the people who held these positions did not entirely suit the fictional character I was looking for. Obviously, I had to go back to my sources. I must have read all Aldington's novels and short stories at least twice during the course of these literary excavations and was therefore digging for the third time when I struck the obvious: Tom Judd just had to be Mr Brown. 'I liked Mr Brown very much. He was a genuine *terrae filius*, as close to the earth as the placid cows and elms of the landscape.'[2] This was praise indeed from Aldington.

Mr Brown in his many guises represented all that Aldington required from his fellow man. He and Mr Brown obviously got on well. 'He approved of most of my horticultural ambitions except in the matter of spinach, concerning which I had imbibed the townee's faith. He crushed me by saying briefly and decisively: "Down 'ere we gives that there stuff to the pigs."'[3] Mr William Brown was Aldington's next door neighbour at Hermitage but from even the very few factual references to him it is obvious that he played a major part in Aldington's novels. Aldington was to use Mr Brown repeatedly but in no more significant instance than one passage in *Women Must Work* where the statement is this time attributed to Mr Crowder.

> 'Enthusiastically Etta began to dig over the vegetable garden, and at night went to sleep over seed catalogues and a book on how to organise a garden. The affable Mr Crowder, always ready for a crack, liked to lean on the wall and enjoy the spectacle of Etta's unhandy struggles.
> Diggin' up the garden like?" he suggested.
> "Yes", said Etta, tugging away at some pestilentially long roots of bindweed. "I want to get it started in good time."
> "Shallots coming along?"
> "Shallots? I haven't planted any. Ought I?"
> "Maybe you don't care for pickled onions?" said Mr Crowder apologetically. "Some ladies finds 'em strong, but I always says they goes tasty with a bit of bread and cheese. They says round here you plants shallots on the shortest day and pulls 'em on the longest, bit of superstition like. But it ain't too late to put 'em in."
> "I wanted to grow some spinach."
> "Ah, spinach, we gives that to the pigs here."'[45]

That the 'affable Mr Crowder' was based on the real William Brown had seemed obvious from the first time I had read that extract but it had now dawned on me that while Mr Judd worked in the fictitious Cleeve, I would have to go back to Hermitage in my quest to find him. In *Life for Life's Sake* Aldington informs us that: 'It was December [1919] when I moved to Hermitage, and for much of the time I was entirely alone.'[5] During the following year the one person who he would be in almost continuous contact would be his immediate neighbour, Mr Brown – not forgetting Brown's wife and family, of course – and a great deal of Mr Brown's rural wisdom would become etched on the author's subconscious later to manifest itself in at least five of his stories and novels in one form or another. Aldington's friend Thomas McGreevy managed to read *The Colonel's Daughter* just before his book *Richard Aldington: An*

Englishman went to the printers in 1931. His impressions of the novel and of Mr Judd in particular, therefore appear almost as a 'stop press' item in the final chapter. 'Mr Judd is the England that Englishmen fought for in the war. Their England is neither the Colonel's Empire nor Mr Purfleet's Bloomsbury. It is Chaucer's England, Shakespeare's England, Fielding's England, the England that had worth centuries before an Irish Peer invented Empire Day.'[6]

Already I was intrigued to see whether my intuition could be proven. It would be fascinating to see if Mr Brown bore any resemblance, for example, to Aldington's description of Mr Judd:

> *'In appearance Mr Judd resembled an upright, cleanly and intelligent porker. It is impossible to say whether this was a protective disguise, hastily assumed by the family on Darwinian principles of adaptation to environment, or whether Judd's Saxon ancestors by long habitation among pigs had become piggy. He was at any rate an unmistakable Nordic blonde. His bristly gold hair was cut short, his blue eyes gleamed with the baresark intelligence of the Northmen, and a line drawn perpendicular to the tip of his turned-up nose would have plunged some distance into his good round belly... He wore a splendid suit of rich brown reach-me-downs with a distinctive lavender stripe, a pair of glorious tan boots which proclaimed rather than squeaked his approach, a brown felt hat one size too large, an imitation malacca cane with a false agate handle... A large, possibly gold, chain was draped across the swelling curves of his waistcoat, and displayed to an impressed and astonished world two Alberts and a Queen Victoria sovereign fantastically secured in a baroque setting.'[7]*

Little has transpired in the time since Aldington left Padworth to change the immediate neighbourhood around his cottage. There are still one or two people around who remember him and practically all the references to village life come from the very small community of Padworth. One need travel no more than a quarter of a mile or so to track down the entire cast of *The Colonel's Daughter*. But it began to dawn on me that I had blinkered myself to the obvious. Aldington tells us that he moved 'from the Hermitage cottage to another about fifteen miles away in the valley of the Kennet, in Berkshire.'[8] The return journey to Hermitage, both in time and space, proved in the end, to be fairly simple. Hermitage, Aldington tells us 'belied its name, for it was a nondescript straggling hamlet without charm or antiquity in rather featureless country. The absence of a parsonage and manor house showed it was of recent growth, and I could never imagine why it had grown at all, for there was no local industry and the farmland was poor',[9] a point with which, I now know, some of the 'hermits' would wholeheartedly disagree. It was unique in one small respect though. It had straggled far enough to warrant two stops on the now defunct railway coming north from Newbury.

Lawrence and Frieda were offered the use of the cottage by Dollie Radford after they were expelled from Cornwall in October 1917 where they had been accused of sending signals to the enemy. It hadn't helped that Frieda was the cousin of the ace German pilot, Baron von Richtoven, The Red Baron, but the accusations were unjust. Their correspondence shows that Aldington took over No 1, Chapel Farm Cottages after Lawrence departed in 1919.

The area around Chapel Farm Cottages is known as Little Hungerford. In Mr Brown's day – more so than now – it had its own separate identity. The brick built bridge that carried Chapel Lane over the railway line at Little Hungerford is still there though and so is Bill Adnams. Mr Adnams lives in Bridge Cottage, where he was born in 1898. When I interviewed him he was 85 and his recollections were leaving him but like a lot of the older 'hermits' he remembered Lawrence walking up and down the lane. Mr Adnams' parents used to be the landlords at The Fox, the pub down the road and they moved to Bridge Cottage just before Bill was born. On the main road, just opposite the point where Chapel Lane joins it is a private house. Still known, apparently, as 'Simonds Plough' this used to be the nearest pub to Chapel Farm Cottages.[10] The mere mention of its name brought back one or two memories for Bill Adnams. 'It used to be run by John Wells and his wife' who, it turned out, were Bill Brown's uncle and aunt. Evidently Bill Adnams 'used to do a bit of singing in those days' a common pursuit in Hermitage at that time, I was to learn later, 'and John's daughter used to play [piano] for me.'

The starting point in my search for Mr Brown had to be Mrs Tucker at No 1. 'Yes,' she had heard of the Browns and knew all about the Lawrence connection with her cottage too. She had even started a little notebook as a visitors' book. I was very proud to add my name to the surprisingly few entered there. In addition to two Japanese men and one or two fellow natives was one name I knew well. Professor Norman Gates of Rider College had come on to us at Padworth almost immediately after he had written his name here. As with all her visitors, Mrs Tucker very kindly showed me round the cottage. Like my own it has been extended in recent years but it was essentially recognisable and retains the tranquillity that Aldington talks of. The room where we all imagine Lawrence to have done most of his writing remains practically untouched. In fact, shortly after she moved in, Mrs Tucker came across a silver teaspoon down behind a cupboard somewhere. Despite the improbability of it all, a monogram on the handle does appear to be an entanglement of the letters D, H and L. As for the Browns, Mrs Tucker could tell me nothing but she promised to ask around the village for me and try and find someone who could set me on the trail again.

Despite the fact that word follows word on the page like this, there are large gaps in time before events link up. Names have been stored away waiting for some key incident or event to bring them to the fore again. I had long been intrigued by the Radford family. I had even opened a small file under their name occasionally adding to it as I read of their significance to the circumstances at No 1. Lawrence refers to the daughter Margaret whose occasional flights from London demanded his and Frieda's exit either to Mrs Lowe, the local shopkeeper, or to Grimsbury Farm at the other end of the village where they camped until the cottage was once again vacated. I learnt that Margaret's father Ernest Radford was a member of Yeats's Rhymers Club, a group of poets who, in the 1890s, would gather to read and discuss each other's poetry. I had become a connoisseur of indexes and in this context I came across a whole column of Radford references in *Eleanor Marx* the biography of Karl Marx's daughter by Yvonne Kapp.[11] Dollie Radford was a friend and confidante of Eleanor Marx. I wrote to the publishers and received a letter from Yvonne Kapp giving details of Dollie and Ernest's granddaughter who in turn wrote telling me that her mother, Dr Muriel Radford, was in good health and living in a rest home in Minehead in Somerset. Then came another letter, from Dr Radford herself, inviting me down to meet her. 'Please be prepared to meet a white haired old lady, aged 92' was how she introduced herself. As far as I was concerned, all the events into which I was prying had all occurred at such a long time ago that they may just as well have been fiction from the pens of the people who I was investigating, but here I was about to meet a lady whose family circumstances were crucial to the whole business at Chapel Farm Cottages.

Armed with books and photographs that I thought might act as *aides-mémoire* I drove to Minehead on 27 November 1981 and met this high-spirited lady. I learnt from her daughter that Dr Radford appeared to gain a great deal of pleasure from my visit but that can be of nothing compared to my own. Here I was talking to a lady who had known D.H. Lawrence and H.G. Wells. Her knowledge and recollections ranged way beyond my own blinkered field of interest. Within minutes of arriving though, Dr Radford told me she had no recollections at all of Aldington at Chapel Farm Cottages and I sensed that I may have entered a cul-de-sac in my search for Mr Brown. However, over the next two hours or so I recorded a conversation that proved to be far from the case. While memories of Mr Brown in particular were slender, the circumstances of life going on around him were to be wonderfully illustrated. Regrettably though these words have to be written in memory of Dr Radford because, she died soon after I interviewed her, in March 1983.

Hardly had I arrived and introduced myself before Dr Radford gave me a book of her husband's poems that she had already signed and inscribed for me.[12] This led on to her vast range of recollections of such friends of hers as H.G. Wells, Eleanor Farjeon, the Meynell family, Edward Thomas, Clifford Bax and many others. It was a tribute to her memory that I took up much more of her time than I had imagined I would and I learnt so much from her. Thankfully Dr Radford must have sensed my pleasure for my responses continued to provoke more and more memories. I only wish I knew that much more as I feel we could have gone on for hours, yet she continually asked whether she was boring me. At one stage I mentioned that I understood that Dollie and Ernest were friends of Yeats.

"Of who?"
"Yeats. The poet."
"Oh, W.B.... Were they?"
"Yes, because I believe that around the turn of the century Yeats formed what he called the Rhymers Club. ... "
"Oh yes. YES!"
" ...and I believe that Ernest was one of the members.

"Well Ernest was, I think, secretary or treasurer of the Arts Society wasn't it? The Arts and Crafts Society."
"Really! I didn't know."
"Yes, I think I'm right in telling this and when Wilde called there and wanted information, Ernest – who was secretary – was always out and so Wilde thought that Ernest must be a very important man, you see. And – I am told – that's how The Importance of Being Earnest was written... Well now, you can take that as only a fable, but that's what I've been told."

Some months later I visited Mrs Tucker again and she gave me the name of someone from Hermitage that might lead me to Mr Brown. I went round immediately and found the lady in question only to have my hopes dashed as she couldn't help. 'Try Mr Rouse over the road though,' she said. So over the road I went. Luckily Mr Bert Rouse was in but, again, his memories were very few. In any event, as I was later to discover, his memory had already been tapped and recorded by Paul Delany in his book *D.H. Lawrence's Nightmare*.[13] By this time I was ready to give up and go back home when Mr Rouse asked whether I had met his brother who lived over the road. So I found myself knocking on the back door of a bungalow two doors away from where I'd started. It was late afternoon and the lady of the house was busy in the kitchen but, from the conversation we had through the kitchen window, I realised that I'd been lucky again. I only hope that Mr Rouse's meal wasn't spoilt as a result of Mrs Rouse's spontaneous recall of practically everyone connected with Chapel Farm Cottages. Not only did she remember Aldington but gave tantalising snippets of information on his sister Margery who, I discovered, had evidently lived nearby. Mrs Rouse also remembered Aldington's companion, Arabella Yorke. There was only one name on which Mrs Rouse needed the slightest prompting. I briefly explained why I thought Mr Brown was so important to Aldington. Suddenly I was engulfed in a loud chuckle. 'I shouldn't be at all surprised because he was a character. Oh yes, he was! Oh dear yes! He used to be the gardener at Southwood – you know, the big house on the Yattendon Road. He was real Berkshire – but he's dead now. They've all gone now except his daughter Hilda. There's no one left around here that could give you her address. She'd be an old lady now, if she's still alive!'

I couldn't help but feel that this really was the end of the search for

Mr Brown. There was just one thing that Mrs Rouse had said that brought out the optimist in me and that *had* to be followed up before I finally gave in. Mrs Rouse thought that Mr Brown's daughter, Mrs Cotterell as she was now known, had gone to live in Slough. It had to be worth a letter to the *Slough Observer*. This is something that I'd done on a variety of other occasions in my search for past Padworth residents but with little success, so I held out no great hopes. But I had found Mrs Rouse and that alone had to be worthwhile. I have to admit that I had to pester her till she agreed to let me come back one evening and talk to her and her husband, John. 'I really can't think that there's much more that we can tell you.' How often that statement had proved to be far from true in the past. The truth is that while people may not have specific memories of those in whom I may be interested, they give a unique insight into the life of the village of the time that does not come across in any academic texts.

At about half past seven the following Wednesday evening, I was settled into a comfortable chair in their sitting room and was introduced to Mr Rouse and their dog. With the approach of Christmas, mince pies and ginger wine came out and I sat back and enjoyed their company. Mrs Rouse's chuckle proved to be dangerously contagious and Mr Rouse's memory, I soon discovered, equalled Mrs Rouse's. I told them that I'd written to the *Slough Observer* but I didn't know when, or even if, they had printed my letter. It had occurred to them that the only person they could think of that may be able to help me was Charlie Sharpe. 'He'd know Bill Brown as well as we did, or even more as he lived closer to him. His sister has just died. She was ninety. Hilda Brown used to write to her every Christmas. Charlie is older than his sister so he must be over ninety now. They were all strong Methodists and all went to chapel.' This, the first real evidence I had of Mr Brown, was not encouraging. If I was to take Aldington literally, the knowledge of Mr Brown as a chapel-goer did not suit my theory about the fictional Mr Judd as he 'rarely attended church and never chapel. The Chapelites, he understood, were no friends to beer, while Mr Judd, in this alone resembling Boswell, liked to promote a friendly glass.'[14] Nevertheless, from an intimate knowledge of Aldington's humour and from what flashed through my mind as Mr Rouse recalled Mr Brown, I became convinced again that I was on the right trail. 'Oh but he was a wonderful character, old Bill Brown was,' he assured me, 'and he had a son, Arthur Brown. He was a terror, an absolute terror.

He was a seaman in the First World War. He got killed on the railway in Reading. He died a very young man.'

Little prompting was needed on my part to release a dam burst of further memories. Mrs Rouse, as I've hinted before, loyal to her village, couldn't agree with Aldington's description of it. 'We've lived in Hermitage all our lives and I don't agree with him. When he was here there was just this road and the two lanes with Chapel Farm cottage on, and very little else but we did have a vicarage. The road wasn't tarmacced though. It was more like a lane – so dusty in summer.' Mrs Rouse had good reason to recall this. At the time I was concerned with – from 1917 until late 1920 – Mrs Rouse's parents, Mr and Mrs Boshier, kept the post office in Hermitage; in fact it is still in the family now. At that time though: 'You could never leave a window or a door open because shoals of dust came in. The post office is so near the road.' The only difference between the post office as it was and as it is to be seen now, is that the army recruiting poster from the First World War has been taken down from the side wall. 'There was nothing then, and when we wanted the roads made up the old man from the railway used to bring a horse and cart and used to leave big flints and the steam roller used to roll them in with water. All up this road here you'd see they'd tip them up on the banks and they'd stay there until they came and repaired the holes. It wasn't till the thirties, I suppose, that we had the tarmac road – early thirties. We used to have a railway here that kept us in touch with people. Apart from that you just had to walk to Newbury.'

Chapel Farm Cottage is really two cottages, or rather a pair of semi-detached cottages, both of which at that time went under the same name. They turn their side to Pond Lane and look down it so that in order to get to the front door of No 2, the Browns would have had to walk across the front of No 1. This shared access is something to which Lawrence, having been brought up in a mining community, would have been totally familiar. The cottages would even have been similar in size to those in which he was brought up. The only difference was that Chapel Farm Cottage was one of a few only, scattered around the lanes. All we know from published sources of Lawrence's Hermitage connection is that it was due to Dollie Radford's generosity that Lawrence was offered the use of the cottage; but why Hermitage, I wondered. In that connection I turn again to the conversation I had with Dr Radford for among the many, many friends she talked of, perhaps her fondest memories were for the Meynell family who, at that time were living at Pulborough in Sussex. 'I've often stayed there… Greatham was the big house. Wilfred Meynell bought it. It was a small estate really and Monica lived at one end; she was a daughter. Another one, Francis Meynell, lived in the converted cowshed. Pru – Viola – lived there and she was our friend really. Pru – Viola Meynell – married a local farmer and their house was quite close to Greatham, the big house. It was a lovely place to stay. There was a very big room downstairs with a parquet floor, so when Monica, Francis and Pru had house parties you were able to have a little dance in the evening and you could walk outside – just under the Sussex Downs.' Lawrence is known to have stayed at Greatham as the guest of the Meynells. Dr Radford recalls that the Meynells 'were very good to Lawrence and in one of his novels he's very unkind about them. He writes very disparagingly… about them… I was rather annoyed with Frieda because she started running down the Meynells. They were friends of ours you know.'[15] Dr Radford together with her husband Maitland once stayed at No 1 shortly after their marriage in 1917. This would have been at the time when Lawrence was still in Cornwall and not too long after Maitland had made a journey to Cornwall to see Lawrence. It was just before Christmas of that year that Lawrence and Frieda first made their base at Hermitage.

Lawrence obviously had a great deal of respect and warmth towards the Radford family, perhaps with the minor exception of Margaret as it always seemed to be her visits to No 1 that made him and Frieda temporarily homeless. On Maitland's marriage to Muriel, Lawrence and Frieda gave them a pair of china Staffordshire dogs which Dr Radford still proudly displayed on her mantle piece when I met her. They are a matching pair of greyhounds each with a hare in its mouth. 'Those were a wedding present from Lawrence and Frieda. They're Staffordshire ware. Maitland said that they were typical of Lawrence's writing, a mixture of cruelty and beauty, and I can see what [he meant] because Lawrence was a mixture like that, wasn't he?' Dr Radford remembered her first meeting with Lawrence: 'It must have been at Well Walk, at Dollie's.[16] But I remember he was very tall and slim… And red-haired… When they were turned out of Cornwall they turned to Dollie to ask her to find rooms for them… You know he was an exhibitionist. I remember him being… at Well Walk – 32 Walk – in Hampstead. He wasn't receiving enough attention so he began doing a sort of *pas seul* around the room you see. He had to be the centre of a party. Well that's the impression I got. Well *you* wouldn't begin doing a 'pas seul' around the room, *would* you?'

With the strength of her memories for other people, I was convinced that Dr Radford would have a well of stories of Bill Brown for me but, again, I was to be disappointed. They only stayed at the cottage on the one occasion and all that she could tell me was that it was Mrs Brown who came in to help out with the housework. It seems that Mrs Brown, as much as her husband, went with the cottage for in a passage from *Life for Life's Sake* that had first caused me to wonder whether Arabella had had help at Padworth, Aldington tells us of Mrs Brown's role at Hermitage. 'While Mrs Brown was clearing up after dinner I stepped into the garden for a few minutes, as I usually do at night.'[17] But in *Women Must Work* Aldington takes us inside his neighbour's cottage. 'The large kitchen, in which the Browns mostly lived, had an open fireplace where Mrs Brown cooked, a plain brick floor and raftered ceiling. The floors of the upper rooms undulated where the wood had warped. Mrs Brown apologized for these defects.'[18] Etta, the heroine of *Women Must Work* 'could hear Mrs Brown's voice scolding and reproving, as she washed and dressed the children, and began tidying up the house'.[19]

Dollie Radford was under extreme pressure after her husband's death in 1919 and the health of Margaret, who was not the strongest of girls. Dollie's son, Maitland, was studying to be a doctor and Hester, her other daughter, was studying art at The Slade School of Art and so both were well able to look after themselves, but this was not quite so with Margaret. Aldington knew her by sight as she had been a student at London University at the time he was there. 'She was a strange, fragile, over-sensitive creature, shrinking from realities and drifting about the college like a wisp of unhappy thistledown.'[20] Dr Radford confirmed this. 'Margaret wasn't at all strong… She was a very delicate person, you know… Yes, but very gifted.' In fact, Margaret was a published poet just like her parents. But under these circumstances, Dollie dreamed of going somewhere the family could get away entirely from Hampstead. Dr Radford told me 'the cottage was really bought for Margaret, for her to get out of London.' In fact, the Radfords didn't actually buy the cottage; they leased it. It was owned by Mr Goodman, a retired builder from nearby Beedon. Mrs Rouse remembers Margaret Radford well. 'You see, they called her Daisy… and I used to go up there to tea with Daisy. She was a grown-up person but she was childish and I used to go to tea and play daisy chains, and things like that, with her. I do remember that. I used to go up there… in the field. There was a field in front of the house in those days and we used to go and pick daisies and make daisy chains. I remember that and she always was a princess… She was a teenager but quite prepared to play with me, and I was seven or eight, on my level, making daisy chains and just playing. She was always a princess, she was airy-fairy… A very attractive girl, I remember, thin and fair, I think… She *was* like a Princess to me. I don't know why.' This suggestion of Margaret as a 'princess' is a link with D.H. Lawrence's short story of the same name. The fact that the fictional princess is American does not detract from the thought that Lawrence laced his knowledge of the Radfords into this story, particularly as he had reason to recall Margaret.

The fictional Urquharts christened their daughter Mary Henrietta: 'She called the little thing My Dollie. He called it always My Princess.'[21] The similarities with Lawrence's princess continue. 'She was a quick, dainty little thing with dark gold hair that went a soft brown, and wide, slightly prominent blue eyes that were at once so candid and knowing. She was always grown up; she never really grew up. Always strangely wise and always childish.'[22] Mrs Rouse again: 'I don't know why… It is easy to read between the lines of Lawrence's text to see the similarities. She was given to wearing cloaks and capes instead of coats… and little eighteenth century sort of hats. Her complexion was pure apple blossom.' One can even see similarities between the lifestyles of the Urquharts and the Radfords. The Urquharts, for example had: 'a tiny but exquisite house in London and another small, perfect house in Connecticut, each with a faithful housekeeper. Two houses, if she chose. And she knew many interesting literary and artistic people. What more?'[23] Colin Urquhart, Mary's father, bears a fictional resemblance to the Ernest Radford that both Lawrence and Aldington knew. In *Life for Life's Sake* Aldington tells us of Ernest Radford in pre-war days. He was 'losing his mind, and his contribution to the talk was an occasional impressive belch, which we ignored like perfect little ladies and gentlemen.'[24] Lawrence has similar recollections. 'Her father however, was ageing, and becoming more and more queer. It was her task to be his guardian in his private madness.'[25]

It is difficult to imagine a more unlikely couple coming to live for intermittent periods in a country village like Hermitage than D.H. and Frieda Lawrence – particularly during war time when all other able bodied men would be fighting at the front. The more so as Lawrence's appearance, by all recorded accounts, was quite remarkable. Everything about him would have drawn attention from his new neighbours. Over six foot tall with ginger hair, blue eyes and a ginger beard 'Lawrence was out*standing*,' Mr Rouse recalls. But what would have raised eyebrows as much as anything was the fact that Frieda was German. They first came to stay at No 1 just before Christmas 1917 and yet with the stoicism of Aldington's Mr Judd the village accepted Frieda almost without question. 'Well I suppose she could speak English but not very well – sort of broken English' Mr Rouse recalled. 'But oh!' Mrs Rouse recalled, 'she and Daddy got on so well. I can see them now laughing and talking over the counter.' It seems that the news of Lawrence and Frieda's hasty exit from Cornwall at the sharp end of a police warrant hadn't got as far as Hermitage by this time and the village was unaware that it was playing host to two refugees. That their appearance caused gossip and chatter at the start of their stay is without doubt though. Mrs Rouse confirmed this. 'Nobody knew who they were for a long time… My sister was working in London at that time. She was in the civil service and came down one weekend and Lawrence was talking to my father in the post office and she said, to me: "That's D.H. Lawrence, surely: What's his name?" So I said, "I don't know his name." And she said: "But it's exactly like D.H. Lawrence." So when Daddy came in, she said, "What was that man's name?" and it was "Mr Lawrence" of course… and she said, "But that's D.H. Lawrence the writer! Well then you see it was all stirred up in the village. People were interested to know who he was and why he'd come and that sort of thing.'

It's odd how often things go round in circles. I had previously traced a Mrs Adams in connection with Aldington's stay in Padworth only to discover that her late husband Wally had lived near Chapel Farm Cottages before they were married. The Rouses remember him well. Mrs Adams remembers her husband talking about Lawrence: '"I can see him now," he would say, "striding away in his walks. He used to go off in a long cape and a big black hat."' This talk of Lawrence's attire brings to mind another delightful memory recounted by Mrs Rouse. Frieda 'would come in every day to have a talk to my father. She was a plump woman – [with a] German housewife sort of style   and I remember them laughing and talking away and then she brought Lawrence in once, because my father used to sell men's clothes and Daddy got him to buy a pair of flannel trousers for 5/- and a blazer with red, white and blue stripes. Nobody else would have been seen dead in it, but Lawrence bought it. I've forgotten what he paid for it… [I heard that] in one of Catherine Carswell's letters she wrote that Lawrence told her that he had to wash these flannel trousers at night and hang them out to dry because he hadn't another pair to wear.' I showed Mrs Rouse the photograph of Lawrence wearing these trousers that appears in Keith Sagar's book, *The Life of D.H. Lawrence*.[26] He and Frieda are standing at the front door of Grimsbury Farm. Below the photo is the Catherine Carswell quote that Mrs Rouse remembered.

Since Mary Rouse had been the one to recognise Lawrence in Hermitage she obviously had good reason to take a particular interest in his fortunes. She read Catherine Carswell's letters and sent her sister 'a cutting about it… The blazer was startling, red, white and blue. It would have been in the shop forever; no one else would have bought it! Daddy used to laugh.' By all accounts Lawrence and Frieda lived on next to nothing during the time they were in Hermitage and I must have said as much because Mr Rouse was quick to tell me: 'But he always had money for beer! He used to drink a lot of beer!' As a boy Mr Rouse used to live near the Plough. 'That's where I used to see Lawrence. He came over there with his jar for his beer in the mornings. He used to come over there – well, daily – for a jar of beer, a gallon jar, yes!' Mrs Rouse remembered him: 'here at the cottage when they used to come to Mrs Lowe's. He used to take the water jug from the basin upstairs to get his beer from The Fox.'

Mr Rouse remembers the effect that Lawrence's presence used to have on another local resident. 'Well, she used to spend a lot of time in the Plough too… She used to drink a few pints! She always said that he reminded her of a walking Jesus. Well, he used to walk simply, very quietly. And she was just an ordinary person – a housewife. Perhaps a little bit quaint, but not what you'd call… soft, and she was always talking about him. "Here he comes again!" she'd say.' But as Mrs Rouse told me: 'Well they were very poor I'm sure because my father used to give them things out of the garden, you know, whatever we had, vegetables or a lettuce or something, and [Frieda] was so delighted. I suppose it was through her that [Daddy] got Lawrence to buy the trousers. I suppose she said, "You go down to Mr Boshier. He'll show you some trousers!"'

From the picture that was emerging of Mr Brown I can't imagine that he would have approved whole-heartedly of the Lawrences getting their vegetables anywhere other than from him if indeed he had failed to get them to undertake any gardening for themselves. If Aldington's experience is anything to go by, Bill Brown would at least have tried. In Aldington's novel *Women Must Work* a stalwart Mr Brown and his wife proved to be a double attraction without even a change of name. Mr Brown becomes the fictional neighbour to two young ladies who make a valiant, yet unsuccessful, effort to live off the land. 'Just look at that garden – we could have more flowers as well as vegetables – and those meadows with the buttercups just coming out. Isn't it all heavenly?'[27] Bill Brown must have left his mark on the garden here in Padworth, too. Aldington says 'I designed the garden myself and stuck to the cottage tradition, i.e. plots for vegetables surrounded with such old-fashioned English flowers as clove pinks, phlox, Sweet Williams, hollyhocks, sunflowers, columbines and poppies. It was really beautiful in late spring and summer.'[28] It still is; the tradition remains – as do the descendants of most of his flowers. Aldington was to pepper his novels and stories with Mr Brown's gardening lore. Despite the fact that he has already fictionalised Mr Brown once in *Women Must Work* the book also features a Mr Crowder – the one that feeds his spinach to the pigs. At one stage in this hall of mirrors Aldington throws up an almost defiant clue to the combined identities of the fictional Mr Brown and Mr Crowder. '"Brown," said Mr Crowder reflectively, "was a middlin smart feller…"'[29]

One passage in *Women Must Work* that I turned to brought John Rouse up with a start. I read: 'pigs, cows, chickens and rabbits can't be docketed "to be fed to-morrow" when something else urgent crops up – they have to be fed to-day. True, the cow-herd, Tom, ploddingly looked after them, but …'[30] Mr Rouse stopped me in mid-sentence; he was that cowherd. His first job, as a boy, had been as cowherd to Mr Cook who then ran Chapel Farm across the lane – immediately opposite the front entrance to Chapel Farm Cottages. 'Well I must have seen him… as, at that time I used to work for a smallholder who kept a few cows, and I used to have to go out into that field in front of Bill Brown's house looking after three or four cows because there wasn't sufficient fencing around.' And indeed Aldington must have seen him too. 'Honest as he was and hard-working, Tom was one of those people who get on with their own jobs and assume that other people know theirs.'[31] John Rouse was delighted. He spent many a day looking after the cows. 'I remember, on one occasion, I was playing [in the field] with another boy and [the ball] went over and hit Lawrence's door. He soon came out to find out what was going on.'

There are so many parallels to be drawn between Aldington's *Women*

Must Work and Lawrence's well-documented Hermitage story, *The Fox,* that Aldington might be accused of plagiarism. The fact that Aldington places two women on an unsuccessful small-holding seemed too much of a coincidence and yet I was puzzled as to why Aldington would choose to lay himself so wide open to such a charge. I felt there must be something more to it than that. I was now getting confirmation though that the rural setting that Aldington uses was in and around Hermitage, as I had for a while suspected, and that only seemed to reinforce the charge. The fictional Browns were after all 'renting a small holding in one of the home counties'. Paddington was the station from which they left London and the two girls in the story, at one stage, 'waited for the local train on the platform of a small junction.'[32] In those days you would leave Paddington and change trains at Newbury for the branch line to Hermitage. I thought I'd try out another passage from the book on Mr and Mrs Rouse: Etta, I read, 'learned how and when to feed the fowls and where to look for the eggs, under the guidance of Mrs Brown's Gladys, a small solemn child pallid from too much potatoes and pork.'[33] Enthusiastically, they told me exactly what I wanted to hear. 'Yes, that would be Hilda, Mr and Mrs Brown's only daughter. She was a little old-fashioned girl.' I hoped that Hilda, now Mrs Cotterell, if ever I found her, wouldn't be hurt by such a description. It was said with no malice.

I knew that the two women in Lawrence's story were modelled on Miss Lambert and Miss Monk who put up the Lawrences at Grimsbury Farm when Margaret Radford came down. I mentioned this to Mr and Mrs Rouse and told them that there are published letters from Lawrence to the two ladies. Mrs Rouse was quick to respond: *'Yes and there was another one! There were three of them! Miss Furlong was the other one. I liked her… Dear old Miss Monk. They were old maids but in the end they got married. I remember Miss Monk coming round to Mrs Lowe one afternoon when we were having tea and she'd brought her husband – or fiancé – and she was about fifty or more! She got married and so did Miss Lambert… As children, we used to think of them as old maids – in their fifties at least."* Mrs Rouse at that time, used to go to dancing classes at Grimsbury Farm: *'Yes, that was with Miss Furlong and Miss Lambert and Miss Monk. Miss Lambert trained us and Miss Furlong played the piano. No! Miss Monk used to play the piano – of course she did; the dark one. [At one time] they got an old army hut… on Cold Ash Common and dear old Miss Monk lived in the most dreadful old shepherd's van. I used to deliver the letters to her… the old Grandfather was there [at Grimsbury Farm] the old Mr Lambert. He was …yes, that's why Miss Lambert lived there. He had to be put in the kitchen when we went to dancing classes.'*

Quite some time after I had written my letter to the *Slough Observer*, long enough for me to have concluded that maybe they didn't print it, or that I was entirely wrong in my assumptions, the phone rang and there, at the other end of the line, was Mrs Hilda Cotterell, Mr Brown's daughter. The fact that she had seen the published letter was pure chance. I don't remember that it even registered with me as, in my excitement, I was already some way ahead of the conversation. In my mind I'd found Mr Brown and couldn't wait to meet him, even though I had learned that it was to be a posthumous meeting. I collected together a mass of information to take with me: books, photographs and, most useful of all, the information I'd already learned. My meeting with Harry and Hilda Cotterell was rather akin to a family reunion. I felt that I knew Mr Brown quite well. Indeed, on this first meeting I could just about recognise Aldington's description of Mr Brown's daughter as 'solemn' but that was only in contrast with a quite disarming smile of welcome. In fact, I hadn't been very long in their company before I plucked up courage and introduced Hilda to her fictional counterpart and that produced a very bubbly chuckle indeed. Mrs Cotterell seemed quite intrigued and immediately produced a photograph of herself at the time that Lawrence and Aldington were in Hermitage. The Chapel, a primitive Methodist chapel, from which both the farm and the lane, and indeed the cottages, derive their name, evidently stood right next door to Chapel Farm Cottages. Sadly, though, it too has had to give way to the pressures of modern development. It was 'a very tiny little chapel. [My father] went every Sunday and after Sunday School about three or four children would come in at the end of service [to leave their books] and we used to go off for a walk with him.' The photograph, which includes young Hilda's cousins, was taken just before setting out on one such walk. Chapel Farm Cottages, in those days, were almost as primitive as the chapel next door. Both cottages, Mrs Cotterell told me 'had two rooms downstairs and two rooms upstairs' but so did most rural cottages at that time. There was no water supply laid into the cottages and it wasn't until some years later that a standpipe was installed and even that was outside in the garden and had to be shared by both cottages. Before that 'everyone had to go down the road to get water out of a well' and carry it back home in buckets on a yoke.

Despite the fact that I have visited the Chapel Farm Cottages a number of times it is very difficult to imagine exactly what they would have been like when the Browns were there. For one thing, I was to learn, the cottages were covered in a mass of ivy which blocked out a lot of the light from the windows and which Mr Brown trimmed back each season. But, naturally, the garden made up for everything that was lacking in the cottage although I was to hear Mrs Cotterell talk of it with the same dispassionate modesty that I suspect Aldington found so fundamentally disarming in her father. 'We had quite a decent back garden [but] not much in front…We used to go up the steps to the back garden and there was a huge garden at the top with a greengage tree.' There was a pig sty there too both in real life and as Aldington recounts in *Life For Life's Sake*: 'Mr Brown knew a great deal about pigs and had interesting anecdotes about those animals, though I am bound to admit that he considered them less as a philosopher than from the point of view of their market value and edibility.'[34] Mrs Cotterell's descriptions were recognisable as the cottage that I had visited as well as being the one in which Aldington had lived. 'The farm was over the road and there was a pond there at one time. At the back of the house was a wood.' This was where Aldington, in *Life for Life's Sake* 'stood listening to the silence, gradually discerning the dark bulk of the knoll behind the cottage with its jagged fringe of larches black against the stars.'[35] But 'in front of the house there was just a field,' (the same field in which 'Tom, the cowherd' had looked after his flock).

It is fascinating now to think of the Browns going about their daily business with little concern for the constant comings and goings next door in No 1. Aldington gives the heroine of *Women Must Work* the same sentiment. 'At dawn she heard Mr Brown get up and re-kindle the kitchen fire before he went out. Then she could hear Mrs Brown's voice scolding and reproving, as she washed and dressed the children, and began tidying up the house. And so they worked the whole day through, never hurrying but going on persistently in a slow rhythm which Etta found very soothing. She envied their placidity and tried to imitate it.'[36] As we are already aware, the walls of the cottage were so thin that the one side could hear a great deal of what was going on next door. Aldington, at least, was well aware of this. 'At first [Etta] was distressed by the sudden sharp quarrels of the Browns which occasionally disturbed the peace with oaths and cries, but they passed as suddenly as they arose, leaving everything as it had been.'[37] Aldington was a far more reserved man than Lawrence and he and Arabella would have kept their disagreements quiet but with Lawrence and Frieda the situation was quite different and would be more in line with the Brown's quarrels. Mrs Cotterell was perhaps too young to be aware of the darker side of Lawrence's nature and has her own unique memories of him. But she does recall her father's attitude to Lawrence. 'Some of the time he thought he was sensible, but a lot of the time he thought he was a fool.'

The way in which Mrs Cotterell recalled these observations seem to echo precisely what Aldington found attractive in her father. Not because of the particular views he expressed, but in the unconcerned way in which he expressed them. Despite the obvious friendship between Aldington and Mr Brown one cannot help but see, on Mr Brown's part, a certain reserve in his attitude and, again, it is that fundamental rural philosophy that Aldington delighted in.

'The subject on which Mr Brown most willingly philosophised was education. He was convinced that the solution of all social problems would be found if all working-class boys went to Oxford or Cambridge. Then, he said, they would all be able to earn the same wages as the bosses... He challenged me to name an uneducated man who had made money. I mentioned Lord Northcliffe and the mayor of Newbury... who had done pretty well in the nail and saucepan business. Mr Brown wouldn't have it. Depend on it, they'd had education, it stood to reason. And when I asked how a knowledge of Greek and higher mathematics would aid the working classes in putting up wages, he said he didn't mean Greek and higher mathematics, he meant education. I used to think Mr Brown would have made an excellent president of a really modern university.'[38]

One can almost hear Mr Brown telling Mrs Brown afterwards what an idiot that chap next door is and even that thought would have delighted Aldington. Mrs Cotterell, throughout the time both Aldington and Lawrence were living next door to her, was only a little girl and the mark of respect that a little girl would have had for all her neighbours still remains. Whereas the whole world refers to them as Lawrence, Frieda and Aldington, to Mrs Cotterell they are still 'Mr' and 'Mrs'. 'We didn't know of Mr Lawrence before he came. He came as a friend of Margaret Radford. We saw quite a lot of her and Mrs Radford. They used to come down occasionally… well, about once a month.' It came as a great surprise to Mrs Cotterell to learn that I had managed to find Dr Radford. While Mrs Cotterell was only a girl at the time she still has fond memories of the Radford family and took down Dr Radford's address. Perhaps it is because of the physical aura that surrounded Lawrence – or just the fact that he was so different – but I am continually fascinated by everyone's powers of recall when they talk of Lawrence. By comparison, their memories of other people are insignificant. This is made all the more remarkable by the fact that most of the people I have met were so young at the time. John Rouse, for example: 'I could see Lawrence and Frieda over the hedge – I was by the gate – and they had no furniture at all [but] used to bring… two very old deck chairs out in the front and they used to sit there… I used to go there daily… Of course, Bill Brown was there. That's how I saw a lot of Lawrence.'

Mrs Cotterell thought Lawrence was marvellous. He came at a time when she was studying for her secondary school exams and one of the first things she told me, quite triumphantly, was that 'He did most of my homework for me!' Lawrence had been a schoolmaster and his instinct was to help. He was keen that young Hilda should go to university and did all in his power to encourage her studies.

It was only as time progressed that Hilda became aware of the circumstances of the Lawrences' removal from Cornwall to Hermitage and that they needed to register their whereabouts with the police. As a result, there were continual visits from the local constabulary. She remembers the first time they came. They didn't go directly to No 1 but came instead to Mr and Mrs Brown. In order to do so they would have walked past the Lawrence's front room window no more than three feet away. Even the two front doors are no more than two rooms apart. To law abiding citizens, the sight of a policeman knocking on the front door can be quite traumatic but the Browns were made of sterner stuff. 'When the policemen came to check on them he said, "Please may we come in?" and we said, "What do you want?" They said, "Do you have a neighbour next door?" so – "Of course we've got a neighbour next door! What do you think we've got?" So he said, "Would you let us know who this neighbour is?" So we said, "Of course! It's Mr Lawrence" and he said, "Oh, but his wife's a German." So my mother said, "Well, but I can't see that she's doing any harm."… And then they came, about every six weeks. They had to check up because she was an alien in the First World War.' Even after all these years, Mrs Cotterell passes on this little story with a sense of deep indignation that the police should intrude upon a person's life in this fashion.

I had worked out that Lawrence's short story *Monkey Nuts* was set largely in one of the two railway yards at Hermitage. It was written in Hermitage and is based on two soldiers, a corporal and a private, who were billeted nearby. I was taken aback to hear that a Corporal George Brewer was billeted at the Brown's during the time Lawrence was there and indeed remained for a while after the armistice in November 1918 before returning to his native Poole. He was a tall, clean-shaven, handsome man. Mrs Cotterell had fond memories of Corporal Brewer. 'I remember when George lived with us there was a tale about some horses that were going to be destroyed. There were going to be four horses destroyed and George was determined that they shouldn't … He threatened all sorts of things … "If these horses are destroyed I shall …" But they were saved.' Lawrence makes strong play of the people and places with whom he was in immediate contact and my feeling was that *Monkey Nuts* holds a little more insight into relationships at Chapel Farm Cottages than at first seems obvious. The third character in the story is a girl from the land army that Albert, the corporal, sets his sights on. The relationship between the two soldiers and the land girl shows us traces of Lawrence's own attitudes as well as what would now seem to be those of the young soldier billeted next door.

> *'Miss Stokes watched the two men from under her broad felt hat. She had seen hundreds of Alberts, khaki soldiers standing in loose attitudes, absorbed in watching nothing in particular. She had seen also a good many Joes, quiet, good-looking young soldiers with half-averted faces. But there was something in the turn of Joe's head, and something in his quiet, tender-looking form, young and fresh – which attracted her eye. As she watched him closely from below, he turned as if he felt her, and his dark-blue eye met her straight light-blue gaze. He faltered and turned aside again and looked as if he were going to fall off the truck. A slight flush mounted under the girl's full, ruddy face. She liked him.'*[39]

The significance of all this struck me only after Mrs Cotterell told me that 'Mrs Lawrence was very attracted to George – *very* attracted.' Mrs Cotterell deemed it prudent to say no more. Essential to the evolution of the relationship between the corporal and the land-army girl is the arrival of the circus at Playcross, the fictitious name Lawrence gave to the nearby market town of Newbury. Mr Rouse told me everyone went to the circus on its annual visit to Newbury and the usual way to get there was to walk. This is exactly what happens in Lawrence's story. During this walk home the relationship between the two soldiers and the land girl reaches its strained climax. That much though must remain entirely fictitious for neither Lawrence nor George Brewer went to the circus. But reading between the lines, it is easy to see how Lawrence constructed his. Maybe there had been a suggestion that Lawrence did go, but in the event Frieda Lawrence took Hilda, the little girl from next door, whose memories of their arrival reflect the finances of the Lawrences as much as her own enjoyment at this special day out. 'Mrs Lawrence asked what price the tickets were. She was told there were two prices, those with cushions and those without. She said, "I don't think we'll sit on the cushions; I expect the animals have sat on those."' On various occasions while they were in No 1 the Lawrences would invite the young Hilda to join them for a meal. 'Mum would say, "I understand you're invited out." I was about eight or nine. Mrs Lawrence would say: "Come in to dinner tonight." Once she made me an evening dress and I went to dinner.' It is generally understood that Lawrence did most of the cooking as Frieda had had so little experience. Hilda disagreed. 'On the other hand, she was a good cook. Oh, she was a good cook. Yes, because we used to have three courses at least.' It was obviously a thrill for a little girl to eat out like this, even allowing for the fact that she had only gone next door. That they all enjoyed it is obvious. 'We all used to wash up afterwards... just like a family.'

There are constant references to the Lawrence's penury during this period and, under the constant threat of eviction, Lawrence's sister had taken out a year's lease on a cottage near her in the Midlands on their behalf. Despite Lawrence's enjoyment of his surroundings at Hermitage, he was obviously under some obligation to move. In the year following the spring of 1918 they managed to divide their time almost equally between the two cottages, but it wasn't until November 1919 that they left England for good and it was in the following month that Aldington took over the cottage. He had been demobbed after a tour of duty with the occupational forces in Belgium and was desperate to get out of the claustrophobic atmosphere of literary London. He was also suffering from shell-shock. With the declining health of her husband, Dollie Radford had presumably given up further thoughts of making use of No 1 and after Lawrence's departure must have wanted to get rid of the place by way of a formal agreement. 'The Hermitage cottage,' Aldington confirms, 'was sublet from the Radford family. I knew one of the daughters, Margaret, very well by sight… Mrs Radford was also a poetess; and Mr Radford, who is mentioned somewhere in Yeats's autobiographies, was a writer or socialist or perhaps both – I forget. In pre-war days I was taken to see the family.'[40] By the time that the lease with Aldington was agreed, Ernest Radford had died and poor Dollie Radford must have been in an extremely distressed state. 'Such were my landlords, and it will surprise nobody to hear that although I paid them my rent regularly they forgot to hand any of it on to the original landlord, so that I was in danger of eviction. In fact, I should have been evicted if I hadn't gone to a more energetic lawyer than my father.'[41]

Of the diminishing number of those I have met, almost each and every one has very firm memories of Lawrence and Frieda and yet these same people have so few recollections of Aldington. Lawrence came to Hermitage with the added attraction of notoriety after his expulsion from Cornwall. Aldington was the antithesis of this; he was shell-shocked and reclusive. His writing shows a decided affinity with the bucolic life, but he held back from his neighbours both at Hermitage and Padworth, with the admirable exception of Bill Brown. Aldington was at Padworth for eight years and yet I can find no one who can tell me anything of real significance about him. 'Old' Dave Wickens the maltster sounds very much as if he might fit the Bill Brown mould but is long since dead and I have found no trace of his family. At the time of his first sojourn at Hermitage Aldington was not long since demobbed. In addition, and as a result of his wartime affair with Arabella, he and his wife H.D. had separated. Under these circumstances the cottage at Hermitage acquired an added dimension. It was, Aldington says: 'secluded and silent, the meadows and coppices near it were full of wild flowers in the spring.' and to a man who had seen nothing but the mud and horror of the trenches 'there was a garden.'[42]

Aldington came to Hermitage in late 1919. 'It was December when I first moved to Hermitage and for much of the time I was alone.'[43] Mrs

Cotterell remembers Arabella Yorke. 'He lived on his own for a while. Well, Miss Yorke was…' Here Mrs Cotterell was a little unsure as to whether she should say any more. Under differing circumstances, it would be only right and proper to respect her confidence but when I explained just how much of these men's lives was known, Mrs Cotterell felt she could expand, just a little. 'We used to look at Miss Yorke sometimes and we used to say, "Well, I wonder who she is?" Obviously 'the Aldingtons' kept their relationship to themselves. Certainly Mrs Rouse was unaware of its true nature. 'I believe he was writing a book while he was up there… Miss Yorke was Aldington's secretary… I've got a feeling there was something about a book and I suppose she used to do the work – writing… They were just there together. You know, she walked around with him and I always thought that… well he's a writer so she must be his secretary.' Mr Rouse, ever one to recall a pretty face, was very much struck by Arabella. 'To us she seemed quite different, yes, she really did… I can remember her having bobbed hair, black hair with a fringe. She was shorter than him – not very tall, no. She had a striking face.' Mrs Cotterell was dismissive when her husband mentioned this. 'She wasn't all that attractive. No! She had a fringe across here. I was a small child then, but she wasn't all *that* attractive.'

Mrs Rouse has distant memories of Aldington. 'I can visualise him still, but perhaps not his features. But I remember he was a very smart sort of man, more so than Lawrence.' As a girl, Mrs Rouse was ideally placed. 'He was very fond of the country, I remember that. I was living at the post office, born and bred there. He used to come into the post office. He was always sending things off. I remember seeing him though – walking.'

Mrs Cotterell has one particularly vivid memory of Aldington. He had retained his army revolver as had most other demobbed officers. 'I always remember he had his revolver he had from the war,' she told me. A very significant passage in his novel *All Men Are Enemies* appears to bear this out. Aldington came out of the war into the 'long armistice' as he was to call it, suffering from the aftermath of the incessant bombardment in the trenches. At times the mental anguish and persistent nightmares that he suffered as a consequence must have driven him to despair and there were times, it would seem from this passage, when he must have seriously considered suicide. This is more than adequately borne out by his first novel *Death of a Hero* but here in *All Men are Enemies* the pistol would have offered a way out:

'In a corner of his room lay his valise; he rummaged in it and found his service revolver and jerked it open so that six heavy bullets shot into his palm. He snapped the revolver shut and laid it on a small table and then took the bullets into the bathroom. When he opened the window, snowflakes and a gust of raw air blew on his face. The silence of sleeping London seemed more silent in the falling snow. He tossed the bullets into the little sooty garden, now turned to a soft brooding white, and saw one of them cut a little jag in the snow where the shaft of light from the window fell.'[44]

On one occasion the Brown's cat caused him to dive for cover when, in all innocence, it took a mighty leap onto his shoulder when he was working. Hilda remembered it well. 'Oh! I shall *never* forget that. "Oh! That CAT!" he said, "I'm going to *shoot* that cat!" I said, "You do! …" and he said, "Oh, when it jumped on my shoulders all sorts of things went through my mind."' Long after the event was over he continued to tease Hilda: '"I don't like cats," he used to say but he was very nice about it. He was very friendly, you know, a friendly sort of person.' Which is no doubt why he and Bill Brown used to get on so well together.

I was surprised to learn that Mr Brown was as young as he was. And neither did he bear any resemblance to Aldington's description of Mr Judd's physical attributes. William Brown was born in 1874. There was an upper age limit of forty in 1916 that meant he must have avoided conscription by the skin of his teeth but everyone tells me he was indispensable and in that respect he and Mr Judd were one. 'There was a dignity in Mr Judd, an air of more than Emersonian self-reliance, which forbade intrusion and familiarity. Even recruiting tribunals had been impressed and throughout the War he had remained indispensable.'[45] It was precisely this air of self-reliance that Aldington gave to Mr Judd. 'This exemption from military brutality confirmed Mr Judd's dignity and increased the clarity and coolness of his judgement, whereas less fortunate men were liable to run off the rails amid explosions of just, but unfortunately ineffective, anger.'[46] Arthur Brown, Hilda's half brother, had served as a seaman throughout the war so Aldington and Bill Brown would have had a lot to talk about. 'At my invitation Mr Brown would sometimes drop in of an evening… we would smoke our pipes and drink ale from blue earthenware mugs and talk of essential things. Mr Brown knew all the things about gardening which you don't learn at agricultural colleges or from beautifully illustrated books. He knew exactly which brand of seeds went with which soil, when and how to plant them, how much or how little nutritive dung should be supplied, how to treat plants as they grew, and many such practical points.'[47] Except when it came to spinach, that is. The Browns crop up again in Aldington's third novel *All Men Are Enemies* in 1934.

'Tony liked them very much, especially the man, a tall dark fellow who had worked hard all his life and had a profound contempt for all socialists and social legislation. Sometimes he sat with them in their kitchen in the evening, talking about the war and their son, not yet demobilised from the Eastern Expeditionary Force, and the news of the day. The carpenter's working-man Toryism was both bigoted and limited, but Tony liked his independence and the entire absence of proletarian whine and grouse which had fed him up for life in the army.'[48] I felt that it was precisely those aspects of Mr Brown's 'working man's Toryism' that attracted and so strongly inspired Aldington. But the final link in the chain that had led me from Mr Judd to Bill Brown comes in a reference to Mr Judd 'who belonged to that haughtiest of all aristocracies – the British upper working-class.'[49] In Aldington's eyes Bill Brown was practically faultless. Whether Aldington was ever aware of it, I don't know, but Arthur Brown died young, not as a result of war service but in a tragic accident on the railway in Reading on 25 January 1925. I may be reading far too much into this but it is curious to note that in *The Lads of the Village* one name on the fictional memorial stands as a tribute to Mr Judd's assumed son, William. We can hardly get much closer to Bill Brown and Arthur, his son, than that.

Bill Brown lived for his garden. For years he worked as a gardener in the big house at the junction of Pond Lane with the Yattendon Road in Hermitage. Mrs Cotterell was delighted to learn that Aldington had immortalised her father in print and underlined his every word. 'His interest was gardening. He grew anything and everything. We used to say that we could go out into the garden no matter what time of the year and we could be sure of getting some flowers.' That Aldington learnt a lot from Mr Brown is without doubt. He couldn't wait to put it all into practice at Padworth. In a later novel, *Seven Against Reeves,* he doesn't even bother to disguise the name of his muse. '"It's my opinion," Mr Brown said gravely to Mrs Brown, "that the boss is a bit off the hooks.

What's he want to give up his business for, all of a sudden like? Tisn't reasonable. If you ask me, he's come to the change of his life, and don't know what's the matter with him. What he wants is something to occupy his mind and leave gardening to them as understands. Next thing we shall hear is that he's been took up in Hyde Park!'"[50]

Harry Cotterell told me that when he came courting young Hilda Brown, he and Bill Brown 'used to go out in the mornings. Evelyn Burgess' farm was overrun with rabbits and Mr Brown would go out there and catch them. At that time you'd get ten pence a skin. It was worth more than the rabbit in those days… He used to give them away all over the shop. There were lots of people then who were short of money and he used to come home and say, "I want you to take two here and two there" so that everybody had some. The place was overrun with rabbits. But no one else was allowed to catch 'em.' Aldington gifted Mr Judd with 'a briar pipe with an extravagant display of pseudo-amber mouthpiece.'[51] Bill Brown was a smoker, too. Hilda remembers this only too well. She had to go to Newbury for her father's tobacco. She used to get it 'at a shop near the bridge in Northbrook Street.' And, as Aldington suggests, Bill Brown kept a pig. Once a year Mr Brown's pig would be sent for slaughter to the butcher in Newbury who would then bring bits of it back to Mrs Brown as the occasion demanded. 'We used to hang the pig and cure it, hanging from the ceiling. It's salted first and then taken to be cured and then it can be hung for as long as you wanted it. We used to have pork for Sunday tea,' said the far from pallid Hilda Cotterell. Bill Brown would surely remain totally impassive if he saw his name in a book as was Mr Judd's response to Mr Raper's rhetoric: 'Mr Judd made no reply, but breathed heavily into his pipe stem.'[52]

There was only one accolade to suit a man of Bill Brown's stoic agrarian nature. On 7 March 1921, three months after Aldington moved to Padworth, when the literary world was buzzing from the publication of James Joyce's *Ulysses*, a general meeting was held in the Old School at Hermitage. The occasion was to lead to the re-establishment of the Hermitage Horticultural Society whose proceedings had been so rudely affronted by onset of the war. Bill Brown was there. A committee was elected to oversee the project and among the members there were a few whose names are familiar to us: W.E. Boshier; Mrs Rouse's father from the post office; Evelyn Burgess the farmer; two more Burgesses and Charlie Sharpe. With the exception of Mr Sharpe and one other, W. Silvey, all the remaining names coincidentally begin with the letter B: Briant; Baden; Boswell, and, of course, W. Brown, Esq. It was proposed that the first of the new horticultural shows be held Saturday, 27 August 1921. At the first annual general meeting after the show, on 1 February 1922, William Brown was elected chairman for the ensuing year.[53]

Almost as an afterthought during my last visit to her, Mrs Cotterell recalled something that Aldington had once said to her when they were talking about Lawrence. Hilda can only have been about ten years old at the time but the memory has remained surprisingly firm. 'Richard Aldington said that Lawrence would be the greatest Englishman that we should ever know.' I suspect, like her father, Hilda was perfectly capable of making up her own mind about Mr and Mrs Lawrence and she liked them, it was as simple as that. For reasons that Aldington would have understood, the feeling was reciprocated. Lawrence and Frieda remained in contact with the Brown family as we see from his published letters, but the biggest surprise came from Mrs Cotterell again. The first time I visited Hilda, she sat with a brown envelope on her lap and continually ignored her husband's insistence that she show it to me, that is until she was ready to do so.

The dramatic moment came with coffee and biscuits and was, as is the best of all revelatory experiences, presented to me in reverse order. Out of the envelope came a series of letters, photographs and postcards some of which she had guarded secretly for over sixty years. The first I was shown was a letter of 29 September 1949 from Frieda Lawrence.

It is a chatty letter in which contact was once again established with the now married Hilda and in which she reminisces about the Hermitage days. She referred to correspondence from her and Lawrence and this is what Mrs Cotterell had been keeping back from me. A series of six postcards, five by Lawrence and one by Frieda, were written to the young Hilda in the months after they left Hermitage. It was obviously a two-way correspondence because Lawrence gives Hilda a forwarding address. But the strength of the correspondence lies in Lawrence's concern for the Brown family and in particular for the future of Hilda. Even the choice of picture postcards reflects the fact that they were to be sent to a young lady. One of the first, that of 6 January 1920 from Frieda, carries confirmation that Aldington was no longer alone at the cottage. The Lawrences had sent Hilda a parting gift of a brooch that Mrs Cotterell still treasures. Frieda said that she was 'glad you liked your present, tell

Fig. 20. Stephen Spender, Frieda Lawrence and another at Lawrence's ranch, New Mexico

your mother I have a coral brooch for her – you will enjoy having Miss Yorke there – mind you work hard for that scholarship.'[54]

Lawrence had been working on his *Movements in European History* when he was at Hermitage and it was published in 1921 under the pseudonym of Lawrence H. Davidson. Boring though it may sound to some, young Hilda – who went on to become a teacher – found it fascinating. Frieda talks about it. 'Soon at last, that history that Mr Lawrence wrote will be finished and he will order you one.'[55] Hilda told me, sadly, that it never arrived and that seems to go against Lawrence's natural instincts towards Hilda. Lawrence's own postcards to Hilda all contain chatty notes of their itinerary through Europe and Ceylon with the suggestion that they may go on to Australia. There are poignant references to the happy times they had together at Hermitage. There was even a suggestion from Lawrence that they may meet up again.[56] The nearest he ever got to Hermitage was his visit to Aldington in Padworth in 1926. Whether Lawrence contemplated popping across to Hermitage will never be known but he must surely have enquired about the Browns.

105

In a second letter of 10 November 1936 – after Lawrence's death – Frieda in writing to Hilda from Kiowa Ranch in New Mexico says: 'I remember it all so well… Mr Lawrence and I were very fond of you and your mother – If I come to England I would certainly let you know and either I would come to see you or you me and we will have a good time together.' She continues, in this reminiscent vein, mentioning all those we have already met and again, giving apparent credence to young Hilda's recollections of Frieda's fondness for Corporal Brewer. 'It was awfully nice getting your letter. I could see us all so clearly, your mother coming in – how is poor Margaret Radford? I remember George too – the lovely walks we had round the country.'[57] Frieda had sent Hilda a series of photographs taken around the ranch in New Mexico which were kept along with these letters and postcards in the brown envelope and from these, Mrs Cotterell pulled out yet another letter, this time from Lawrence. It was written on 30 July 1920 from Taormina, Sicily where he and Frieda were staying.

'Dear Hilda,
'The holiday is come, and we think of last year and Pangbourne, and hope that this year you'll have a good time. We are just going away also: first to some friends in the mountains near Rome – then Mrs Lawrence is going to Germany again to see her mother. I shall go with her as far as Milan – and from Milan to Baden is only about twenty hours. We rather dread the journey from here to Milan about thirty-six hours direct. But thank heaven the weather is cooler. It has been hot blazing sun for week after week, day after day, and so hot lately it was too much. I have lived for weeks in a pair of pyjamas and nothing else – barefoot: and even then too hot. Now thank heaven clouds have come from the north, welcome and lovely. It has rained a tiny spattering today. Everywhere is burnt dry, the trees have shed nearly all their leaves, it is autumn. Only the vines are green. The grapes are just about ripe, hanging purple under the broad leaves. Vegetables are all gone – except melanciane – egg plant, purple things. But there are tomatoes in abundance – two pence a pound, fresh from the gardens. And the second lot of figs and peaches just coming. We had a nice lot of apricots – quite cheap for once. Potatoes are twice as dear as apricots, and about the same price as peaches. But Italy is very expensive nowadays, for ordinary things, worse than England.*

'We often wonder about you, and the cottage and the garden. Are there many greengages? – will there be apples? – how are the potatoes and marrows, and the good beans? Is there a black pig in the sty? What news of Hermitage? Does your Dad still trudge across to Oare, and your mother ride on Polly Wernham's bicycle? And is Mrs Allan better? – remember us to her.

'I send you a pound for your holiday. Put your name on the back, and anybody will cash the cheque for you: Mr Boshier or Mrs Lowe. It is for you to spend exactly as you please, on as much nonsense as you like.

'Have we told you that Peggy has a baby sister – born about a month ago. There's an addition to the family. Send a line and tell us how you are and address it to me: presso Signor Juta.

'Mind you write decently or heaven knows what the Italian postmen will say to me…'

He then goes back to the first page, turns it upside down and continues:

'A lovely moonlight night, tonight, with a moon bright on the sea, and a few moving dark cloud-shadows. So nice to see clouds and their darknesses.'

But, in the knowledge that he is writing to a little girl he adds:

'Are the phlox out?'

At this point he must have read through what he had written and realised that he hadn't mentioned what, to an ex-teacher, would be foremost on his mind. So again he turns his letter through ninety degrees and adds another 'P. S.'

'I'll bet you've never got that scholarship, you careless young baggage. Peg of course has got one – sharp-shins that she is. They say no news is good news: but not about scholarships. – Kindly say what the flower garden looked like this year, if any of my efforts came to anything and if your Dad was any less scornful than usual.
DHL.'[58]

Chapter 6

Women Must Work

At some point during my investigations, my attention became held by the name Anna Munro. She was, I learnt, a suffragette who had lived in Padworth.

I assumed that the suffragettes had passed into the history books by the time Aldington arrived in Padworth and that, as my cardex was restricted to 1918-1930, Anna Munro had long since moved on, but after talking to one of the senior citizens of the village who told me he came to live here in about 1930, I realized this was not the case. He had been a chauffeur to the people who bought Bridge House. He also mentioned parties he used to go to at Venture Fair, home of the Ashman family.

Mention of parties took me back to *The Colonel's Daughter* but by now I could read an entire novel into the slightest remark. I then learnt that Mrs Ashman was Anna Munro or Mrs Munro-Ashman as she was better known, at which moment her husband – Donald Ashman, who had owned a house in nearby Bucklebury that I had been investigating – dropped into context. The Ashmans, I was being told, were renowned for the wild parties they threw in the thirties and they had been in Padworth since the middle of the 1920s. Anna Munro's parties reminded me of those described in *Women Must Work* particularly as Vera Wraxall was herself something of a suffragette. It all seemed worth chasing. I went back to *The Colonel's Daughter* where Georgie Smithers is horrified at the exuberant activities of Margy Stewart, a fictitious 'bright-young-thing' of the twenties. Margy 'had a peculiar talent as a hostess. She liked to have a couple of stars for a week-end performance, but owing to a somewhat superficial observation of human life, she frequently invited two sub-eminent persons who were violently antipathetic to each other. Them she would surround with a miscellaneous collection of youth, picked up more or less at hazard over the telephone at the last minute, and usually so ill-assorted that the stars hated the chorus nearly as much as they loathed each other.'[1]

Fig. 21. Anna Munro, suffragette

The Colonel's Daughter contrasted the destiny of Georgie in those post-war years with the implied solution in *Women Must Work* that provided a circumstantial link to Anna Munro. It was around this time that in transcribing the details of the parish council minute book, I learnt that Mrs Ashman had joined the parish council. Someone must know something about her I felt but all I picked up were the usual platitudes about a village elder. But one intriguing fact emerged. No one seemed to know her married name but Mrs Ashman's daughter was the current owner of June Rose Bungalow opposite Malthouse Cottage on the north bank of the Kennet and Avon canal. Then, early in 1982, an advert in the local paper announced the forthcoming auction of June Rose Bungalow. A letter via the estate agents produced a very fulfilling reply from Margaret Ridgway, giving me a potted biography of her extraordinary mother. It soon became obvious that in 1920s Padworth, Anna Munro represented a threat to the old order. Her name is conspicuously absent from anything Aldington ever wrote, so to link her with Aldington's fiction is pure speculation on my part and yet she occupies a significant presence between the lines of *The Colonel's Daughter*. It beggars belief to think that they did not know each other, particularly in view of the Capper connection with June Rose Bungalow and Venture Fair. I find it particularly interesting that two such similar intellects should live within yards of each other and yet pass without comment.

Anna Munro's influence in Berkshire is extensive. In any era she would be a remarkable person but in those post-war years she would have been thought of as positively Bolshevik. In the context of these notes, it is difficult to know precisely how to describe her. The memories of her daughter, her son and her housekeeper deserve a place in future editions of the *Oxford Dictionary of National Biography*.[2] Mrs Ridgway told me that her mother was born Anna Gillies MacDonald Munro in Scotland in 1881, she was therefore eleven years older than Aldington. She first came to London in 1902. By a delicious irony I found she was descended from Robert Adam, the architect whose draughtsman, John Hobcroft, designed Padworth House and nearby Wasing Place. Her husband, who remained Mr Ashman despite his daughter's advice that he should change *his* name to Munro-Ashman, was born and brought up five miles away at Thatcham where they lived until coming to Padworth in about 1925.

Anna Munro was organiser for the Women's Social and Political Union in Dunfermline and became a founder member of the Women's

Freedom League in 1907 and was on the committee for the remainder of its fifty-year life. She was never a militant suffragette and she did not approve of the undemocratic and violent protests of the Pankhursts. She was not, in her daughter's words, 'anti-man' but wanted equality, each sex having its own contribution to the common good. She was a beautiful woman with brown curly hair, and large dark eyes, always elegantly dressed in the Edwardian manner, she retained a life-long liking for furs and silks. She always liked the best, I learnt. She had a melodious, outstandingly clear voice with just a trace of a Scottish accent and she was a very powerful speaker. She was imprisoned four times for periods of up to six weeks each time and indeed spent her honeymoon in prison, 'leaving father on the steps of Caxton Hall, so to speak,' recalls her daughter. She was once arrested while addressing a meeting. With her husband's skill in leather work he was able to smuggle letters to her, sewn into bananas. On one occasion she was jailed for chaining herself to the railings outside ten Downing Street. During her time at Padworth she collected classical gramophone records, English china and paintings, she even had a painting by Rossetti.

Throughout her life she formed lasting friendships with fellow socialists such as Keir Hardie, Ellen Wilkinson (the first woman Labour MP) and Maude Gonne (the Irish socialist and friend and muse of W.B. Yeats). I was later to learn from her housekeeper of her friendships with Hugh Gaitskell (the leader of the Labour Party), Lord Pethick-Lawrence (supporter of the suffragettes) and practically everyone connected with the Women's Freedom League which grew out of the suffragette movement including Charlotte Despard, Earl French, the Knight sisters, Mrs Schofield-Coates and the writer Israel Zangwill (who is praised by Aldington as one of the only three authors known by him to have repaid a publisher's advance when the subsequent book failed to earn).

In 1938 after being blocked for some years by a chairman 'who would not have a woman on his bench'[4] Anna Munro was finally appointed a magistrate, one who would be well aware of the inside of a prison. She helped found the Newbury Labour Party and later became chair and life president.

Ms Munro remained a radical to the end, a rebel and young in heart. It is interesting to speculate – for at this distance of time that's all I can do – on the reasons for the apparent lack of contact between Aldington and Anna Munro. Mrs Ridgway has 'a recollection that mother knew an author in Padworth but that's all'. I believe it to be the case that while Aldington had every sympathy with the concept of political equality for women – the fact that Anna Munro was, in her daughter's words, 'perhaps lacking in a sense of humour' would distance her from Aldington who was always prepared to see himself in the same satirical light in which he cast others. Neither of them would be any good at small talk so when they met around the village there would be no more ready chatter than was minimally necessary.

Fig. 22. Anna Munro, Labour politician and magistrate

Aldington had every sympathy with Anna Munro's take on life but repressed as he was by his dominant mother he shied away from strong women as much as he avoided the warmongers among men. The entire novel, *Women Must Work*, is centred on the struggles of Etta Morison to live life on her terms, to break her dependency on both men and *her* mother. Aldington was well aware of his mother's attributes. She had achieved a great deal and, as he saw it, for them to survive in that post-war world, women *must* work.

By the middle of 1922 Aldington had been at Padworth for eighteen months, eighteen months of relative peace and tranquillity that helped banish the stark horrors of trench warfare. Had the pleasures to be obtained from living in Padworth been prescribed they could not have been more beneficial. He and Arabella spent a few weeks in late summer in Rome. The memories of Armistice Day back home that year would be lessened. But to judge from a letter of 17 December 1922 to F.S. Flint, his peace was about to be shattered. 'We have been very quiet and happy down here but over Christmas we shall be visited by my sister and her friend (a Whig of the worst type) and Mrs Yorke, the champion of Americanism. Donc, my attic tranquillity will be temporarily suppressed.'[5]

He was faced with a houseful of women who would disrupt his routine until the beginning of March. There is something in Aldington's attitudes towards his sister's friend and to Mrs Yorke that bears comparison with what I guess to be that towards Anna Munro and indeed towards his mother, too. Writing subjectively many years later Arabella confirms that Aldington's father Albert Edward, was studious and weak and that his mother, Jessie May, was a very egotistical sometimes maternal barmaid. Three years later, in January 1925 he told Flint that his mother was 'coming down here on Thursday and will probably want to take us "ridin' abaht in 'er moter-cah" for a few days… I don't think she will enjoy the quiet and solitude of this place for very long.'[6] The entire Aldington family felt smothered by Jessie May. In 1913 the strains on her husband proved too much and he had a nervous breakdown that was to affect all of their lives. Aldington had to leave university without a degree. Neither Aldington nor Margery ever forgave their mother. It is reflected in that telling line of his poem: 'only because I need it know I love.'[7]

It was while searching for Mr Brown at Hermitage that I turned up something that brought the entire plot of *Women Must Work* sharply back into focus. Now that I knew of her existence, I had imagined Anna Munro between the lines of every page but that presence was immediately usurped by two people much closer to home. During my first meeting with Mrs Rouse she had told me (through the kitchen window) more in a few seconds than I could immediately take in. One brief statement brought me sharply to attention. 'His sister Margery used to live over at Oare. Margery put down roots in the village quickly. [She] lived with Miss Salter. She was a writer. I believe she wrote under the name of Stewart "Mary Stewart". They were all connected, I suppose.' In the time that it took her to utter those few words, Mrs Rouse had given me the primary source for *Women Must Work*. What's more, the name of Margy Stewart in *The Colonel's Daughter* sprang to mind.

Mrs Rouse had no idea how closely those two names *were* connected. The fictitious Margy Stewart was obviously an amalgam of *Margery* Aldington and Mary *Stewart*. My mind was racing far too fast for comfort; and all this amid the noise of traffic, and through Mrs Rouse's kitchen window. I was puzzled though, for despite the fact that I had accumulated some knowledge of Aldington's life I could not see how his sister could have been there at the same time. I said as much to Mrs Rouse who immediately put me right. 'She came here after he'd gone. That's extraordinary because that's how I felt I knew Aldington. No, they weren't here together… I knew him because he was Miss Aldington – the singer's – brother.'

This was a revelation. As I have said, the disturbing similarities between certain passages in *Women Must Work* and Lawrence's story, *The Fox*, had niggled for some time, particularly as I had already concluded that both centred on Hermitage. The parallels had been too close for anything other than a disquieting subjective analysis. But, while those parallels cannot be denied, I now had reason to believe that Aldington's experience was totally dissociated from that of Lawrence. Norman Gates had told me that Margery Lyon-Gilbert, Aldington's sister, still lived in Rye where the family had established themselves in the early years of the twentieth century. I felt I had to meet her. There was some trepidation on my part though for, almost in the same breath I had learnt things which I would hardly dare mention.

Having discovered the whereabouts of Oare and its proximity to Hermitage I had a more pressing urgency to find the cottage where Margery and Miss Salter lived. I went back to *Women Must Work* again. Etta Morison the heroine was brought up in Dortborough. I was now able to recognise that as Dover, the Aldington's home town. Certainly some of the fictitious circumstances fitted what I knew of Aldington's childhood in that seaport town. Etta even has a brother – Teddy. Despite their reversed ages, there is no reason why Teddy could not be Aldington himself, nor indeed why the aspirations of Etta should not be those of the author. 'By the time Etta was nineteen [1914], she made two unsuccessful attempts to get away from Dortborough.… there were girls who wanted to get away, not with a man, but on their own.'[8] But Etta was not on her own, she went off with Vera Wraxall, the mere mention of whose name in the Morison household brought forth the denunciation with which we are all familiar in one form or another. 'Vera, dear, I wish you wouldn't always be running around to her, filling your head with all that suffragette nonsense. One of these days she'll be arrested by the police, and then think of her poor mother.'[9]

At the time of writing I still know precious little of Miss Salter let alone Mary Stewart and as she wrote in a somewhat autobiographical manner of a fictitious child, it was prudent not to delve too deeply in the course of meetings that followed.

But from an article of hers of February 1927 uncovered from the archives of *Good Housekeeping* magazine Olive Mary Salter has a sound knowledge of the business acumen of what appears to be Jessie May Aldington and an equally sound knowledge of the south coast. My feeling therefore is that she too came from Rye or Dover and that, as in *Woman Must Work*, she and Margery had known each other since their childhood days. Even before I (later) discovered these facts there was obviously every reason to believe that Miss Salter was the fictitious Vera Wraxall in *Women Must Work*. Aldington's description of Vera was to become firmly associated in my mind with what I was to learn of Miss Salter. 'At first glance it seemed a naif sort of face, more round than oval, with a very clear virtuous skin, large childish eyes, and fluffy yellow hair which always looked very fluffy in spite of Vera's despairing efforts to screw it into a practical bun. Vera isn't pretty, Etta thought to herself, but she certainly makes the worst of what looks she has – whatever makes her wear those floppy tweeds and that mannish-looking blouse and collar and that awful old hat?'[10] A complete re-reading of the book was hardly necessary to trigger off further associations with Hermitage. They were already firmly fixed in my mind from the chase I had to find Mr Brown.

Within days of that first meeting with Mrs Rouse I had sent off a further spate of letters to places as diverse as America and Oare. As a result, I was now being shown around what might be termed a very desirable residence in Oare by the present owner, Roberta 'Bobbie' Hards, who told me that 'Wallins', as it was called, was 'a smallholding before my folks bought it.' The cottage had 'belonged to the old people called Wallin.... He died in 1928... It had belonged to the estate of Sir William Mount... We called it "Wallins" because it was the home of the old people for a great many years.' The cottage has changed considerably for the better since the time Miss Aldington and Miss Salter lived there, but I was still able to endow it with fictitious traits from the old photograph that Mrs Hards showed me. 'It was once two cottages,' she continued, 'with two front doors and two staircases.'

The front cottage had one up and one down and the rear cottage, two up and two down. 'It only had cold water [from a pump] and no sanitation.' Drainage came later when Mr and Mrs Hards married and moved in. At the time the two young women were there it was however, 'one cottage with an open fireplace and square-backed fireplace.' Mrs Hards knows as she was living 'over the road at the time. That would have been in the early twenties.' She was only a young girl at the time but remembers her neighbours well. 'Aldington was tall and fairish and the other one, Salter, was darkish – dark haired, brown hair. They were nice looking girls and, if I remember rightly, Aldington was tall. Salter was small and had [her hair] in earphones' – exactly as Aldington described Vera Wraxall. John Rouse has even stronger memories. Obviously as a young lad he was very impressed by Margery Aldington.

'She was a very fine, beautiful girl. I was only a boy but… She was tall and very stately. She was *fantastic*! She had a lovely face. She was a lovely girl.' All the more reason for me to meet her, I thought.

Although they had never met, Norman Gates had been in correspondence with Margery Aldington and gave me her address. It was only a matter of time before I was knocking on the door of a very beautiful cottage in one of the older streets in Rye, Sussex. A very distinguished lady made me very welcome and almost immediately introduced me to her younger sister Patricia. Margery was born in 1898 and Pat, as she preferred to be known, ten years later. Only Aldington himself was absent from the very lengthy conversation that followed and yet his spirit was there in the personality and strengths of Margery and particularly in her phraseology. To hear her talk brought to life the words and emotions of her brother in a direct and often alarming fashion. Margery Lyon-Gilbert is herself a published poet and showed me an unpublished novel that has been gathering dust for fifty years. Her brother was evidently impressed by the novel as was a family friend, Havelock Ellis, to whom Margery referred in the same breath as that in which she talked in intimate terms of the friendship between her father and Henry James. Like my meeting with Dr Radford, the time spent in Margery's company was totally captivating and yet for reasons often totally disconnected with the purpose in hand. The overriding impression that I brought away from that meeting was the bond and similarities between her and Aldington. It was only natural that we talked about Richard, rather than Aldington. It was during the hours of conversation that both Margery and Patricia talked about Malthouse cottage as it was more than sixty years before.

I had written in advance telling Margery briefly of what I had turned up at Hermitage and Oare but it wasn't until I got to Rye that I urged the suggestion that in *Women Must Work* Aldington expressed his aspirations for his sister. I sensed a slight hesitation before Margery told me it was so long since she had read the book and couldn't recall the story well enough to judge but she talked spontaneously about her time in Oare. Early on I mentioned Miss Salter's name. Margery was surprised. 'Oh you know all about her, do you?' It was a rhetorical question. 'All I can remember is the girl who worked at the post office. She rejoiced in the name of Louis Flitter and I remember the post-mistress but not her name. [The cottage] was on the farm estate at Oare. The farmer was awfully good to us. In fact, the whole of the neighbourhood was terribly sweet to

us. I went there with a great mutual friend of us all. She was a writer.'
This confirmed my theory: *Women Must Work* was based on Margery
Aldington and Miss Salter and both the story and what Margery told me,
contributed insights into her brother's life and attitudes as well as to her
own. The fictional Etta was a few years older than Margery. It suited
Aldington's particular purpose. He was able to put some of his own
expectations into the role that Etta was to take on in the novel. 'And this
was just the beginning!' he wrote. 'She would have to go beyond that –
to reach something really interesting – she had no idea what – her efforts
would not be wasted. And with age creeping on like this, she had only
about two years to do it in – certainly it mustn't be later than 1915.'[11]

These were Aldington's own expectations, for by 1913, then aged
twenty-one, he was making inroads to literary London. We know that the
times coincide as Margery told me 'Richard came back from abroad' and
that this would have been after his trips to Italy in 1912 or 1913. The war
was to bring all his hopes and aspirations to a sudden halt and we see in
practically all his work a bitter resentment against the attitudes that led
to its outbreak and the effect that had on his career. In *Women Must Work*
we see his sister's point of view, or rather what he imagined her view to
be. While Richard's natural gift was as a writer, his sister Margery foresaw
a career in one form or another on the stage. At the time Richard was
touring the continent, fifteen-year-old Margery had enrolled at a drama
school run by a German woman in London.

As a lawyer, her father had rooms at the Temple and Margery would
stay with him. Quite how much more tolerant their father was compared
with their mother, can only be judged from the words that Aldington
attributes to Mrs Morison after comparable events in the novel. 'I'm sure
I was against it from the beginning, but your daddy always would spoil
you, and after all our trouble and paying all those fees, you only stopped
one term.'[12] Margery's real talent lay elsewhere. She had always had a
good voice and there was nothing she wanted more than to be given the
opportunity of receiving a proper musical training. The chance came from
her drama teacher. At the age of seventeen, Margery told me, she was
given 'an introduction to the conductor Percy Pitt... for an audition in the
foyer at Covent Garden. I'd got my pigtails still which I used to tie at my
throat. Elderly people of about twenty-two were there for the audition,'
Margery said with a smile. 'I walked about half a mile [across the foyer]
to a rostrum and sang. When I'd finished he said "Well now, what

experience have you?" I said "None"… Well I was sent away and went over the road for a glass of milk and a bath bun at the ABC and went home. That night I got my contract… I was the youngest chorister at Covent Garden!'

I was enthralled as Margery's story unfolded. 'I was very wrapped up in that part of my life… and it was about that time… that Bun Salter and I shared digs with another woman somewhere in Empress Gate.' For whatever reason, Margery couldn't recall the third name. 'So why "Bun" Salter?' I asked, as if I did not know. 'I've already told you! She wore her hair in earphones.' No, I thought, those were Richard's words. Two events though had a disastrous effect on Margery and her brother. Margery confirmed that in 1911 their father '… slipped up badly. He had a nervous breakdown.' Family finances fell away. The rug of security was pulled from under them. Richard was forced to leave university without his degree. The repercussions are evident in his 1934 novel *All Men are Enemies*, too. Henry Clarendon, the father of Tony Clarendon 'withdrew into a silent brooding, which Anthony was unable to break down' forcing him to face the 'suicide of his father's deadly apathy.'[13]

That Richard and Margery did survive is surely down to their mother's stubborn streak. In their individual ways, they each rose to the occasion. In 1913 Jessie May Aldington bought the famous Mermaid Inn at Rye no doubt giving rise to Arabella's comments about her as a maternal barmaid. Richard was conscripted in 1916. Despite the fact they only saw each other occasionally there was a strong bond between brother and sister. It was only natural that Richard took on a protective role towards Margery and yet he knew that she must not be dependent upon him any more than she had been upon their father. He foresaw what would happen to his sister; there would be no call for talented singers in wartime. Margery would be entirely unqualified for anything other than her musical career and yet she would now be called on to eke a living from whatever source she could. As her brother urged, *Women Must Work;* if they were to have any measure of independence they must never again be dependent upon men. In *Women Must Work* Ada Lawson, perhaps the nearest fictional parallel to Anna Munro speaks for him.

'She began by talking of the status of women under Roman law, which only recognised them as daughters, wives and mothers – a male always had to be responsible for them. This had been perpetuated right down to the eighteenth century, even if the rigours had been softened. The women of Provence, of Renaissance Italy and eighteenth-century France had attempted to create something better, but all failed. Yet in the pre-industrial world women had certain privileges and compensations now lost. They were undisputed mistresses of the household, and the men gave their consciences over to the women's keeping – they lived their lives as men, but rarely behaved in such a way as to alienate or destroy the women's lives. Moreover, women were not then cursed with idleness – even queens worked at the distaff. The men fed the world, but the women clothed it. There was a balance of the sexes, both materially and spiritually; and if men might rightly be proud of their share, so might women. Neither could exist without the other.

'This delicate balance, she went on, was destroyed in one respect by the rapid introduction of machinery. "Spinster", instead of meaning a woman who span, became a sort of joke. Women were defrauded of a large part of their most interesting work. So far as working-class families were concerned, the job of producing was dumped entirely on the men, and the women were left to be household drudges – the men now never thought of sharing this work as they had done. In the well-off classes it was even worse. The middle-class lady was invented. She was forbidden to do anything useful or sensible. Her job was to lie on a couch and be sexually attractive in a clinging please-protect-me way. She was instructed in "accomplishments", not for her sake or their sake, but because they were supposed to charm men. And these futile accomplishments plus a little household management were often her only preparations for the realities of marriage and maternity. Was it any wonder, she asked, that sensible and self-respecting women of all classes were in revolt against a state of affairs which made them parasites or drudges? Wasn't it reasonable to ask that the balance should be restored, that one half of the human race should not be defrauded of the right to its share in human activity?'[14]

Margery had to abandon all thoughts of a serious musical career. Until then she had: 'thought of nothing. I dreamed of nothing, I lived for nothing but my voice, my singing.' Had it not been for her determination Margery may well have had to go back home. Aldington takes up the same theme in the novel. Vera Wraxall, Etta's friend tried to help.

'She said: "It isn't easy to make any really practical suggestions, but if you're serious I'm sure we can find some way out. Look

here, we're frightfully hard up for voluntary suffrage workers in Dortborough – why not make a start here? It could easily lead to something else." "No, thank you," said Etta decisively. "To be quite frank I've no love of work for work's sake, unless of course I could find something which was fascinating. Working is only a means of getting away from Dortborough." "It is a shame your father won't give you an allowance," said Vera helplessly. "Mother won't let him. I might try being a chorus girl – I've got rather nice legs." A flippant suggestion it may seem, especially to her friend: "Don't be beastly," exclaimed Vera. "Fancy showing yourself half-undressed to a lot of pigs of men! You're really not fit to make a stand for equal rights and independence." [15]

Not surprisingly, it was one that in reality had to be considered. Even Margery though admits that it was not entirely satisfactory or appropriate *'so, down the hill I went – to the Gaiety [Theatre]. George Edwardes saw that I'd the great asset of long legs and I'd got this fine voice… so I got lots of jobs at the Gaiety'* that, once Richard became aware can only have hardened his resolve that his sister – any more than any other woman – should not have to gratify men's desires in whatever form in order to earn a living. Added to his fears for his sister, he, as much as anyone *'was half suffocating with anger for the selfishness of men, who wanted from their women only their own pleasure and submissiveness to their wills. Let the woman choose her way, let her cease to be a pleasure-gadget, let her want a little disinterested affection and kindness … Va donc, bonjour! mais va-t-en, sale femme!'* [16]

Women Must Work more than adequately displays the problems facing a single girl's attempts to make a liveable wage in London during the war years. 'Quite rapidly Etta became acquainted with the realities of poverty in one of its lowliest forms – that of a poor middle class girl looking for a job. Only youth can engage in this struggle and survive as a vital human entity. For the older ones it is death, death of spirit, because the pittance, the bit of bread and drink, the wisp of clothing, the flicker of fire must be begged of business, not even as charity but as a gracious boon in exchange for the best waking hours.' [17] The effects of Aldington's war were felt long after hostilities ended and that same anguish is evident in his sister's feelings. 'You try to earn a living in the London of the 1920s when you walked the streets with ex-soldiers walking in the gutter playing instruments and begging. There was no work. I got the sack from one job because I looked so shabby.' Aldington, however, was one of the lucky ones. Neither his talent nor his contacts had entirely deserted him and within a short time of his demobilisation he had managed to gain work from various periodicals. There was no reason why he should remain in London. He could write equally well in the country and, at the same time, gain materially from the tranquillity of his surroundings. His heroine, he felt, would similarly benefit from and appreciate a change of scenery. Etta, he felt, would be very glad to get away from people.

In the ensuing years Padworth and the surrounding countryside came to represent so much of value to Aldington both in the psychological and the fictional sense that great tracts of the Kennet Valley can be seen throughout his fiction. He gifted Etta the fictional means to acquire 'Dymcott' the house that had previously belonged to her mentor, the suffragette, Ada Lawson. But in reality, as is so often the case, circumstances were not quite so opportune. Nevertheless Aldington wished upon his sister the same peace of mind that he found in this strategic little cottage. It is at this point in the story that Vera Wraxall comes into her own. She manages to find a place in the country where she and Etta can seek refuge.

Margery told me what actually happened. 'Country air I longed for; country air I needed. Richard helped us and we found that cottage at Oare.' Among Margery's fondest memories of the time she and 'Bun' were at Oare was the long walk between there and Padworth that bound them to Richard and Arabella whom she dubbed Dolkins. '… She – funny little thing – looked rather like an Indian – wore a hard cut black, bang and short cut hair and walked with a funny tottering walk but she did that sixteen miles that we used to do. We … with our long English legs and little 'Bun' scuttling along, and Dolkins scudding with her and Budge, the dog, behind. That was how we commuted together between these two places.' Margery remains very relaxed about this interlude. So, too did Etta and Vera in *Women Must Work*. 'The house delighted Etta at once, it was an old six-room cottage with barns and stables, which evidently had once gone with more land that the seven acres worked by Mr Brown.'[18] As Mrs Hards told me: 'The theory was that these small holdings were given to Yeomen after the battle of Newbury as a sort of "thank you" for fighting for the King.'

What Mrs Hards showed me of Wallins exactly fitted Aldington's description of it as a six-roomed cottage. Even after all these years it is not difficult to picture the place as it was in Margery's day. Upstairs the rooms follow the raking ceiling way up into the roof and are only stopped by the tie beams holding the cottage together; and the floors, as in most cottages of this age go every which way. So too, in the novel: 'The floors of the upper rooms undulated where the wood had warped.' The fictional cottage is obviously based firmly on Wallins but nevertheless linked to the geography of Chapel Farm Cottage at nearby Hermitage. 'The idea was that Etta should try to learn about running such a place while she stayed [next door to the Browns]...' Rather in the fashion of the author, Etta '... envied their placidity and tried to imitate it'[19] exactly as Aldington himself did. Etta and Vera '... went up the hill at the back of the house and sat under the edge of the copse ... near the crest of the hill looking over the fields and watching the golden evening sunlight throw longer and longer shadows.' And in the rural way of things '... there were hosts of little things she scarcely noticed when she was with the Browns. For instance – the wood fire. Etta loved the wood fire, but hadn't realised how it was fed. They omitted to shelter the wood-pile properly, so it got soaked, and the logs hissed and smouldered, instead of burning. Trying to saw logs with too much energy Etta strained herself inside, and had to lie up for a day. Then came the question of a fresh supply of wood. Brown, they discovered, had paid so much for the right to cut down firewood in a copse about a mile away; but they had neither the strength, nor the tools, nor the time to do this. So they had to pay heavily to have wood cut and brought to them. Thus it happened with numbers of things – they had to pay out, instead of getting in. There was the earth closet, for instance, which was in a little hut twenty yards from the house, in summer covered with roses. It had seemed engagingly primitive and picturesque then. But now it was a penance in wet weather, and then they couldn't find anyone to empty it, until reluctantly a neighbour consented to "oblige them" – for a shilling a week. They discovered that all odd jobs had to be contracted on the "oblige" principle.'[20]

The parallels between truth and fiction cropped up quite fortuitously. Margery told me for example that they bought a goat from 'Louis Flitter's boss at the Post Office ...' and in the novel, Etta learned to milk after a fashion but had to give up because it strained her back. It is difficult even with hindsight to judge who enjoyed themselves the most, Margery and Bun Salter or Etta and Vera. Certainly Margery and 'Bun' entered into the spirit of things in a vigorous fashion that says as much of their own free spirits as it does of the bucolic life they were living. Margery told me with a knowing smile that an ' …old lady gave us six old hens and … a chicken farmer across the road … said "Poor old hens. They want a cock to cheer them up!" so he gave me a fine cockerel, *MacHeath*!' I wondered how their neighbours looked upon them and what role Margery and 'Bun' played in their small community. In the novel they were fairly well isolated from everyone except the fictitious Browns: 'Nobody called on them, except the vicar, once – an embarrassed duty visit.'[21] It was Margery herself that suggested, quite unwittingly, what lay between her brother's lines. 'Awful adventures we had. Those six old hens. We made a marvellous sort of fencing for them by the barn. And having got the last nail in, we found we had nailed ourselves in and at that moment the vicar called. We had to call him. "Would you mind going into the dairy and looking round. You'll find a pair of pliers. Then we'll come out and make you some tea!" Terrible adventure!'

Practically everything that Margery told me mirrored the fictitious lives of Etta and Vera. At times the four young women become one and yet I was soon to meet another. The fictitious 'Elizabeth Rollo' was created by the pen of 'Bun' Salter, and in common with both 'Bun' herself, and Margery; 'The strange passion in her life was music.'[22] Margery confirmed that Bun Salter '…was my accompanist [and] we used to make music.' This immediately brought back fragments of the first conversation I had had with Mrs Rouse. Even at ten years old she had judged Margery to be 'a great singer.' When I went back later Mrs Rouse told me how 'Miss Aldington and Miss Salter' used to come down to the post office in Hermitage. Mr Boshier obviously played a fundamental role in the well being of Hermitage's cultured guests. 'Margery was a great singer … a contralto I think. When they first came to Wallins their spinet hadn't turned up or something, so she came to the post office and asked my father if they could hire a piano and he said, "Oh, you can come here and use ours." So she used to come down about three times a week and practise her arias and arpeggios.'

Spinet, harpsichord, piano, whichever is which, it occurs to me that this may well be the one that finished up in Padworth in July 1922, for it was somewhere around this time that the two girls left Oare and much to John Rouse's disappointment were never seen again. In any event though it did arrive eventually at Oare and played a central role in the social life at the time. It meant everything to Margery as it brought together a little band of like-minded friends. 'We had a little spinet [and] there was an old man who used to play the violin and his son in law who played the cello and his daughter who played the viola … and we all made music together – all eighteenth century.' Mrs Rouse told me of one lady who used to sing with Margery, 'voice training' was how she had described it. Margery's voice was very much admired: 'I think she was a professional singer.' It was that very professionalism and her stage experience that prompted Margery and Bun to suggest that they do more than just entertain themselves. 'We toured the district there. We called ourselves "Mr Gay's Players" after Gay who wrote "The Beggars' Opera"…' which brings us right back to the chicken farmer over the road and the reason why the cockerel he gave them couldn't be called anything other than 'MacHeath!'

Practically the whole of *Women Must Work* is written from a feminist standpoint and the fact that it is written by a man makes it all the more remarkable for it represents, as it were, the sympathetic centre and an alliance of male-female attitudes – all men are *not* enemies. And yet the direction from which Aldington arrives at this standpoint is entirely understandable given the slightest insight into his nature and his family upbringing. What pulls the novel together though seems to be the feminist aspirations of his time and obviously the covert presence of Anna Munro and Bun Salter. It was within minutes of first meeting Margery that she told me Miss Salter 'wrote one novel that got a very good review… but she did an awful lot of magazine writing; things like *Nash's Good-Housekeeping* – on all sorts of subjects. In those days they were getting round to an interest in women's problems, health problems and that sort of thing. Oh, Bun was a versatile sort. She'd write about anything if she got an idea.'

I never thought to ask Margery how Salter spelled her pseudonym. It was a more straightforward task, however, to make contact with *Good Housekeeping* magazine. To my good fortune, almost by return of post, came photocopies of the six articles that Miss Salter had written for them during the 1920s. For the first time I learnt her full name – Olive Mary Salter. As Margery had suggested, these articles touch upon the achievements of women, two in particular were pertinent to my own conclusions. Her February 1927 article 'Running a Country Hotel' suggests that Salter knew of Jessie May's purchase of The Mermaid Inn at Rye. 'I know a courageous woman who took over the leading hotel in a well-established coast resort, without having a single penny to her name… This was a more desperate adventure even than it sounds, for in addition to the anxiety of having to start the whole concern upon borrowed money, she had no experience at all of hotel management, and for the first few weeks was even reduced to asking her visitors to help make out their own bills.' The Mermaid at Rye acquired a certain renown during the First World War as a refuge for servicemen on leave from the front and the laxity of concern that was shown towards their behaviour. Without the slightest hint of irony Miss Salter continues: 'I am thinking of an hotel run for many years by a woman who possessed to a very marked degree the power to dispel worry out of the atmosphere, as it were, simply by the influence of her own placid personality. Her house was hardly ever empty of hard-working politicians, newspaper men, artists and similarly highly strung types, who would run down for a few hours, whenever they could spare the time, admitting that they came largely for the sake of the restful atmosphere which she could provide for them.'[23]

But it was a second article of March 1926 that seemed to have a more direct bearing on life and circumstances of the two young women at Oare. I had become aware of the possible significance of one passage in *Women Must Work*. 'They two wenches up where Browns used to be were commented on acidly – if rich, why were they taking the bread out of honest people's mouths… and if poor, why messing about with good land they couldn't work.' His answer, in broad terms, is a continuing theme throughout Aldington's fiction. '"Let me think," said Etta reflecting, "First I want a life that is full and interesting. I should like to work at something which had a purpose beyond mere moneymaking. I should like to mix with people who would make my life fuller. I want to live near a man I love and who would love me, and I think I'd like to have a child."'[24] That this liberated credo was written by a man is interesting, but that Aldington was expressing it is perhaps telling. HD produced a daughter by another man while Aldington was in the trenches.

Aldington did not find it easy to take on the responsibility of the women who were dependent upon him, whether his mother, his wife, his mistress of the moment or indeed, as we see here, his sister. He chose to unburden himself in fiction. Etta Morison sought to take her emancipation that one stage further and have a baby on her own, she wanted to live near a man, not necessarily with a man. She claimed her right to decide when she might have a baby or indeed to choose not to have one at all, to both of which views Aldington's concurrence can again be seen in his novels. *The Colonel's Daughter* is as much about the problems of Lizzie Judd's unfortunate pregnancy as it is about the plight of poor Georgie for an essential aspect of women's emancipation was that power to choose.

Contraception, even in the 1920s, gave women as much power over their own destinies as the vote. And yet, despite Aldington's apparently generous nature, there may be another more singular reason for supporting the cause. Aldington's personal crusade against the cant of the Victorian age applied to their sexual attitudes as much as to their jingoism. On both accounts Aldington was judge, jury and prosecuting counsel and it is when he gets on this particular hobby horse that we see him let fly with a vengeance that makes the 'angry young men' of the 1950s positively tame by comparison. A passage from *Death of a Hero* for example, is not only pertinent but is expressed with a fierce passion the justification of which is even now as relevant as it was in 1929 when it was written. 'I have shown, with a certain amount of excusable ferocity, how devilishly and perniciously the old regime of Cant affected people's sexual lives, and hence the whole of their lives and characters and those of their children. The subsequent reaction was, at least in its origin, healthy and right.

'There simply had to be a better attitude, the facts had to be faced. And nobody with any courage will allow himself to be frightened out of saying so, either by the hush-hush partisans of the old regime or the doing-what-grandpa-did-and-let's-pretend-it's-all-lovely, or by the fact that numerous congenital idiots have prattled and babbled and slobbered about sex until the very word is an exacerbation. But the sexual life is important. It is in so many cases the dominant or the next to dominant factor in people's lives. We can't write about their lives without bringing it in; so for God's sake let's do it honestly and openly, in accordance with what we believe to be the facts, or else give up pretending that we are writing about life. No more Cant. And I mean free-love Cant just as much as orange blossoms and pealing church bells Cant. '[25]

The first four of Aldington's novels follow a very logical sequence each one throwing light on the times and each telling of the effects on the generation that followed their Victorian predecessors. In *Death of a Hero* young men's lives are sacrificed on the altar of Cant. Georgie Smithers in *The Colonel's Daughter* remains bound by Victorianism in the twenties. In 1933 Aldington contended that *All Men are Enemies* and in *Women Must Work* he poses a way out of their dilemma. In February of 1925 Miss Salter's article, 'Stocks and Shares in Adversity' (the first of a series) appeared in *Good Housekeeping*. 'Many women will find the solutions of their personal problems in this stimulating article' is how it is flagged.[26] This was followed in August 1925 by 'Out of Touch,' in which the author 'sums up a good deal of post-war "frightfulness" and reaches some new conclusions.'[27] 'The Human Equation' a month later, is a deep discussion on marriage relationships and voices the new emancipation of women compared with the old Victorian ideals. We are, Salter writes, 'all looking out for something that will last, in love as well as in more material commodities, and we do not, if we are wise, allow the mysterious attraction of passion to hoodwink us into a bad bargain. It may be romantic to love we know not why, but it is also confusing, perhaps a trifle undignified, and frequently leads to complications which the modern young person is extremely disposed to avoid."[28]

Further pitfalls are suggested the following April, aimed at those who may still find an attraction in 'Marrying for Money'.[29] That wealth 'does not always bring the truest balance to the matrimonial scales' is the theme of this article but it was the article of March 1926 that held my attention. Contrary to the theme set by the others 'A Prodigal Singer' is a short story in which the son of Salter's heroine, Elizabeth Rollo, is brought up unaware of the true identity of his father. The story is remarkable not just for the autobiographical undertones it shares with the musical lives of the author herself and Margery at Oare but for the parallels with *Women Must Work* that was written eight years later. In *Women Must Work*, Etta Morison makes a conscious decision not to marry the father of her child much against his desire to be seen to do right by her.

    ' *"The life of an illegitimate child in England is unthinkable. – disabilities and humiliations at every turn. Besides, if this were to be known, my career would be ruined."*
    "If it's only that which worries you, I give you my solemn word of honour nobody shall ever know it is yours."

"But a child has to be registered by law," Francis almost screamed at her. "Get that into your head to start with."
'Etta tried an appeal: "Don't let us quarrel, my dear…"
"I'm not quarrelling, I'm trying to knock a little common sense into your obstinate lunacy."
"I'm not going to let you make me angry, Francis," said Etta wistfully. "I love you, and you're the father of the child I'm going to have."
"You're not!"
"I am! I've planned it all out. I shall go the country with Vera and the child, and work there for it and bring it up."[30]

Here, I must hasten to add, despite the numerous parallels with the life of his sister Margery, Etta's baby is entirely fictitious. The fact that both Aldington's Etta and Bun Salter's Elizabeth both appear to be firmly based in Oare follows from their fictional circumstances. Wallins is one of the last cottages on the north side of the village, the otherwise magnificent view of the Downs only recently spoilt by the imposition of the M4 motorway in the foreground. That the Downs hereabouts are often known locally as the Newbury Downs confirms this as Elizabeth Rollo's cottage. '"Maybe the Lord don't see our cottage, so small and hid away as it is," said Elizabeth under her breath preoccupied (rather melodramatically) with soiled dishes. "You can see as there's a cottage here as far as from Nelsonbury Downs when the smoke's going up good," murmured the boy.'

That Elizabeth Rollo is a musician is a reflection of Salter's talents in that direction. As Margery confirmed, 'The strange passion in her life was music.' But the remote nature of their surroundings played on Salter's mind. 'Their lives were lonely and self-centred, especially during the winter months.'[31] As the two young women were more accustomed to life in London, this is not surprising. It was during the winter months at Oare – the concert season in London – that Margery and 'Bun' would do the rounds of the local village halls in company with Mr Gay's Players and, before their spinet arrived this would surely be when they would be down at the post office practising. Elizabeth Rollo, Bun Salter's heroine, followed in their footsteps. 'When winter came she got permission to use the old piano that stood in the vicarage rooms.' Margery and Bun would give singing lessons to some of the locals, the chicken farmer and the cello player for instance, very much as did Elizabeth Rollo. Elizabeth 'taught Yew to pick out his notes, and played song after song for him, often until their candle gave out and they must fumble their way out through the dark, her hand caught, like a palpitating moth in his great fist.'[32]

One common thread binds these narratives. Aldington expresses Etta's circumstances quite simply. 'She thought she knew all about Francis Leigh, and she didn't. She knew about the wife and children, and she knew that Francis held "modern" views about the sexes; but she was completely deceived by the hypocrisy of respectability which is forced on men in any public position.'[33] In Bun Salter's story, there immediately follows an appropriately torrid sequence worthy of Mills and Boon and an equally romantic separation during which time the inevitable happened. Elizabeth's aspirations to become a 'music teacher in Nelsonbury' are dashed. There was 'no sign of Yew for three years, and life goes hard with unmarried maids in country places…'[34] exactly as Aldington takes great pains to explain in *Women Must Work*. But, in the best tradition of Edwardian melodrama, Elizabeth is subsequently widowed and after many a long year, Yew finally comes back to the village and all went happily ever after. Not so in real life. 'Bun' Salter and Margery Aldington upped sticks one day and, as far as the village is concerned were never heard of from that day to this. Aldington echoes the fact in *Women Must Work*. 'They were an anomaly, puzzling to the village, and by no means above suspicion. Two young women from London… and no man about were enough to rouse the suspicions of anybody.'[35]

And there the matter must lie for the present, except that is, for an intriguing series of established facts. While Aldington was in the trenches on his second tour of duty, his wife H.D. became pregnant and in 1919 when the marriage was in a state of flux she gave birth to a baby girl. Despite the fact that he was not the father, Aldington initially offered to bring up the child as his daughter. That offer was rejected and he and H.D. separated. He came to live at Hermitage with Arabella and H.D. formed a life-long relationship with Winifred 'Bryher' Ellerman, the enigmatic daughter of the financier, Sir James Ellerman to whom Aldington himself had turned for introductions following his demobilisation. H.D. chose to bring up her daughter in the company of Bryher and along the matriarchal lines propounded by Aldington in *Women Must Work*. It wasn't until many, many years later that H.D.'s daughter learnt what is generally accepted to be the true identity of her father.

The intimate personal details of the breakdown between Aldington and H.D. may, quite rightly, never be known, but at the time Aldington and Arabella were living at Hermitage a great deal of correspondence had passed between husband and wife. 'Piles and piles' of paper was how it would seem to the young Hilda Brown next door. 'Nobody's supposed to know about that,' she told me '…but when he left, he left a lot of papers, and all the things were left behind [suggesting] what [might] happen to him in war time.' This would seem to be a reference to the arrangements that any soldier had to make for the well-being of his wife under those circumstances. But Hilda Brown's recollections go deeper than that. There were more than just these wartime arrangements, 'there were letters about him and his wife… from her to him… I don't know what the exact [nature of them was] … but there were piles and piles of papers left. He left the whole lot behind and Mother said "What's the…?" and he said to my mother "Would you burn that for me?" so she said, "Yes, certainly."' But of course nobody, but *nobody* would do so without giving them a cursory glance at the very least. It must have proved quite an eventful afternoon for the Browns, and the end of an equally eventful few years for them too. No doubt Bill Brown was quite pleased to see the back of them all. No more shenanigans going on next door. He would be able to get down once more to a bit of serious gardening.

Chapter 7

The Squire

Aldington could not tolerate pretentiousness, falsehood and insincerity in whatever form. His sister told me that: 'If Richard saw anything… he put his head down and charged like a bull.' When Heinemann brought out a uniform pocket edition of his books in 1934, they decorated the pastedown and the dust jacket with a colophon derived from a prehistoric drawing of a bull in the caves of Altamira, head down and charging, that C.P. Snow saw as 'a shorthand symbol of the author's credo.'[1] It was the falsehood and insincerity of literary London, as much as his desire for tranquillity and solitude, that drove Aldington to Berkshire in the first place. He persecuted false idols with an ardent intensity that can be seen in his collection of short stories, *Soft Answers*, in which he attacked Nancy Cunard, Ezra Pound, T.S. Eliot and the male species generally. In contrast, however, he worshipped eccentricity; the further off centre, the more Aldington was attracted. The definitive, whimsical, unassuming self-ridiculing traits of eccentricity were the natural foil to everything Aldington found intolerable. Eccentricity is synonymous with the image of the English country squire and two such gentlemen in particular can be seen to have intrigued Aldington. His book *The Strange Life of Squire Waterton* was expanded from an essay of the same title, one of *Four English Portraits* published the year before.[2] and Aldington was evidently drawn to the explorer's eccentricity.

Aldington might have added, as here he implies, that the eccentric is as often as not the man who knows what he wants to say and simply and openly *says* it. For indeed in a literal rather than derogatory interpretation of the word, bigotry was a further facet of the eccentric that attracted Aldington. We have already seen evidence of that in his fictional images of Mr Brown. While he may have objected to a viewpoint, he would admire the strength of the conviction with which the view was held. At the time Aldington wrote the introductory essay on *The Strange Life of*

Squire Waterton, the eccentric was as extinct as the moa and the passenger pigeon, which had saddened Aldington. He felt that the English eccentric made a valuable contribution to the world's human fauna. That was in 1948 but Aldington had also held a fascination with another eccentric squire from his time in Padworth.

He tells us that 'Padworth House was a treasury of family heirlooms, museum pieces which were in great demand for national and international exhibitions. There were even two bedrooms with 18th-century wallpaper – pretty coloured patterns like the flowered muslin gowns worn by the ladies. But the greatest museum piece was the squire himself, a genuine English eccentric.'[3] Indeed, Holly Lodge, the fictional home of the colonel's daughter 'had probably been a dower house alienated from the Manor in the reckless fashion of the old Squires' precisely as suggested even now as you look down from Padworth House to what was its Lower Lodge.[4] Despite the implied folly of the squire's action, one senses that Aldington couldn't help but admire the 'reckless fashion' in which it was carried out.

Major Christopher William Darby Griffith was an inspiration to Aldington; he, together with Bill Brown, represented the embodiment of what Thomas McGreevy sees as 'Chaucer's England, Shakespeare's England, Fielding's England, the England that had worth centuries before an Irish peer invented Empire Day.'[5] It is equally plain from *Life for Life's Sake* that Aldington and 'Major Darby' as the squire is remembered, knew each other fairly well, for in addition to the times when they met on the train to London, Aldington talks of at least one occasion when he was invited to Padworth House. It is therefore not unreasonable to assume that Aldington's 'too tender regard for the honour of the eccentrics' flourished as a direct result of his acquaintance with the major and led him eventually to his ever-enlarging studies of Squire Waterton. Major Darby and Squire Waterton had a lot in common and it is evident that Aldington's aspirations for the one ran parallel to his findings on the other. 'Unlike his neighbours', he tells us in *Life for Life's Sake*, Major Darby 'was of an old country family, the kind of people who scorned a title because they were prouder of their names than of any "honour"'[6] whereas: 'The Watertons of Walton Hall, like the Evelyns, the Landors, the Blunts, were too proud of their family name to accept titles, even when they were offered.'[7] Certainly at the time of writing *Life for Life's Sake* in 1940–41 Aldington had already read the Waterton book because he uses a quote from the book, referring to the King as 'our Royal Goat' when describing Henry VIII's hunting expeditions at nearby Aldermaston Park.[8]

Within a matter of days of learning that Aldington had lived in this cottage, I had read *Life for Life's Sake* and had managed to acquire a copy of *The Colonel's Daughter* but at that time my knowledge of 'the fauna' of Padworth of the 1920s was absolutely minimal. I naturally concluded that Sir Horace Stimms, squire of Cleeve, the archetypal villain of *The Colonel's Daughter*, was founded on Major Darby. It took quite a while before I could be shaken from that foolishly entrenched inference as I ran into evidence that strengthened, rather than weakened my resolve. The more I learned from the people of the village, the more I realised that throughout *The Colonel's Daughter*, the author had used real events and circumstances with very little licence that would lead anyone to jump to some very disconcerting conclusions. Padworth House was no longer the Darby Griffith family home but a finishing school for young ladies and I had therefore cast aside all thoughts of learning anything of him from that quarter and yet quite unexpectedly I did learn one day that the principal and his wife were themselves curious about the history of the house and were as interested as I was in finding out about Major Darby.

Two phone calls, and about the same number of days later found me taking tea in the slightly decayed but original elegance of the drawing room at Padworth House. We had a lot to talk about, and for the first and only time I found that I was to be saved an immeasurable amount of effort in taking things that one stage further. I was invited back a second time to meet a very important person: Major Darby's housemaid, Mrs Hilda Hearn (formerly Hobbs). Hilda's mother had come to the village nearly a hundred years ago. She took a post as nanny to the then rector, the Reverend Clinton and married William Hobbs, head gardener at Aldington's favourite Elizabethan house, Ufton Court. The Hobbs family were caretakers for the absent owner and had the run of Ufton Court, exactly as Aldington wished upon his heroine Etta Morison.

To Aldington's obvious regret he tells us that Major Darby 'was unmarried and the last of his long line.'[9] This led to speculation in *The Colonel's Daughter* on what would happen after the Major died. In *Life for Life's Sake* he tells us that 'within a few miles of my cottage… existed relics and fragments of English history, terminating in that singular human relic, the squire of Padworth. To someone with a sense of the past, it was fascinating; a great book, with many blanks and torn pages indeed, but

Fig. 23. William Hobbs, head gardener at Ufton Court

more vivid that the written word.'[10] He is, of course, correct on all counts. His descriptions of Major Darby as an eccentric are underlined by practically everyone I've met. All their memories, Aldington's included, are tinged with affection for 'the old major'. Major Darby was very tall – 'six foot four or five' – and wore a moustache with an air of shrewd abandon that complemented his circumstances at Padworth House. Mrs Hearn recalls ruefully that her wages were 'twelve shillings a week plus keep' and that normally 'in service you were usually allowed two shillings or half a crown a week' to cover laundry expenses but, the major 'wouldn't allow anything for that because he said that the tips we got [when guests stayed] more than covered that amount. He was right of course!' And yet in other ways and at different times the major could be more than generous. Mrs Hearn fortuitously recalled one such occasion when he 'once gave me a pound note for putting a loop on his Ulster that had a hood on it and that he used to go up to Scotland in. He needn't have done that. It was nearly twice my week's wages. That was my job. He didn't have to give me anything.'

I'm pleased though that he did and that this story has remained with Mrs Hearn for all these years. It could well be that on this particular morning Major Darby was off to London for the day by train. As a young boy living in Mill Lane Leslie Austin recalls that he would often see Major Darby on his way to the station. 'He was a nice old boy – dressed in a big white moustache. He always dressed in plus fours. We'd be on our way to school and he would stop and give us a penny.' And that was an aspect of Major Darby that Aldington liked. He was not so overloaded with his own importance or imposed social position that he couldn't give away to Leslie Austin the odd penny that he hadn't paid Hilda Hobbs. The fact that he was in effect buying respect from the local children would never have occurred to the major. By contrast there was one old dame 'up-the-village,' as upper Padworth was referred to, Miss Froude, who would annually give the school children a tea party at her house as a treat and who according to the daughter of the then headmistress made the journey to school one year in order to withdraw the invitation from one little girl who hadn't curtsied to her that morning. But the day on which Major Darby set off for the station could well be the morning when Aldington too was off to London for the day, perhaps a Wednesday, for that was the day Aldington reserved for his London business.

'One morning when I was on the station platform waiting for the

London train, the squire turned up, having walked the two miles to the station to save gasoline.[11] He was astonishingly dressed for a visit to the Empire's capital, but seemed totally unaware of his curious appearance. On his head he wore an old fishing cap with flaps and a couple of ragged trout flies still stuck in it. His suit was of shabby tweed; and over it he wore an immense rusty Ulster with a set of flaps, like those worn by Dickens' coachmen.' But that was not all. 'Round his neck was knotted a large white silk handkerchief which fell over his chest, and into this he frequently sneezed, for he had a bad cold – doubtless due to some ill considered economy. I could not avoid travelling with him, as he also had a third-class ticket. In between his uninhibited sneezes, he discoursed of the cupidity of the workin' classes and informed me that the coal miners were bleedin' the country white.'[12]

This would have been just before the general strike in 1926. Rumour still has it, among those who were around at the time that the major was

Fig. 24. Major Darby's study at Padworth House

supposed to be a very wealthy man. It was certainly a firm recollection of Mrs Hearn's. 'I don't think he had any special interest other than the stock exchange. He spent a lot of time in [his study]. That was his rather special room. People used to come to him for advice about money. He was really good on that – telling them how and where to invest his money and when to take it out.'

This ties in well with Aldington's account of their shared journey to London. 'By an easy transition he then went on to say that he had just cleared forty thousand pounds by a deal in sugar. The money was on deposit in the bank, as he couldn't discover immediately another safe and profitable investment. He understood that I was connected with The Times, and therefore presumably on the right side and in the know. What did I suggest as a nice comfy investment? I nearly said: "Sell all that thou hast and give it to the poor". But he was impregnable to satire, and would merely have told me I was a rotten socialist.'[13]

With all this talk of money I was not entirely *un*-convinced that Aldington had based the fictitious Sir Horace Stimms on Major Darby. Ron Bates had told me that part of his father's duties at the Mill House involved the maintenance of the sluices that drove the turbine providing power to Padworth House. Geoffrey Hunter-Payne, in *The Colonel's Daughter* noticed this and was talking to Colonel Smithers about it. 'I noticed the other day that there's a very neat little dam and power-house on the river with a wire leading up to the Squire's house. Why don't you get him to let you run a wire along here – we could install all sorts of things. I could do most of the installation myself if we only had the power.'[14] Sir Horace though was possessive about his power. 'He thinks the river's all his because it runs for a mile or so through his land, and he wouldn't dream of allowing anyone else to use his electric power.'[15] In *Life for Life's Sake* Aldington tells us that Major Darby (despite his supposed wealth) was astonishingly parsimonious far more so that Bill Brown who, it will be remembered, gave away rabbits 'all over the shop'.[16]

Not so Major Darby. Obviously speaking from personal experience Aldington says that: 'Although his coverts were crowded with pheasants, at Christmas he bestowed on each family of the parish exactly one rabbit apiece.'[17] It was the association of such statements that continued my belief that Darby Griffith and the fictional Sir Horace Stimms were one and the same person for in the epilogue to *The Colonel's Daughter* – a most splenetic piece of satire – the author attributes such generosity to Sir Horace: 'when men cry 'Noel, noel!' and neighbourly love and charity soften the heart, upon each and every one of his tenantry doth he bestow a coney from his own broad acres.'[18] No more than four pages before this Aldington similarly but quietly admonishes Sir Horace over his 'sin' that we know to be that of Major Darby. 'The electric lights which had been shining haughtily over the dark village from every window in the distant mansion were suddenly extinguished; the wealthy but thrifty host possessed a switch to turn off every light in the house at twelve sharp. Waste not, want not.'[19]

Mrs Hearn told me, as if confirmation were needed, precisely what Aldington was saying. Aldington was however being over generous even to the hateful Sir Horace by allowing an extra hour and a half of electricity for Mrs Hearn tells us: 'At a certain time of night you would be plunged into darkness because the turbine was stopped. We knew that and I'm afraid we used to delight in staying downstairs until half past ten. You got a bit of warning because it was a distance away, but as soon as the light began to dip you just raced like mad all up those stairs. I slept in the very last bedroom of all but … you could just make it to your bedroom before the lights went out.' These parallels between fact and fiction are so misty. Another story that Aldington reports, struck me as so apocryphal that it never occurred to me that there could be any truth behind it. I remember reading it to Mrs Hearn as much for a smile as for any ulterior reason. 'At the Restoration the heir of the family recovered his lands and married a wealthy heiress. The new house was lavishly stocked with furniture, silver, glass, lace, and objets d'art of the period, much of which had been preserved, while the collection was added to during the eighteenth century and later. Unhappily the squire I knew had not inherited the artistic tastes of his ancestors, though he appreciated the financial value of his inheritance. Even this developed tardily. With a curious mixture of pride and regret he told me that as a youth he had used old family portraits as targets for archery practice, only to discover that he had done thousands of pounds' worth of damage to authentic Romneys, Gainsboroughs and Reynoldses.'[20]

By the time I met Mrs Hearn I had written all over the place in a fruitless hunt to track down these pictures. I needn't have bothered as the matter of fact tone of Mrs Hearn's next pronouncement confirmed Aldington's veracity. 'I always thought it was his father that did that, but

Fig. 25. Major Derby at the 1926 re-union of The Old Comrades' Club at Padworth House

I only know what [the Butler] told me so I couldn't swear to this. But I always thought that it was his father and a pal of his. The oil paintings then – the ancestors – they were all up in the attic and they used to shoot at their eyes – you know – bull's eyes.' While I was on this tack I was delighted to learn of Major Darby's god-daughter and was doubly pleased to be offered the opportunity to visit her in the original Griffith family seat at Malden in Yorkshire. By now I had lost most of my initial trepidation in asking direct questions and it was not long before I was being given a guided tour of the house and heaving huge portraits away from the walls. Sadly, too few of the family possessions have found their way back to Yorkshire to enable our search to be definitive and all that have returned have again been recently restored.

There are still far too many loose ends for my total satisfaction. Everyone I met, though, has photographs and Mrs Hearn was no exception. Two she showed me were the first photographs I had seen of Major Darby. The first one, it has to be said, only went to illustrate Aldington's description of him as the greatest museum piece of all those at Padworth House. Taken in 1926 on the occasion of the Annual Regimental reunion of The Old Comrades Club, Major Darby is seen sitting disconsolately in the centre of this typically formal portrait with the entire village ranged out along the steps on the north side of Padworth House.

The second photograph showed Major Darby, similarly bored to distraction by the company of those around him taking tea in front of the carriage house. The first photo seems to suggest that the old major was doing no more than fulfil the obligations of his incumbent position by allowing everyone – which on other occasions would include those attending the various village hops and even the temperance fete – to prance about in his grounds. The second seems to express his mixed fortune at having his friends close to hand. I wondered about the circumstances of this latter event and the identity of his friends. With an alacrity that could only be matched by that of Mr and Mrs Rouse, Mrs Hearn was immediately forthcoming. 'It always seemed to be a nice day and tea was always held in the coach house. The gentleman in the centre of the photograph is Major Crook.'

Major Crook! I wondered immediately if this could be the father of the colonel's daughter. I had the name in my cardex but all I had been able to add to it was the fact that he lived in The White House in Mill Lane. Could he be the 'rude, red-faced soldier, a retired sergeant-major of the guards, who served under the squire in good Queen Vicky's golden days' to whom Aldington refers?[21] Certainly the photo showed evidence

Fig. 26. Major Crook seated (centre) taking tea in the coach house, Padworth House

of that supposition. Mrs Hearn agreed. 'Yes that makes sense. That's Major Crook!' He's also in the first photo, sitting in the foreground, third from right, wearing a bow tie. My mind was already racing far ahead and jumping to conclusions. Obviously even in the short time he was here Aldington knew Major Crook well enough to know that he had served under Major Darby, any story against Queen Vicky would have held his attention.

Aldington recounts one of Major Crook's stories:

'This old man had some instructive stories of cite vieille caleche qui s'obstine a s'appeler Victoria. At Windsor the sentries had to march up and down the battlements at night, and one of these walks passed close to the queen's bedroom. If the sentry kept rigidly to a narrow line of flagstones his step was inaudible in the Queen's room, but if he accidentally made one step to the right or left the echo woke her, she would put on the light, make a note of the exact time, and the sentry would be punished. Moreover, if she

141

passed any troops in the neighbourhood the officer would be reprimanded if he didn't halt his men, fix bayonets, and give a royal salute to the empty air, for the manoeuvre took too long to be executed before she had disappeared. A lady in waiting was instructed to look back from the receding carriage and make sure that the salute was properly forthcoming in every detail... Well, the squire readily gave his old friend and servitor full permission to fish for trout in the Kennet, assuming that he would use the fly, by which method a fisherman seldom landed anything much over half a pound. But the sergeant major wasn't a sergeant major for nothing. In defiance of all the sporting rules he dabbled succulent worms in the dark pools of small tributaries, and yanked out four and five-pounders, to the squire's dismay and wrath. When my old friend, General Mills, chaffed the squire about "worm fishin' goin' on, bad as poachin', what?" the squire went so purple in the face that I thought he was about to be smitten by apoplexy. Even that eccentric Achilles had his vulnerable heel. Perish the Romneys and the Restoration silver, but let it not be said, O Lord, that there was worm-fishin' on The Estate.'[22]

I remembered Ron Bates telling me that he had the best fishing, living as he did at the Mill House. There are now numerous fishermen on the river Kennet between Padworth and Aldermaston but not then. Major Darby was 'not keen on fishing' and Ron had strict instructions to 'tell everyone else to go away...' leaving him and Leslie Austin to fish pretty well where and when they liked. The only problem they ever encountered was from another source altogether. It was always 'Smith, the agent, and old Lawrence, the gardener who were always after us.' I already knew that 'old Lawrence' was head gardener to Padworth Estate as his son is chairman of our parish council. Mr Lawrence is there in the first photo too. The left of the two drainpipes seems to descend down the back of his neck. The young Ron Bates and Leslie Austin also had a penchant for the particularly forbidden apples in the orchard at Padworth House and Mr Lawrence saw to it that their success rate was low. But I had to delve into my cardex again to see, if what I had just learned might allow me to identify that particular Mr Smith from the many I had listed there.

In those days the mill used to belong to Major Darby and Mr Smith,

'Alfred John Smith' as my records showed him to be, lived at the mill before the Bates family. In fact, in 1902, his occupation is given as miller at the baptism of his son, Geoffrey. But, by the time Geoffrey married in 1929, his father's occupation is recorded as 'Estate Agent' a term that has been distorted over the years. With what Ron Bates told me I was able to clip together the two cards in my system. A.J. Smith, 'miller' and A J Smith 'estate agent' were the same man. Not only that but Mr Smith had also taken on the roll of clerk to the parish council in 1917 under the chairmanship of Major Darby and had represented the major at a variety of meetings and functions connected with the school. Furthermore the records suggest that, as 'overseer to the poor,' Smith would be required to play a fictitious but minor role in Sir Horace Stimms manipulations in the life of poor Lizzie Judd. An eccentric old squire he may have been, but Major Darby seemed to have held a fairly tight rein over the affairs of the village. Hence my confusion over the relationship between Colonel Smithers and the true identity of the fictitious squire, Sir Horace Stimms. 'Smithers liked shooting, but Horace owned the shoot. Smithers liked fishing, but the fish existed by kind permission of Horace. Smithers and Alvina would still have liked to hunt, hoary old vulpidices that they were. But whereas twenty noble steeds champed in the stables of Sir Horace, only cobwebs occupied the melancholy void of Smithers' outhouses.'[23]

Was this photograph revealing the identities of Colonel Smithers and Sir Horace Stimms? In a great many ways Major Darby comes across as a very tragic figure. Mrs Hearn assures me that he had a very lonely childhood. He was an only child and the nature of his position would have made it impossible to run round to friends next door. In later life the major lived alone and often must have longed for companionship, which by virtue of his position, he could not fully accept from those who looked after him and yet he would surround himself in the company of those he knew. Mrs Hearn remembers that he would even invite his old army batman out from Thatcham five miles away to wait at table when he had weekend parties. 'The major didn't like strange faces round here – he couldn't bear strangers.' Every week throughout the summer season he threw lavish parties at which his guests were all close friends. Sir Eustace Fiennes, Lady Winifred Henshaw, Lord and Lady Invernaim, Lord and Lady Inverclyde, the Barclay-Harveys, the Vickers shipbuilding family and the Wills tobacco family (who were related to royalty) were among those whose friendship the major treasured. What staff the guests brought supplemented Major Darby's servants.

But before the war the most celebrated of all of these occasions was the Ascot week festivities, for guests from all over the country would come to Padworth House for the entire week and would daily make the twenty-five mile journey each way to and from the racecourse. This was the social event of the calendar for miles around. Rising to the sense of occasion Major Darby would send his old stagecoach down from Padworth House – complete with his horn-blowing coachman – to the station each time he knew his guests were due to arrive. Florence Downham, the sister of postman Frank Downham, worked at Beenham Grange for the Freelings in those days. She told me that 'Mrs Waring was Major Darby's favourite lady. Every race meeting he used to have a big "At Home" and the coach used to come down to the station to pick up [his guests] and the man used to sit up there blowing his horn and go along the Bath Road and up and over the Padworth arch and up to Padworth House. Mrs Waring acted as his hostess. Captain Waring, of course, was in the army and wasn't home all that much.'

Major Darby's closest friend though, and one to whom he entrusted the care of the house during an illness which took him to a nursing home in Reading, was Sir George Holmes. Despite the fact that his home was in London, Mrs Hearn remembers that 'Sir George was often here.' He was ten years older than the Major and distanced somewhat from his wife by being hard of hearing. 'I think he was so deaf he used to get on her nerves and when you've got money you can live apart if you want to', Mrs Hearn speculated, but they 'always had tea together when he was in London.' The major was one of the founders of the now defunct Bachelors' Club in London that suggests an acceptance of his circumstances in life rather than his aspirations. Mrs Hearn believed that in his younger days, the major was in love with Mrs Waring. However, she married the squire of Beenham House which stood in full view of Padworth House on the opposite scarp of the Kennet Valley.

Sir George Holmes' death therefore on 13 February 1926 must have devastated Major Darby. He immediately arranged for Sir George to be buried in Padworth churchyard. He now had no one other than his servants for company and yet, with the retirement of his butler and his wife even their numbers were sadly diminished. Hilda Hobbs and her sister were two of the faithful few left. It was in this context that I found

I had to make judgements about the part that Major Crook may or may not have played in Aldington's scheme of things.

It seems reasonable to assume that Mr Smith's promotion to the position of Estate Agent had coincided with his retirement as miller rather than his replacement, for the business of milling at Padworth ceased when he went. The extent of John Edward Bates' responsibilities to Major Darby when he took over the tenancy was solely that of maintaining the electricity supply. Otherwise he was free to keep his cows, run the milk round or anything else he chose to consider. Given that the date of Smith's accession to the post of parish clerk in 1917 probably coincides with his new career as Major Darby's agent, an understanding of the general state of Padworth Park can be gained. The fact that, unlike some neighbouring estates, Padworth never regained anything of its former glory is due undoubtedly to the retiring nature and the death in 1932 of Major Darby but the evidence seems to suggest that the sorry state of upkeep may well be due to the fact that practically the entire labour force was on active service. There wasn't really a great deal that Mr Smith would have been able to do about it.

The then heir to the nearby Wasing Estate, Sir William Mount, whose family had originally come to Berkshire at the same time as Major Darby's, watched it all happen from the touch line, as it were. 'He had no proper agent,' Sir William told me. 'Padworth Gulley was always an awful mess… Home Farm was very rough and tumbledown… Darby Griffith didn't have a farm properly in hand.'

Obviously Major Darby was not a forceful man. In many respects he and Aldington had a lot in common, hence the appointment of Mr Smith as his agent. They had presumably got on well for years and, as the miller, Mr Smith would have had some degree of business acumen. For a while, obviously, all had gone reasonably well. The major can have made no great demands on Mr Smith and he in turn was left to enjoy his active retirement in whatever way he might consider appropriate. His fictional counterpart even turns up at one of Margy Stuart's parties along with Purfleet and Georgie. It may well have happened for all I know. Then, according to *Life for Life's Sake*, along came the 'rude red-faced soldier' Major Crook. My cardex suggested this would be sometime in 1924 as his name first appears on the electoral roll of 1925. For whatever reason Major Darby gave Major and Mrs Crook the use of the White House. Whether Crook had intended to stay permanently in Padworth I don't know but from the moment of his arrival things went wrong and relationships at Padworth House were severely strained. Mrs Hearn well remembers the effect his coming had on Major Darby and Mr Smith. It would seem that Major Darby's social obligations had backfired on him. Crook, it seems, knew precisely what needed to be done and made his feelings known to Major Darby in no uncertain terms. He frightened Mrs Hearn. 'He had risen from the ranks and it had gone to his head.' Within presumably a very short time of his arrival he had noticed that Major Darby was desperately in need of his particular ability to organize things and had suggested that he take over the job as agent. Sadly, from what Mrs Hearn recalled, that may have been right for the estate but it was entirely wrong for Major Darby and poor Mr Smith. If Crook 'could have got rid of Mr Smith, the estate agent, our lives just wouldn't have been worth living. [Major Crook] stayed [at Padworth House] before he went to the White House. I suppose the major must have let him have it [but] I think he really got a bit beyond himself when he got there.'

The school log book records that on 18 December 1925, for example, Major and Mrs Crook in the company of Major Darby, who as school governor had long been very philanthropic in that direction, paid a visit to the school. Other than very local dignitaries and of course the clergy and the governors themselves this was a privilege accorded to very few people only. It seemed that Major Darby's obligations were being tested to the limits. Quite what did eventually happen to Major Crook, Mrs Hearn was unable to recall. Neither could she offer me any suggestions as to his continuing role in Aldington's life. In any event though, Major Crook's presence here offers an insight into the state of the Padworth Estate during the nineteen twenties, precisely when Aldington was making his own judgements. Needless to say, Mrs Hearn's recollections of her time below stairs made for an intriguing afternoon's listening. There was so much to be told and it seemed so right and proper that she held audience in the major's old drawing room. We were surrounded by so many ghosts and her stories had a very familiar ring to them.

So much of Major Darby's court at Padworth House had been apparently laid bare in *The Colonel's Daughter*. The lifestyle of Sir Horace Stimms seemed personified by the man at Padworth House and yet there remained doubts. It was more than that, something sinister even.

To hear, for example, of the illustrious guests at Padworth House brought to mind one particular passage in *The Colonel's Daughter* and it shows far more about the author's attitudes towards business than it did about Padworth. 'Now "in the evening of life", as Insurance Companies call old age, [Smithers] dwelt in a ruinous nook of England on about £600 a year. Meanwhile, Horace had absorbed at least three estates which had been intended for the nurture and comfort of warriors, defenders of the Throne, and he had done it all on grease. This, in fact, all Smithers' hoity-toity never-stooping-to-anything-unworthy-a-gentleman had resulted in his being the paid bravo in the international quarrels of a successful Camberwell tradesman and his pals.'[24]

I hope that Major Darby never read *The Colonel's Daughter*.

Chapter 8

The Businessman

The first time I read *The Colonel's Daughter* I was startled by the vehemence of Aldington's attitude towards business as personified by Sir Horace Stimms. Sir Horace may be the symbolic capitalist but the plot needed an emblematic businessman and he was to be found much closer to home. Craigie, the fictitious factory owner, just had to be the proprietor of Padworth's local brewery. The names Malthouse Cottage, The Malthouse and Brewery House all gave credence to a sizeable enterprise for such a small community but neither Craigie's features, nor the nature of his business are detailed in the novel. Aldington's plot needed an entirely fictitious business and that he had one nearby was sufficient in itself. I assumed that as Aldington lived in Malthouse Cottage, 'the impoverished gentry' to whom he paid his weekly rent, must be the brewer. In the intervening years the cottage had become detached from the brewery but there were no such clues to its provenance in my deeds. I use the word 'clues' advisedly though because the true significance of some of the names and facts contained in those deeds only became clear as time passed. Only after finally seeking a legal opinion on my deeds was I able to be more conclusive about their relevance to Aldington's fictional Cleeve in *The Colonel's Daughter*. By the time I arrived in 1971 the brewery had long since been sold to Sterling Cable Company, part of the Sterling Greengate Company, an American organisation manufacturing sophisticated cables for the international communications network.

The enterprise is now far larger than it had been in Craigie's day, but Sterling Cables nevertheless inherited the brewery cottages and the odd parcel of land around The Wharf as Aldington's neighbourhood is colloquially known. The true identity and nature of Craigie and his business can be seen in the beer bottles that turn up in our gardens: 'Strange & Sons, Aldermaston'. The fact, too, that the bottles place the brewery in Aldermaston whereas Aldington puts Craigie's factory firmly in Cleeve also confirms the interplay between the three parishes, in fiction as well as fact. I learned from Norman Gates' research that the Beenham postmark on Aldington's correspondence has confused American scholars no end; they imagined Beenham to be a separate town whereas his local post office was yards away only, in the neighbouring parish.

As Aldington tells us that Mr Judd 'was chief foreman… of the small factory at Cleeve' it does suggest that he would be living in one of the nearby cottages. So too, logically, would his colleague and Sunday morning companion, for while Mr Judd supplied 'more than half… the rest of the brains of the establishment was supplied by his clerkly friend Mr Raper.'[1] Once more I was convinced that I had to look no further than the end of my drive to find Mr Judd when quite by chance, I came across 'Mr Raper' or rather, his son. I had written to the *Newbury Weekly News* outlining what little I knew of another of Aldington's near neighbours and asking if anyone could help. Leslie Austin phoned and his recollections proved invaluable. Obviously I was well aware of his name and even during that first phone call I was delving into my cardex system. I saw that he was still at school at the time but he was the first of many to remember Aldington as 'a great walker'. But what caught my attention was that his father, William John Austin, was chief clerk at Strange's Brewery. Looking out as its name suggests, over the squire's land, the Austin family home at No 1 Park View was nevertheless one of those in Mill Lane that belonged to the brewery. Within seconds of putting down the receiver I was turning to the novel again for a full account of the relationship between Mr Judd and Mr Raper. 'Mr Judd was on the production side and was an optimist. The rest of the brains of the establishment was supplied by his clerkly friend, Mr Raper, a bitter pessimist struggling gamely against an annual decline in revenue. Mr Judd was not interested in accounts – his job was to produce the goods; Mr Raper was not interested in production – his job was to balance his books and perform the superhuman feat of showing a profit.'[2]

As was William Austin's role at the brewery, Mr Raper's fictional role was a supportive one, the author tells us: 'this rustic Gog and Magog propped up a staggering concern' while the 'nominal owner' got on with other things. William John Austin was an equally reliable man. Messrs Frames, the clothing manufacturers in Reading, had entered a lean period after the end of the Boer War as the demand for army uniforms had practically ceased. George Earley, the then company secretary to Strange's Brewery knew William John Austin – they were fellow choristers – and offered him the job as chief clerk. According to Bill Austin, the family 'emigrated' to Padworth in 1900 and moved straight into the newly built cottage in Mill Lane. Life must quite suddenly have taken a turn for the better and Mr Austin very soon put down roots in the village for, by the time Aldington came along, he had been appointed school manager and his name appears alongside that of Major Darby and the local farmers on the list of parish councillors, indeed he was at the eventful meeting at which the war memorial was discussed at Padworth House.

I spent the best part of a longish afternoon talking to Leslie and Mrs Austen. I am sure I exhausted them in an effort to glean from them every-thing they could recall of Padworth. Only as I was preparing to leave did they suggest that I may be interested in meeting a neighbour of theirs with whom Leslie had continued a close, lifelong friendship. The remainder of that scorching day in 1981 was spent enthusiastically in the company of Ron Bates, who was brought up at Padworth Mill. It was a bonus I had not anticipated. What is surprising looking back on that day is the fact that it no more occurred to me to enquire, than it did Leslie Austin to suggest, that his eldest brother Bill was still around. It was not until the following June that I found him and only then did I realise they were brothers.

One detrimental effect of the male orientated society in which we live is that women, generally speaking, drop their maiden names when they marry. It wasn't until I questioned the name Pam Strange that cropped up in conversation with Leslie Austin and Ron Bates that I realised that a woman whose married name was known to me and who lived no more than a mile or so from me was indeed the sole surviving member of the Strange family I was seeking. Needless to say I arranged another meeting very soon afterwards, and it is entirely due to the generosity and broadness of mind of Pamela Gardner that a part of what follows may be written down. As a result, I am able to make what, at face value, may seem to be uncharitable comparisons between fact and fiction. It was from Mrs Gardner, too, that I learnt the history of Strange's Brewery. It had been founded in 1792 which immediately ruled out the fictional suggestion of a mortgage from the squire. Frederick Gerald Strange, Mrs Gardner's father was the fifth generation of brewers. The initials of previous generations are inscribed on the cottages in Mill Lane. "JTS" – John Thomas Strange – Mrs Gardner's grandfather, built the Austin home 'He's on the village hall at Aldermaston, too,' Mrs Gardner reminded me. In

1876 W.J. Strange – J.T.'s father – built the two rows of four cottages in Mill Lane (that Aldington dubbed 'infamous' in *Life for Life's Sake* as well as others along the Bath Road towards Theale. So Strange's Brewery was well established by the time that Aldington took up residence in what had once been their staff cottage. It would seem that Craigie was purely fictitious. Not by any stretch of 'fancy and caricature' could Aldington have considered Francis Gerald Strange guilty of the crime of arrivisme attributed to Sir Horace Stimms. 'Nevertheless', I hear Aldington saying to the colonel's daughter, 'This grotesque anachronism, Miss Smithers, is run on patriarchal lines. That means that Craigie employs non-union labour (which he can still get here) and pays his men about half a crown to five shillings more than the standard agricultural wage of the county.'[4]

Mrs Gardner told me that a woman who I already knew well enough around the village had been nanny to her and her elder brother. It was hardly worth getting the car out to pop round to Mrs Hissey. I recall Bill Austin telling me that Mrs Gardner's father served in the Royal Berkshire Regiment but Mrs Hissey talked freely of him as 'Major Strange' thereby introducing yet another major within Aldington's reach. Mrs Hissey introduced me to another teatime guest, a silver-haired lady, Miss Violet Mills. Quiet as she was for most of the time 'Vi-vi', as she was known in the household, went into service in 1920 as housekeeper to Major Strange's wife, Marjorie Blanche Strange. At times they expressed a delightfully blunt assessment of their master while retaining a staunch loyalty to the mistress of Brewery House.

The extent of the brewery's land and business empire was substantial.

The brewery itself was built on the south bank of the Kennet and Avon canal and gave purpose to Brewery Lock alongside. In the 1980s Brewery House and the stables alongside were demolished to make way for road improvements and the construction of the new bascule bridge over the Kennet and Avon canal. Nowadays there is an undeniable tranquillity to the malthouse and Aldington's brick-built Malthouse Cottage, two hundred yards to the east of the bridge. The old clapboard facing has been removed revealing the nineteenth century timber framed structure of the original malthouse. The old wharf now has a lawn fronting the canal. In its heyday the hops and barley for the malthouse would have arrived by barge and been off-loaded onto the wharf but by the time Aldington arrived, the canal had long since fallen into disrepair. But he would nevertheless have looked out onto a decidedly industrious scene. There would be the clatter of draymen bringing in their wares by horse and cart to the malthouse alongside and 'Young George Hale' would be stacking willow hoops destined for the cooperage alongside Mr Albury's coffin workshop on the opposite bank. The wharf provided an altogether substantial buffer preventing Major Darby's park from reaching down to the canal for quite a considerable distance along its passage through the lower end of the parish.

Fig. 27. 'Young' George Hale stacking hoops on the wharf

There were those who were proud to be have worked for Major Darby and those, like Mrs Hissey, who were equally proud that they didn't. He may have had his drawbacks but Major Strange was in no way dependent upon Major Darby and that pride reflected in those who worked for him: 'Lower Padworth didn't have anything to do with those up there! [Major Strange] was independent. That's Padworth estate up there, but not down here.' In Aldington's time there were more servants in the Strange household than at Padworth House for in addition to Mrs Hissey and Violet Mills there was a cook, a parlour maid, a serving maid and a housemaid. Brewery House though, wasn't a country seat as may be imagined. It sat, urbanely, right in front of the working brewery itself and would be constantly subjected to the sights and smells of the business. There would be constant movement between the brewery and the nearby Malthouse and the sight of Major Strange coming down the lane would be a familiar one to Aldington. I wondered what he was like. Despite their loyalty to him, his servants were objective enough to realise that not everyone would have felt the same. He was, after all, an employer and would personify the frustrations that the brewery workers had. Showing extremes of tact and prudence, Mrs Hissey told me: 'I really didn't think that he was a well-liked man.' 'Vi-vi' was less inhibited and her response was immediate. 'Here's one who didn't like him. He was a type – like there is today. If you didn't do as I told you to do... look out for yourself.' This prompted Mrs Hissey to expand. 'He was a little short, dapper-dick, he got his good ways, he got his bad ways' and as if it would explain everything: 'Well, it's army, isn't it?' No doubt Aldington would concur.

Frederick Gerald Strange would have had much in common with Major Darby as both had retired from the army with the same rank. At one point the British Army must have been overrun with majors and most of them it seemed had ended up in Padworth, and this the slow realisation would no doubt have distressed Aldington somewhat. I was even to learn that Major Strange's cousin, Christopher Draper Strange, was also a Major. Major Darby Griffith, Major Crook, Major Strange and Major Draper Strange all lived within barking distance of Aldington. One of these had to be the model for Aldington's eponymous colonel, my ultimate goal, but if I was so far correct then I could exclude Major Darby and even Major Strange. Not only were all the officers back from the front but so too, as we have seen, were all the 'other ranks' and in converse fashion to that of Aldington's profiteers, the brewery business would

153

presumably pick up again. While Messrs Judd and Raper were propping up Craigie's 'staggering concern', Craigie '...the nominal owner fussed about in a car and performed upper-class Tartarin feats with Sir Horace Stimms.'[5]

The prospect of such a meeting between Craigie and Stimms is loaded with melodramatic connotations. Aldington created them to illustrate not only his own uniquely inclined disposition towards business but, as I was now beginning to learn, as a direct contrast to the life he wished upon both Cleeve and Padworth itself, that of 'Chaucer's England'. That there was at least some social discourse between Major Darby and Major Strange is without doubt as is the existence of Major Strange's car. Mrs Hissey recalls that 'he was one of the first to have a car.' But those at the bottom of the village sensed a difference that was perhaps more the direct result of the stature of Major Darby as much as anything else. 'Vi-vi' used to answer the door when he called at Brewery House. 'I used to hate asking him in. I was frightened of him. I didn't like him. He was a funny man. He wasn't very popular [down here].' No doubt Major Darby, a sensitive man, would have every reason to be apprehensive on those occasions when he chose to walk down to the station, for coming down the same path as Aldington and Eliot took on their way up to the church, the major could not avoid walking down Mill Lane, the very spine of the brewery territory. As 'Vi-vi' says, the 'Stranges monopolised Lower Padworth.' Major Darby would have to run the gauntlet as it were, past 'that infamous block of cottages' to which Aldington refers.

I met a woman who preferred to remain anonymous as her husband used to work at the brewery for Major Strange. She told me that they found him a very difficult man from an employees' point of view which is perhaps to be expected. Her husband, she told me, had to take a lot from him. It was impossible she said to speak your mind with someone else's roof over your head. Her husband used to go into work on a Saturday morning to collect his wages. He had to go in until 12 o'clock and the major would – purposely it seemed – keep out of his way. On another occasion Major Strange threw the money down where he was working. It seemed as if he begrudged it. £2 a week! He was charming to people who mattered, but not to his employees.

There was one subject though towards which Major Strange displayed unequivocal enthusiasm and that was cricket. One of the most pleasant open spaces for miles around – the sports field at the corner of Mill Lane with the main road and directly opposite Brewery House – was created largely by the strenuous, personal efforts of Major Strange himself. He turned a previously open field into a broad green frontispiece to his own house and a welcoming mat for the neighbourhood. Despite the occasional threat by his successors to erect a factory extension there, it is still in use today by their employees much as I guess it was in the 1920s.[6] Cricketing stars and celebrities have played charitable matches here in recent years. Major Strange thought the world of his cricket and that had to be to everyone's advantage: 'He got his good ways, he got his bad ways.' Such a philanthropic gesture is presumably an illustration of the Victorian values of which we hear so much these days; a gesture though, in this particular instance, that one might more normally attribute to the squire. Aldington took a less than charitable view of such matters in the epilogue of *The Colonel's Daughter*. 'Bim and Bom sat facing each other inside a pair of Soccer goal-posts, situated in a small outlying field of a large park. Sir Horace Stimms, the grease prince, had with reluctance ceded this otherwise useless field to keep up the spirit of manly sport in the village hobbledehoys.'[7]

In 1916 when some of the worst battles of the War were being fought and most of the initial glory had worn thin the government introduced conscription for married men. Duty called and Aldington, albeit with reluctance, obeyed. There were those, though, who didn't and with what appears to be equivocation elsewhere in his writings, they too are severely censured by Aldington. His friend John Mills Witham, with whom Aldington passed so many indecisive weeks at Hunters Inn before accepting the call, was one who refused and seems only to have escaped Aldington's ire because of their friendship. Generally speaking, Aldington resents those who objected on the grounds of conscience for taking precisely the stance that he could not and then damns himself forever for taking the dutiful way to his particular hell.

Anna Munro's husband, Sidney Ashman, was a conscientious objector. He was born in August 1884 and was therefore eight years older than Aldington. They were respectively thirty-two and twenty-four years old in 1916. Sidney was the son of George Ashman, a saddler and leather merchant whose business stood at the junction of Church Street and the High Street five miles away in Thatcham. When their father died, Sidney and his brother Frank took over and expanded the business. Sydney was first drawn to his future wife by the power of Anna's speaking voice at a rally. Their daughter writes that Anna Munro 'could be heard from one end of Newbury to the other!'[8] Sidney Ashman and Anna Munro married in August 1913 a year before war was declared. The Ashman brothers obviously had a good head for business but in Aldington's eyes, Sidney Ashman was a profiteer and made money from the circumstances of war as they stayed behind while others were away at the front. Mrs Dorothy Adams their housekeeper during their days at Venture Fair told me that he used to buy and sell army surplus goods.

Sidney Ashman joined forces with his brother-in-law Wilfred Street, an engineer, and from a small yard, part of which still stands at the eastern end of Thatcham's small by-pass, started up Thatcham Road Transport Services with one lorry in 1921. In its time Colthrop Transport Company – as it was eventually to become – would be operating a fleet of about a hundred lorries, a far cry from his days as a cobbler in the First World War. At the time that TRTS was started Aldington would have been at Padworth for a year or so and would no doubt have been as familiar as we are with the *Newbury Weekly News* and would have seen a regular advertisement placed there by Sidney Ashman, the cobbler, such as this one of 24 February 1921.

ASHMAN'S BARGAIN LIST.

WRAF chrome boots	18/6
gum boots	12/6
part worn ditto	8/6
cased toe, Army's	18/6
repaired Army's	7/6
FMS Boots	14/6
Ladies tan brogues	14/6
Box calf shoes	12/6
Gent's boots	20/-

Ashman's Boot Stores, Station Approach,
Newbury and at Thatcham.[9]

Aldington would be appalled that someone could turn other people's misfortunes into money, particularly as he may well have fought alongside the men whose boots Ashman was selling. This would reinforce his strongly held view that half the problems facing his world could be laid firmly at the feet of profiteers whom he fictionalised as Sir Horace

Stimms. The epilogue to *The Colonel's Daughter* is a bitter indictment of the power and position that Sir Horace was able to buy with profits taken from the backs of the soldiers during the First World War. 'Intelligence doesn't pay here – they go in for high hats and low cunning. But listen to me, Bim, and don't drink so much of that Bass or you'll go to sleep. As in many similar instances, the foundations of yonder stately home were laid by the son of a needy military adventurer who joined the Crusade of William the Bastard. There his descendants abode, living and hunting on the land for which they performed military service or paid scutage. Sir Horace, I may say, had invariably paid scutage, particularly during the years of 1914-18.'[10]

It was inconceivable that the estate of Major Darby could be displaced by business but that was what Aldington prophesied. The coming of Major Crook to Padworth, albeit soon followed by his rapid disappearance, allows a glimpse into the state of affairs at Padworth House and further demonstrates the tragicomic nature of Major Darby that so aroused Aldington's imagination and sympathy. The more I knew of Major Darby the more I am aware that he was not the model for Sir Horace Stimms. Major Darby in person is conspicuous by his absence from the novel. Major Darby's age as well as the nature of Padworth Park was causing Aldington to speculate about the future of the estate and it is a common theme throughout his work. We see it, for example, in *All Men are Enemies*. Tony Clarendon 'was distressed by the sight of Scrope dying; For him the death of Scrope meant the death of something in himself and in England. Once that orderly ideal was gone – and it was on its death bed – nothing was left but confusion and anarchy, the base struggle of plutocrats or a tyrannous ant-hill organisation for paltry ends. There would be no more great characters, no more plenitude of life.'[11]

Aldington was an idealist, his idealism delivered with a finely honed but often disturbing sense of humour. He was paranoid that Major Darby's estate might be taken over by a profiteer. The very title of his third novel, *All Men are Enemies*, seems to be explicit of so many of his fears. Despite the fact that Major Darby was alive and well right up to the time that Aldington left Padworth, Aldington needed to make his point and in the highly fictitious epilogue to *The Colonel's Daughter* he contrives a very convenient way of removing the squire from his home. 'Thrice that house has been rebuilt – when it was turned from a fortress to a mansion under

Elizabeth, after it had been burned by Essex's pikemen, and finally in 1765 when the Lord had grown rich on English farming. Unwisely for them, the family stood out against the Whig industrialists. The last scion of that noble house, an orphan, served in the European War as aide-de-camp to a general of specialised morals. In 1921 he was served in his turn with a *lettre de cachet* of exile.' Then comes an expression of Aldington's worst fears: 'The mansion was on the market – dirt cheap, for the young laird was a bloody fool in the hands of crooks, and there was a hell of a trade slump. In comes me master Horace, and snaps it up with an easy and shark-like grace.' What happens next we hardly need say. 'Behold our grease merchant, who sells his axle-grease as margarine in packets, and his margarine as axle-grease in tins, installed as Lord of the Manor, duly seised of the manors of Pudthorp, Cleeve-on-the-Hill and Maryhampton.'[12]

The 1920s marked the end of an era. Aldington's prime bone of contention was with the politicians who had brought on the destruction of war. They had not only failed to keep the peace but as a result of their slow but certain persuasion throughout the nineteenth century had caused the nation to become intoxicated by the '*Boys Own'* glory of war. There was a common assumption among those at the front that those left behind were suffering almost as much as they were. It did not dawn on them fully until they returned home that the hardware of battle, every bullet they fired, had put money into the pockets of those who had manufactured them. Your average Tommy Atkins in general, and Aldington in particular, loathed and despised the profiteers. Despite the personal fervour with which he expresses his sentiments, Aldington's views were common to the majority of men returning from the front and not just in the ranks. In speaking of his own experience of the Second World War, Brigadier Charles Stuart Mills, who later plays his own part in this narrative, agreed with Aldington. 'We all hated those who had made money from the war whilst others had been away fighting… Those with Victorian parents were unfitted and untrained for any form of business other than being "gentlemen". The war forced that change on those who remained behind with the result that the returning soldiers were totally unequipped for commercial life when they returned. They had been left out of things. Those in business had a head start on them.' So, in that respect Aldington was typical. But, whereas the majority attempted to make up on the head start the others had over them and perhaps overcome the challenge, Aldington didn't. He expressly avoided commercial life like the plague and became scornful of the City, business, and all connected with it. 'I too could have earned ten pounds a week' he wrote. But he didn't.[13] He withdrew to Padworth along with Arabella and his pen and spent the rest of his life trying to write the war out of his system.

Chapter 9

The Church

Although innumerable yet compounding small changes have occurred since Aldington's day, Padworth still has a rectory even though it is now a substantial private house.

Tradition dictated that the church as good as belonged to the squire as though if was a private chapel appended to his house. Padworth House and the Church of St. John the Baptist had an interconnecting gate and they stood at the geographical centre of the parish, occupying the strategic high ground which emphasized the house's superiority to the lower orders clustered around the working wharf. During Aldington's time he could see Padworth House from his back door. The rectory however, still stands at a discreetly amenable distance from both the church and the squire. Close enough to enable the rector to have easy access to his church and yet far enough for him to realise to whom both he and his church owed their existence. Padworth House looked over the shoulder of the church and

Fig. 28. Rectory House, Padworth, 1920

gave a clear view of practically everybody who came through the lychgate and into the churchyard. Alongside the rectory and still used occasionally for its intended purpose as a meeting place for certain parochial bodies, stands the rectory room almost in the fashion of a lodge to the imposing rectory itself.[1] For the rectory is as imposing as Padworth House albeit in a more genteel way. Both are Grade 2 listed buildings. Indeed at one time a considerable acreage of the land surrounding the rectory went with the living. It follows, therefore, that the rector would be a man of modest means, a scholar and, moreover, a gentleman and in this respect the Reverend Clinton was no exception.

When Aldington arrived in Padworth, the rectory together with its outbuildings, land and stables was in the incumbency of Rev William Osbert Clinton and it had been since August 1888. It is still a proud boast among one or two of the longer established residents that the Rev Clinton (1850-1921) was related to Captain Marryatt, the author of *The Children of The New Forest* whose home at Lymington, Hampshire, was close to Ashley-Clinton where the Rev Clinton's family estate was to be found. In 1911 Rev Clinton edited notes prepared by Mary Sharpe at Ufton Court leading to the privately printed history of the village, *The Parish of Padworth and Its Inhabitants*. Emma Thoyt, from the neighbouring parish of Sulhampstead was the central figure in a local history circle in the 1890s and inspired the circulation of a manuscript book between the incumbents and local historians in the neighbouring parishes. Rev Clinton's contribution was to record items of Padworth's history that he picked up around the parish. He too, along with Major Darby – we learn from the introduction – undertook to read the proofs of the Padworth portion of the *Victoria County History of Berkshire*. Reverend Clinton was a man to whom his parish was everything. Mrs Hearn's mother came to Padworth as nanny to Clinton's children, Walter and Frances, and so we find that Mrs Hearn's recollections are again invaluable, particularly as they relate to the circumstances at the rectory.

'There were sheds and quite a granary at the back of the Rectory in one of the meadows and that does rather speak of land. Lots of the rectors did supplement their livings with glebe farms. They did at Ufton, but that was before my time.' Rev Clinton was there very much under the grace and favour of the squire and yet he had to maintain a sizeable rectory. There cannot have been much financial reward to be had from the parish itself. Mrs Hearn again: 'Well I don't think there could have been *any* really. There wasn't a great deal asked of them in those days. No one bothered too much whether their sermons were good or not. They would christen people, marry them and bury them but there wasn't too much asked of them.' Rev Clinton was eight years older than Major Darby. At the time Clinton arrived in Padworth on 18 August 1888, their respective ages would have been thirty-eight and thirty and therefore by 1920, they had spent thirty-two years of their lives closely bound in comfortable compatibility by the ties of their situations. Each would know the other's strengths and weaknesses and they would rely on each other. Major Darby was not a dominant man in the sense that he could command men; and neither was Rev Clinton a forceful man in that sense. Mrs Hearn suggested Clinton suffered from nerves a lot 'always hummed and hawed a lot before he could get any speech out… "m.m.m.m" – a lot of that before he could get a word out… but then they often put the rather dull one into the ministry.' At different times, different families in the village were struck by tragedy and the Clintons were not exempt from this. In 1905, the rector's wife, Margaret, died, aged forty-nine leaving the rector with his son, 'Mr Walter,' born the year after they arrived at Padworth and then aged twenty two, and 'Miss Frances' who, I believe, may have been a year or two younger. Then came the First World War and the death of Walter Clinton under the futile circumstances we have seen recorded in the churchyard.

A third and equally significant member of the community completed this triangle of authority. Mrs Albury was the headmistress of the village school and had known both the rector and the squire from the arrival of her family in 1900. Mrs Albury was due to retire in 1920 but delayed the occasion at the rector's personal request to coincide with his anticipated retirement due to take place on his seventieth birthday the following August. A commemorative photograph was taken to celebrate the occasion (that has subsequently been lost) and, on 1 September 1921 Mrs Ollis took over as headteacher. The rector, however, didn't retire immediately. It would seem that it was proving difficult to find a replacement and that Major Darby had perhaps asked the rector to stay on. Two months after Mrs Ollis took temporary charge of the school it was her unfortunate duty to have to record in the school log book for 17 November 1921 an event which nevertheless helps us to understand the confusion that follows in *The Colonel's Daughter*: 'I regret to record the death on 12th inst. of the Rev W.O. Clinton.'[2] The Reverend Clinton had been rector of Padworth for thirty-three years. He was one of very few rectors whose incumbency was terminated by his death rather than by his retirement. He had been here longer than any other rector in the recorded history of Padworth. He had either baptised married or buried everyone in the village but with his death came a time of uncertainty and instability following which a long time was to pass before the community was to recover and even then the recovery was not permanent.

Aldington had been at Padworth for almost two years when the Rector died and his understanding of the situation can be judged from the fictitious parallels in *The Colonel's Daughter*. In the novel it would have been about this time that the evil Sir Horace enters this cautionary tale by buying the squire's house with his ill-gotten gains. Although no more than a mile as the crow flies separated the squire and Aldington, their views of their parish would differ considerably. The squire sat firmly in the middle of his own parish and while Malthouse Cottage is in Padworth, it does look out onto the jigsaw boundaries with the neighbouring parishes. 'When Sir Horace Stimms took possession of his estate, he was horrified by the spectacle of a clergyman driving an ordinary farm cart from the station. This was the unlucky Rector of Maryhampton, whose "living" was ninety pounds a year, plus thirty pounds from Queen Anne's Bounty.'[3] There are parallels in *The Colonel's Daughter*. 'Since the Rector had a wife and three children, and was unwilling to see them starve, he did a brave and sensible thing – rented some land and worked it himself.'[4] While they may be fictitious, the agrarian nature of the rector's activities does fit the history of Padworth. Aldington would have been familiar with the maps of his own backyard showing the 'Rector's Field' immediately alongside the rectory but Sir Horace's reaction is entirely fictitious.

'Why Sir Horace should have been so frozen with horror may seem strange, since holy men from St Peter (who was a fisherman) and St Paul (who was a tent-maker) down to the religious orders of today have worked with their hands yet lost nothing in sanctity.'[5] Indeed as Mrs Hearn confirmed, that was the way of the clergy of the past. 'But in Sir Horace's scheme of things, the clergy were merely part of an ingenious system for keeping the rich rich, and in his opinion manually working clergy were less efficient than gentlemanly ones'[6] the Rev Clinton being the last from that mould. 'Sir Horace solved the problem with characteristic energy. He persuaded the aged and comparatively wealthy vicar of Pudthorp to resign. He repaired the rectory and got permission to unite the two livings and let the vicarage, thus bringing the rector up to £310 a year, to which he added £90 annually, on condition that the farming was given up.'[7] Aldington was suggesting that the parishes of Aldermaston and Beenham might combine. Except in his timing he wasn't far wrong; it was Padworth and Mortimer West End that eventually did so by which time too, the sight of the Rector farming his own land had long since ceased. 'It was given up gratefully, but the Rector found to his dismay that he had merely exchanged toil for servitude – Sir Horace meant to get his money back in servility.'[8] A little harsh, I thought, when I first read this but Mrs Hearn was quick to correct me. 'Oh yes. I think they rather had to do what *he* said.' While the appointment of the living wasn't entirely in the squire's hands – there are the church authorities after all – Mrs Hearn told me nevertheless that Major Darby did have a considerable say in the matter. 'He … had a good deal to do with it. …Half [the rector's] stipend came from the squire. Certainly he could make it uncomfortable for them if they weren't quite what he thought they were.'

In a few lines of fiction, Aldington had set the scene for the succession of rectors of Padworth that came and went with disconcerting regularity in the years following the Rev Clinton's untimely death. A list of past incumbents is displayed in the church porch showing the dates of their accession but it doesn't tell us how long they stayed; only that they all retired. One of the prime functions of any new rector is to make himself known at the village school so the dates upon which their names appear in the school log book gives a good indication not only of the speed with which they adapted to their task but the rapidity with which they can all be seen to have disappeared.

Six months after Rev Clinton's death came Rev Owen Randall Slacke. He stayed about a year and ten months. His last visit to the school was on 29 March 1923. The lack of evidence on the electoral roll suggests that Slacke didn't even take up residence at the rectory. There was a further gap of about eight months before Rev Michael Longridge took office on 1 November 1923 but he had moved on by the summer of 1924. Then followed another three-month gap. For the remainder of Aldington's time here, Padworth was as frequently without a priest and in the interregnums we see a whole variety of neighbouring clerics presiding over all manner of births, marriages and deaths at Padworth church. All this would obviously affect Major Darby. At the age of sixty-three Major Darby was uncomfortable without Mrs Albury, Rev Clinton and Mr Smith. He would be under pressure to show leadership and that was never one of his strong points. Aldington's obvious affinity with the man is not to be wondered at. A question was forming in Aldington's mind: what would be the fate of the village when the squire passed on? In *The Colonel's Daughter* this had all come to pass by the mid-1920s. Sir Horace Stimms was established in the Manor House at Cleeve and he wielded his dexterous power over the surrounding parishes. 'Remained Cleeve, where the living was somewhat better. Sir Horace added £100 a year and gave it to a Congregationalist.'[9]

On 1 November 1924 Rev Lancaster was appointed rector of Padworth and once again the village had high hopes of settling back into a familiar routine. As was custom, the new rector was invited to stay at Padworth House for his induction not so much out of a sense of duty on Major Darby's part but perhaps, as Aldington judged, to see how they might get on together. 'But, such are the aristocratic traditions, nobody liked a parson who wasn't a gentleman, especially since he tried to hide his plebeian origins with all the Anglo-Catholic clobber he could acquire… [He was] a distressingly High Anglo-Catholic (of Congregational origins), who had given offence by the introduction of incense and a crucifix, and by calling Holy Communion "the Mahss".'[10] It was all too familiar a picture for Mrs Hearn. Nothing seemed to be going right for the village or the church, and certainly not for the squire. 'I can understand it regarding Mr Lancaster,' she confirmed, 'because he was "High Church" and that *certainly* wouldn't have suited here.'

Given that the congregation was faithful in the past, that allegiance had been towards a given rector as much as to the faith itself. Now, as Aldington says, the 'insurance system didn't work here, because the working people went to Chapel – and hence might drift into the Liberal interest – and the gentry stayed away or went to Maryhampton.'[11] In a revealing turn of phrase Ron Bates agreed. 'We went to either church or chapel – wherever the cake was best for Christmas.' Certainly the Strange family went to Aldermaston as Brewery House sat uniquely on a very small but perhaps significantly detached portion of that parish. It seemed almost as if it was so as a result of representations made in the past. Miss "Vi-vi" Mills knew exactly why *she* went to Aldermaston; 'because it was better,' she told me. But, while Aldermaston and Padworth churches are almost equidistant from the wharf, Aldermaston would be far more easily accessible by car. To anyone nearby without such modern luxuries however the options were wide open. 'Sir Horace was chagrined but not defeated. He wangled a transfer for the Congregationalist, and then found he could get no substitute. £250 a year, plus Sir Horace, scared the few candidates who presented themselves.' And so, once again, for a period of nearly six months – it would seem from what may be learned of the rector's attendances at the school – the church was once again in the doldrums. 'Finally, Sir Horace saved the situation – and himself £100 a year – by appointing Carrington, who had a private income, and was a widower.'[12]

On 22 September 1926 The Rev Lord became rector of Padworth. It had been nearly five years since the death of Rev Clinton during which time – and due in some respects, it would seem, to the best efforts of Major Darby – the church had drifted like a rudderless ship. The fictitious Rev Carrington is given an important role in *The Colonel's Daughter*. He finds himself party to one of the divisive factions at the heart of the novel prompting the choice of Cleeve as Aldington's ambivalently named village. Carrington stayed long enough to make his mark on Cleeve but did not however become a permanent member of the community. Reverend Lord stayed in Padworth for about two years before he too resigned leaving the taste of rumour in the air.

Chapter 10

The Colonel

I have to remind myself that there was a time when all I knew of *The Colonel's Daughter* was Aldington's hint that it was set in Padworth. The connection between Major Darby and Sir Horace Stimms was entirely fictitious but having uncovered so many links between the characters in the book to the people of the village, I still felt that I would one day come across the real colonel. The nature of the novel obviously precluded Aldington from naming the colonel in his autobiography but my instincts were firmly fixed on Major Crook, the eponymous 'Sergeant-Major of the Guards'. It was quite by accident that I had been able to identify Major Crook and yet his whereabouts remained unknown. Despite the impetus given to me by Norman Gates' visit in 1978 and my promise to write up these notes for him, it seemed that the colonel was to remain no more than a gleam in the author's eye.

Norman had been engaged in the mammoth task of editing Aldington's letters and wrote to ask if my cardex system had anything on a Brigadier-General Mills, a name that cropped up in Aldington's correspondence. I did not know then of the brigadier's attendance at the meeting to discuss the war memorial. All I had were two Mills households on record but no mention in either of them of a brigadier-general. But neither were there any mentions of the officer status of Darby Griffith, Strange, Draper Strange or Crook on the electoral rolls that I had first consulted. As Norman had looked in the available reference books I thought my best bet was to write to the British Army as it must have something on the man. I received in reply the briefest of letters from the National Army Museum but enclosed with it was a photocopy of a synopsis of the career of General Mills. At the bottom in tiny print were the magic words 'Address: Bridge House, Padworth, Reading' and the date of his death, 19 September 1927.

I had to smile as Norman 'doubted' if information on General Mills could be found in 'the usual sources (Who's Who, etc.)' and yet the photocopy before me *was* from *Who Was Who*! The clues were sufficient to persuade me that this was the breakthrough I had been looking for. There was, of course, only one person with whom the excitement of the find could truly be shared and trying hard not to gloat, I wrote to Norman accordingly. General Mills was worthy of note and one of the local newspapers must have carried his obituary. I found it in *The Reading Mercury* of 25 September 1927. 'Brig. General George Arthur Mills C.B. of Bridge House, Padworth who died on Monday, was born in 1855, educated at Clifton College and in 1873 gazetted to the Royal Madras Fusiliers (102nd).' The obituary continued along similar lines to the *Who Was Who*. Here at last, was the identity of Aldington's landlord. Norman told me in that same letter that Aldington had written to Glenn Hughes on 10 March 1928. 'Old General Mills, the owner, died some months ago, and his widow is trying to sell the place.'

That was all I needed to send me back to *Life for Life's Sake* for now it was obvious that the Mills household was the 'impoverished family of gentry' to whom, Aldington says, the cottage belonged. All the problems of searching for Major Crook were now put entirely out mind. That General Mills was the fictitious colonel seemed beyond question. That I was now absolutely positive can be judged from comparing what I already knew of the fictitious colonel to what I had now before me on these two small pieces of paper. It was almost as if Aldington himself had sat there with them in his hands, as he wrote the book. Perhaps he did. In fact, the more I thought of it the more it seemed to be a strong possibility. If the information was so readily available in *Who Was Who* then the obvious could no longer be overlooked. Aldington must, at some time, have looked up General Mills for the fictional parallels are too close for him to have imagined them. Neither did he exercise an excessive amount of licence in what he found. In *The Colonel's Daughter* he asks: 'Is the name of Smithers aristocratic? …Perhaps it is written in Debrett; certainly it has been inscribed in the Golden Book of the Army List.' He continues in a manner that certainly suggests he knew his man well: 'Yet it has more kinship with the nameless Three Hundred of Thermopoylae than with the Four Hundred of New York, the creme de la creme. Though "Smithers" invokes rather the ringing of anvils than the glitter of coronets, yet it is marvellous what two generations of Army can do… Smithers was pukka Army.'[23] He certainly was. 'Tell me, O Muse, the Saga of Smithers' Aldington commands. We can do no more than make the comparisons.[3]

Lieutenant Colonel Frederick Smithers, Aldington writes 'had been borne on a troopship, in consequence of a small arithmetical misunderstanding between Smithers mere and Lucina.'[4]Whereas, we see from *Who Was Who* that Brigadier General George Arthur Mills was 'b. 28 March 1855. s. of Captain George Longley Mills, Bombay Army; m. 1885 Helen Henrietta, d. of John Garland Baker of Mahagastotte, Ceylon.' Smithers, we are led to believe was 'never a bright child'. General Mills, though perhaps not attending the very best of schools was nevertheless 'Educ. Clifton College.' Smithers 'early gave unmistakable signs of his military vocation, signs which filled his parents with honest pride.'[5] General Mills was 'Gazetted to Royal Madras Fusiliers (102nd), 1873.' Here Aldington let loose his imagination. Smithers, for instance 'delighted to flee away from his amo and tupto, to the brook, the fell and the butts. The Gradus ad Parnassum was abhorrent to this British Hippolytus. The gun and the rod were the symbols of his deity. With that delicate dissociation of feeling only possible to a born sportsman, he contrived to love horses and dogs with a tender passion while waging ruthless war on all wild things, from grouse to trout, and, in later years, from tigers to foxes. Yet when he had passed his salad days of catapults, he never slew tom-tits and never assaulted tom-cats, however plentiful and tempting the game. Every honourable scruple of the chase was his. For the gentle and timid roe-deer he used a rifle with telescopic sights… he condescended to execute the mallard with Number 5 shot; but the fox, albeit cousin to the dog, he disdained to touch and abandoned to fratricidal teeth.'[6]

But the comparisons with General Mills are always there. Smithers again: 'Nor plied he Todhunter and the then unspotted Euclid. Rather would he urge the flying ball than compute the formula of its trajectory. Therefore, the Artillery was out of the question. Too poor for the Guards or the Cavalry, he entered a Line Regiment, and on the plea of some remote and hypothetical Keltish ancestry, was gazetted to a Scottish Battalion.'[7] General Mills became attached to one such 'Keltish' regiment. He became 'Major 1st Royal Dublin Fusiliers, 1888; Lieut Col, 1898; Lieut-Col. commanding 1st Bn. Royal Dublin Fusiliers till 1902; served with 1st Bn. during South African War, 1899-1902.'[8] Smithers: 'Up and down the Empire and to and fro upon it this gallant officer sailed, marched, trained, shot, hunted and fought for his country. He jabbed the butt of a pig-sticker into himself and broke two ribs; he came a purler at polo and broke an arm; a Fuzzy-Wuzzy nicked him in the ham with a spear, and brother Boer broke his omoplate with a well-aimed Mauser bullet.'[9] General Mills served in 'Gibraltar, Ceylon, Egypt, Baluchistan, and South Africa' where he was 'severely wounded (left hand and arm disabled) at the battle of Alleman's Nek, 1900'[10] Smithers 'was always conscientiously two years in debt, promotion avoided him, and in 1910 he retired to the half-pay list, a mere Captain with the consolatory rank of Major.'[11] General Mills 'commanded No. XI district, 1906-10; retired, 1910.'[12]

After a lifetime in military service, Colonel Smithers' frustration has to be imagined.

'What then? For nearly five years he abode at Bath, in a small rented house, while Georgina attended school and learned to keep young. Or rather, learned little, and was kept young... Der Tag was a great day for Smithers. When he learned that the European War was definitely "on", he pranced about the streets of Bath on an invisible high horse, while the unseen spurs jingled more evidently than ever. He was in a fever of apprehension lest England should be "disgraced" by staying out. Not that he had made any close study of British international policy or had any clear conception of how the situation had arisen. His feeling was that England must fight and therefore England would be right, for would not Smithers get a job? ...Smithers was rejuvenated by the declaration of War... For some weeks he had thought of going over to Ireland to defend the Curragh against Redmond's devils, to act as a sort of Runner to Galloper Smith; but a European War was far more satisfactory. As he told Alvina on the night of the 4th, when they sat up late, too excited and happy to sleep: "There'll be plenty of fun and plenty of pickings. Kitchener will make a long War of it..." Next Monday morning Smithers was in London, tapping at the doors of a perturbed and anxious War Office, which perhaps was rather more conscious of its responsibilities than capable of discharging them. The more earnestly the War Office resiled from his civilities, the more eagerly did Smithers press them. The War Office knew about him and was not impressed. But they had to take him on. Then came the question of what to do with him? ...Fortunately, someone recollected the famous Smithers love of animals – demonstrated by many a skin, brush

and skull – and he was set to look after remounts, and later given nominal command of a hospital for horses and mules.'[13]

Indeed, General Mills did join up again. This time though 'commanding 7th Reserve Brigade, 1914; combatant member Travelling Medical Board to 20 Jan. 1917.' He continued to serve throughout the First World War. He landed in France on 17 October 1917, was area commandant at Vraignes in March 1918 and was with O.C. Corps Troops, Cavalry Corps the following month. He was with the special service 4th Army B.E.F. and throughout 1912–1919 when he finally retired, was attached to the headquarters of the 4th army staff, 'B Branch'. General Mills was mentioned in dispatches four times and possessed an array of medals of which he was no doubt justly proud. But there was one item in the *Who Was Who* entry that finally and positively linked him to Aldington's Colonel Smithers, for listed among General Mills' declared interests of 'racing (India), shooting (big and small game) fishing, hunting, polo, etc' was that of 'pig-sticking' in which field he had evidently 'won the Gujarat pig-sticking cup in 1897'. [14] This obviously raised a canny smile on Aldington's face for Colonel Smithers is immediately transposed to far flung places where he too: 'Stuck spears into wild pigs, while disdaining the more succulent porkers of his native heath.' Aldington, though, wouldn't allow Colonel Smithers quite the same measure of success. 'He jabbed the butt of a pig-sticker into himself and broke two ribs.'[15]

Having now established exactly who was the inspiration for Colonel Smithers I was somewhat apprehensive about what I may uncover for even allowing for the 'fancy and caricature' he mentions in *Life for Life's Sake, The Colonel's Daughter* was proving to be founded on fact. All Aldington did was move things around a little. Holly Lodge, the fictional home of Colonel Smithers was recognisable from my very first reading of *The Colonel's Daughter*. It suited the author's intentions to move General Mills and his family into the Lower Lodge in full view of the squire at Padworth House and then move the whole lot back to a situation somewhat midway between Sir Horace Stimms and Craigie. The novel demands it.

My quest for the writer and his village, the links between fact and fiction were knitting together like three-dimensional noughts and crosses, up, down, sideways and diagonally, practically every line was complete – except one. There was one person though, whose possible existence had tantalised me for ages – the colonel's daughter. And yet without having to give it much more than a moment's concentration, that evidence was before me. I should never have doubted Aldington. There, squeezed between a semi-colon and a full stop in *Who Was Who* and marking her relative significance in her father's life was the inconsequential abbreviation 'one d.' Brigadier General George Arthur Mills C.B., and his wife Helen Henrietta had an only daughter! Nothing else. No mention of her name or anything at all about her. Assuming that she too may have achieved something of note, I too consulted just about every reference book I could lay my hands on but all to no avail. The fact that I now had a name to go on would make my task that much easier but the obvious had occurred to me. Whichever way I looked at the figures they all led to one conclusion; that the daughter of Brigadier-General George Arthur Mills would by now have passed on. I had come so far and, I suppose, in my optimistic way, never imagined that I would be unable to meet her, it seemed so just that I should.

It was the chauffeur to the Baker family who had mentioned Anna Munro's parties and who told me that Donald Ashman had bought the house on The Avenue at Bucklebury, the arcadian splendour of which had so impressed Aldington on his walks to Yattendon and beyond. Donald, I discovered, had bought the house from Mrs Mills and her daughter and as a result of a chinwag between the postmaster and one or two customers I learnt that Donald had died a few years earlier in Australia and that after her mother died – 'years ago' – Miss Mills had moved to Crowthorne, some twenty-odd miles away. The house she lived in is still there but no one could tell me of her fate but at least I had the general himself well within my sights. As I've said before, there were five 'Mills' on the electoral roll but only two households. Now that I knew which one to concentrate on I could look again and add that bit more to my cardex. The first and most disconcerting fact to emerge was that Miss Mills herself, being unmarried and therefore ineligible to vote at the time, is conspicuous for her absence from the electoral register. 'Mills, George Arthur' for so he appears on the electoral roll in 1918, was 'a' for 'absent' during this, his first supposed year of residence at Padworth. Presumably his wife, 'Mills, Helen, Henrietta' had come on in advance to set up base camp. But entries for the following year took me totally by surprise for while General Mills was still not yet back home, there was another, one 'Mills, Charles

Fig. 29. Brigadier General George Arthur Mills with his brothers William and Charles

Stuart' the sight of whose name jolted me back to the first page of *The Colonel's Daughter* for there living with the family at Holly Lodge, was 'Cousin Robert (an elderly Will Wimble relative of Alvina's)… known as "Coz".'[16] I had been so distracted with the general and Miss Mills that I had totally forgotten about 'Coz' and yet here he was in front of me: Charles Stuart Mills. Was *no-one* immune from Aldington's pen?

With the general's return due some time during 1920, the family was setting up their first ever home together. Their story may have ended there, had they not let this cottage to what they judged to be a very personable twenty-eight-year-old ex-soldier and his 'wife'. Aldington's description of them as impoverished gentry didn't quite fit the picture, as I perceived it in the 1980s. Even in the 1920s, Bridge House with its two supposed staff cottages and four acres of adjoining paddock would surely have been a substantial acquisition. Perhaps though, the fact that the Aldingtons rather than servants occupied one of the cottages did say something after all for when Craigie's employees were being paid £2 a week, the eleven shillings rent Aldington paid for this cottage would go some way towards balancing any deficit that may have existed. There again, as I understood things, the Bridge House estate had remained intact until just before the time I bought the cottage in 1971 at which time the Malthouse itself had been divided into three units for conversion into separate houses. That meant that the general may well have owned a malthouse that was still being worked by Strange's Brewery. Indeed, there is a clause in my deeds that still allows the successors to their long since abandoned horses and carts a right of way across our strategic frontage to attend to the old communal septic tank in the paddock alongside.

It slowly dawned on me that I had left one stone unturned and I approached the building society for a copy of my deeds. There I found names with which I was now becoming familiar. I felt it worth the small investment needed to get a proper legal opinion on what I read. This is what I am told by a solicitor in Newbury. 'It would appear that a family trust was set up on 26 February 1918 which provided a mortgage sufficient to enable General Mills to purchase the Bridge House estate. The trustees were W.B.S. Mills and Rear Admiral, Julian Alleyne Baker [b.1845] who died on 1 June 1922.' Presumably therefore General Mills *did* need funds to repay his dues to the trust and that eleven bob a week from Aldington was useful after all. But it was those other names on the deeds that intrigued me. Who were they and what was their relevance? It didn't take too much to discover that the said Julian Alleyne Baker – no relation to the Baker from whom I bought – was the nephew of Sir Samuel White Baker the great explorer who discovered Lake Albert. Much later I was to learn that Sir Samuel Baker was the uncle of Mrs Mills. Mrs Mills' father, John Garland Baker of 'Mahagastotte, Ceylon' was married to the twin sister of Sir Samuel's first wife. Julian Alleyne Baker was therefore Mrs Mills' cousin. General Mills was confirmed, in Aldington's terms, as 'impoverished' and his wife's family was providing the mortgage enabling him to buy Bridge House.

Lovers on The Nile by Richard Hall is a biography of Sir Samuel Baker. It gives a fascinating glimpse into Mrs Mills' side of the family as well as into the eccentric aspects of Sir Samuel. Lest I be accused of cynicism, I quote from the blurb on the dust jacket:

174

'In 1858, frustrated in his wish to join Livingstone in the exploration of Central Africa, he set off with the Maharajah Duleep Singh on a tamer but still ambitious foray across the Balkans to Constantinople. While passing through what is now Bulgaria he attended a slave auction, was struck by the appearance of a slim, fair-haired Hungarian girl among the victims offered for sale and, on an impulse, bought her. He was then 38; she was 17. Florence became his mistress and soon his beloved companion, but he could hardly take her home and present her to his sisters as a bargain snapped up in a Turkish bazaar. Instead he set out for the Nile and mounted his own expedition into the Interior. "I am going to Khartoum, and thence, God only knows where, in search of the sources of the Nile". There followed a prodigious journey. Wild animals and hostile tribes, hunger and disease – the hazards of untamed Africa – dogged every step. Once Florence emerged from a week-long coma to hear men digging her grave. But this indomitable pair discovered Lake Albert and the Murchison Falls, then returned at last to Europe, where they were feted as heroes (and secretly married.) Sam was knighted and so the girl from the slave market became Lady Baker. But Queen Victoria was outraged on learning the truth about their seven-year liaison. When Sam became a friend of the Prince of Wales she did her utmost to break up the relationship. And finally as the Bakers were at the peak of their fame, came a scandal that seemed to endorse all of Victoria's doubts.'[17]

The dust-wrapper continues; 'Richard Hall recounts this bizarre epic with wit and humanity' by which means his view of Baker holds a great deal in common with Aldington's view of the general. General Mills seems as unconcerned about the repercussions of his actions as his wife's uncle was of his. 'Samuel Baker was typical of those upper class Victorian eccentrics who devoted their lives to the cause of adventure and patriotic enterprise.'[18] Maybe Aldington had known that all along.

From the same source we learn that the introduction of corridors in railway carriages was as a direct result of the amorous intentions of Sir Samuel's younger brother, Colonel Valentine Baker, himself a prominent member of the Prince of Wales' inner circle. In 1875 Valentine was found guilty of indecent assault on a young lady during a train journey to London. Richard Hall tells us that Sam Baker came from 'a rich family in the West' of England. He was the eldest son of a merchant and banker whose fortunes derived from sugar plantations in Jamaica and one of his ancestors, Sir John Baker, had been chancellor of the exchequer to Henry VIII. Another was an admiral who had fought some spectacular battles against the French.

With the parallels I had so far found between the village and the novel, it would not be stretching the imagination to assume that General Mills, like the fictitious Colonel Smithers, had servants and by asking around I was finally given names. 'The Roberts girls' had all evidently worked for the general at various times, all I had to do was find them. The electoral register showed that the only Roberts were Arthur George ('absent') and Flora Matilda but that they didn't come along until 1929 after Aldington had left. On file though, I had a note of one or two Roberts that I had seen on the marriage registry but none of these were connected. It was a while before I got to know some people well enough to be put in contact with a Mrs Norris who might be able to trace them. A letter from Mrs Norris – the president of the local Women's' Institute in the 1970s hence the chain – telling me that her brother Charles married Florence Roberts and gave me their address. More than a year had passed since I had heard of General Mills but the letter I got back from Florence Pigg was more than encouraging. Not only was I invited to meet her but her two sisters would be there too. All three of them had worked for the general at various times during the 1920s.

But then again I started to worry. So much else Aldington had written was proving to be based on fact. I realised one of the ladies I was about to meet could be the model for Lizzie Judd, and I wasn't at all sure that I wanted either to find out or to let them know of fictional Lizzie's 'indigestion'. The meeting however was set for 1 September 1982. Before that day arrived, something happened to make me wish that I had started out on this search at least ten years before. My letter to Mrs Pigg had evidently led to a buzz of memories between the three sisters, the eldest of whom, Mrs Daisy Hale, had been at Bridge House for most of the 1920s. She, most of all, was intrigued to find after all these years, that someone was interested in the general. But only a matter of days before I was due to travel north to meet them, Mrs Hale fell ill and died.

Under those circumstances the generosity of Mrs Pigg and Mrs

Sambells in refusing to postpone my visit was as warming as the welcome they gave me. I felt worse than ever and anxiously sought clues to dispel my anxiety. Mrs Pig's daughter-in-law offered coffee and biscuits. Much to my relief it was evident that her husband would be far too young to stand as evidence of inspiration for Lizzie Judd's misfortunes. Imagine too, my relief to learn in the course of conversation that Mrs Sambells had no children, but yes! Daisy had a son! I dared not ask. 'Yes, John was born just after they all left Bridge House… Miss Mills was his Godmother.' 'Yes. … When did Bill and Daisy marry?' 'Oh, that was about 1924.' 'So John was born about 1929' by which time Aldington had left, meaning that Lizzie Judd's child was pure imagination and did not have a real-world counterpart. I began to relax and, during coffee, explained my predicament as well as the reasons for my visit. Thankfully both sisters thought it all highly amusing and very soon, sixty years were rolled aside in their recollections of Bridge House. Daisy's absence and what she could have told me had she been there, was nonetheless diminished by what her sisters told me of her reminiscences.

She would have liked that, I was told.

'Daisy was there long before us. She went as parlour maid. Old "Wiggy" Wickens ['old' Dave Wickens' wife] was cook. Then she left and Daisy became cook.' The Roberts family home was at nearby Baughurst and Violet and Florence had gone into service as did most young girls at that time. They had 'previously been housemaids… and somehow drifted to Bridge House.' They were very soon made to feel at home… [The] family were very friendly. Didn't treat you like servants. They would pour you out a cup of tea when you took tea in. We were like one of the family.'

All of which goes to reinforce the unaffected nature of the general that so obviously appealed to Aldington.

The fictitious colonel, for example, came down so heavily on the side of Lizzie Judd and Tom Strutt in the novel that, despite their fictional existence, I couldn't help but read a little of their life into what the sisters told me of Daisy. Bill Hale who lived over the canal from Bridge House would occasionally 'do a few odd jobs' for the general and so met and married Daisy Roberts, after which time he worked full time for the general. By today's standards, any household employing three or four full-time servants would be considered positively wealthy but in the context of his times and seen as the reward for services rendered by the general to his empire, his was not. Worse still, for a man of his nature and after an entire lifetime devoted to the British Army, he was now dependent upon the finances of his wife's family for the home in which he lived, both in fact and in fiction.

As the 'Roberts girls' confirmed, General Mills would have found it extremely difficult to keep up the sort of appearances that with some justification, he would have felt his situation demanded. 'I think that the General just lived off his pension. ... I would have thought that Mrs Mills had the money. I think it was tied up in such a way that the General couldn't get at it.' Seen in this context, the eleven shillings a week he would receive from Aldington takes on an even greater significance. My deeds confirmed that Mrs Mills was taken care of. After the general's death, the trustees were the vendors of the estate to their namesakes, the Baker family.

The general would have felt he had earned the right to a few home comforts. One can understand that Colonel Smithers being a 'little testy' when Hunter-Payne made reference to his 'non-existent garage'. As Aldington says of Smithers: 'A family in their position ought to have a car, even if it was only a Ford or a baby Austin runabout.'[19] After all, Craigie over the road had one. It would be only natural too for General Mills, having spent his life tramping the empire to wish to impart some of his experiences to anyone who showed the least inclination to listen or indeed those who, like the Roberts girls, would have had no option. 'He used to tell us long, long stories of his life in the army. He would go on and on! He used to hinder us an awful lot. If he caught you it was hopeless; you were there for about half an hour and he would talk and talk.' *The Colonel's Daughter* too, seems to suggest that Aldington would also get caught. 'With the *Morning Post* slipping gently between his relaxed knees, [Smithers] pondered a campaign... Under these circumstances the Colonel... would [branch] forth on a long story of complicated manoeuvres whereby he had worsted the administrative side of the Army Remount Department.'[20] General Mills, though, had far more interesting stories to tell. Violet recalls being very impressed by one in particular relating to his *Who Was Who* entry about the South African War. 'They were taken prisoner of war together – Churchill and General Mills. There were quite a number of officers taken prisoner of war and they had all planned to escape together. They'd worked it all out and planned [it] but, unbeknown to the others, Churchill decided to escape first and he came back home and wrote of his escape and General Mills and all the other officers, of course, were left there in the camp, and they had to suffer for that. He never forgave him for it. He said that if he ever came face to face with Churchill he would shoot him! He was bitter, very, very bitter about it.'

Who Was Who informs us that General Mills was injured at the Battle of Alleman's Nek in 1900 and mentioned in dispatches a few times. The Roberts girls told me that 'he was carrying a carbine under his left arm and felt a blow which twisted him round.' There was blood coming from his left hand but there was no pain from it. He had been shot. 'The bullet had hit him between the thumb and first finger and had run up and come out about his wrist.' His hand never healed fully but Mrs Mills made him a 'special glove to keep his finger and thumb together... He wore part of a glove on his hand. It came up to his wrist and left his fingers showing.'

Now that Major Crook was out of the frame I was able to go back to others I had met for their memories of the General, and common to all of these is his stature and military bearing. No one was left in any doubt that they were in the presence of a General. Mrs Hissey recalls that he was 'a tall, fine superior man.' To the Roberts girls, he was 'a good-looking, stocky man. Smart. Handsome.' whereas Mrs Smith, the postman's sister, recalled his commanding presence, saying he was 'a big, tall man, up-together-sort-of-thing. He gave orders and expected them to be carried out.' Which is exactly as Aldington described the colonel. 'Colonel Smithers was undoubtedly a gentleman. As he stamped along with his military gout waddle, invisible spurs jingled at his heels: the very houses sprang to attention and the trees presented arms. The Marcia Reale from a distant barrel-organ immediately became the British Grenadiers. Smithers was pukka army.'[21] Imposing as he was, it seemed that the general had met his match in his chosen partner, Helen Henrietta Mills. She was also tall, 'very tall' the Roberts girls told me. Tall, but 'very stately, more like a Queen Mary type. Rather tall and very severe.' 'Amazonian,' if we are to believe Aldington's descriptions of the colonel's wife, Alvina Smithers. 'Experience had taught [Colonel Smithers] that he could not compete with Alvina in domestic invective, whatever his triumphs on the parade ground and in the Field.[22] ...Never in all her huntin' years had Alvina forgotten the place, time and hour of a meet, but rare indeed were the weeks when she remembered everything for the house. Alvina was terrifying to quiet men who liked their meat chopped for them.'[23] In later years at least, as Mrs Gardner recalled, a certain vanity overtook Mrs Mills. 'I remember the old lady – with her black dyed hair – thinking, that hair can't get any blacker!'

Aldington also suggested a contrast between the woman he knew with the way he imagined she had been. Alvina 'laughed a laugh which once might have been pretty but now was a trifle harsh.'[24] Mrs Mills is seen by Aldington to have far too much in common with his own mother but we can get some idea of the bearing and social ambitions of Mrs Mills from a quite fortuitous photograph in the Reading Mercury. In 1936 King Edward VIII was on an official visit to Reading during which time he made a tour of the town and finished up at the Royal Berkshire Hospital. Here he was introduced to glittering array of VAD nurses (volunteers who trained to be nurses to cope with the demands of war) among whom was Mrs Benyon the wife of the local landowner and MP. But, at the moment the photograph was taken the King was chatting to a lady to the right of Mrs Benyon – Mrs Helen Henrietta Mills.

From the evidence of *The Colonel's Daughter* and from what I was hearing from the Roberts girls, Aldington was a frequent visitor at Bridge House. Despite his affinity with the Mr Judds of this world, Aldington's middle class background and war service would have allowed him at least some small measure of social discourse with a general, but the suggested relationship between Aldington and Mrs Mills seems to be little more than mutual tolerance. Nevertheless though, the Mills would have been intrigued to hear of the intended visit of D.H. Lawrence and Frieda to Padworth. Without identifying who, Aldington says that a 'neighbour of ours, an intellectual climber, had begged to be allowed a glimpse of him, and we contrived some excuse for a brief meeting.'[25] It is not, therefore, beyond 'a little fancy' to imagine that this took place in the lane that leads to Malthouse Cottage for, as Aldington continues, in *Life for Life's Sake*, he and Lawrence 'went for walks and it was fascinating to see how quick he was in noticing things and making them seem interesting.'[26] The general and Mrs Mills just happened to be out for a morning constitutional, the general himself almost certainly dressed in his standard issue plus fours and perhaps sporting the monocle he wore on occasions. Anyone meeting him for the first time would be struck by his military bearing and, of course, his gloved left hand. As if by accident on this morning, the Mills would have encountered the two writers. All four of them were equally as tall as the other and, while Aldington's build would have matched the general's, Mrs Mills' slender physique would have had more in common with Lawrence's skinny frame.

It is with obvious delight that Aldington reports Lawrence's reaction to the meeting. Lawrence, he reports 'could be devastating in his judgement of human beings... After she had gone Lawrence merely said "Dreary little woman."'[27] Mrs Mills was, it seems, quite a remarkable woman. In the best traditions of an army wife she had taken to VAD nursing with the evangelical vigour of Florence Nightingale. Her fictional counterpart, Alvina, 'positively hunted men back to health'.[28] Equally as imposing as the general, Mrs Mills was nevertheless far more intimidating. The Roberts girls remember her around the house in the uniform she would wear as commandant of the local branch of The Red Cross. 'She just lived for that.' Mrs Mills was obviously the social climber that Aldington referred to. Lawrence, I feel, confirms this. It would be some years before Aldington fictionalised these events but for Lawrence the process was more immediate. Within weeks of this meeting in June 1926, Lawrence was creating the character of Sir Clifford Chatterley for *The First Lady Chatterley* among whose traits he includes one very significant aspect of General Mills. Sir Clifford was 'every inch a gentleman – even to the half of his little finger that the bullet blew away.'[29]

The Roberts girls' recollections brought home just how seriously Mrs Mills took home nursing. 'Mrs Mills' room was in the very large room up another flight of stairs all laid out like a hospital.' In fact, the layout of the rooms upstairs at Bridge House seems to sum up the relationship between the general and his wife, as much as their geographical positions in the house. The general 'had the end room, nearest the canal, Miss Helen was in the middle. Then there was a spare room and Charles was over in [the] corner, on the landing facing the garden. We [the servants] were up in the attic.' There was a distance between Mrs Mills and the general that cannot be summed up in a few sentences. 'She was very aloof [towards the Roberts girls] and aristocratic. She came from a better background than the general and more or less treated him that way. They weren't very friendly towards each other; not by any means. They were not friendly to each other. She was a very aristocratic lady and he had no time for her

Fig. 30. Brigadier General George Arthur Mills wearing his glove

job.' Feelings must have been reciprocated though because, on the other hand I learnt from Mrs Gardner, that to the general 'a wife or a daughter was a sort of chattel' a point that Aldington puts across on the opening page of *The Colonel's Daughter*. Georgie, he says, was 'father's dear little bottle washer'. Despite that though 'Georgie honoured her father and her mother, particularly her father, who was quite a dear, and still had rather graceful ways with nearly all women except his wife.'[30]

Harsh words indeed, from one who knew the general well. Furthermore, Aldington would have us believe, the colonel 'escaped the dullness by an occasional little run-up-to-town-and-a-night-at-the-club. With whom did he spend those nights? He was elderly but…'[31] He obviously wasn't where he was supposed to be. A brief mention of that suggestion produced a spontaneous response from Mrs Sambells. 'No, no! He wasn't! No! No! *Definitely* wasn't.' Whatever the general was doing was done with apparent indifference to the feelings of those around him, it's no wonder that Aldington held him in high regard. Mrs Sambells again: 'I can't remember what her name was, I knew at the time, but he definitely had a lady friend.' The general's nephew told me of the occasion when, as a youngster he was 'driven past the Army and Navy Club to see Uncle George at the window… and then had to keep "mum" about it as I don't think he was supposed to be there… He was a bit of a rogue.' Uncle George was stood there 'in his matching jacket and trousers. I don't think he had a suit…' In that guise General Mills makes a fleeting appearance in Aldington's short story *A Gentleman of England* where over dinner, everyone was 'mixing wines like false metaphors' and 'there was Blenthrop, wearing a staff uniform and a double row of ribbons, with slacks.'[32] In his unique way General Mills was to leave an impression on Aldington very much as did Bill Brown and Major Darby — and upon his servant girls too, particularly Florence Roberts. 'He was a gay old man! He used to love girls! He *loved* girls! Yes he did… He was a charming old chap really. He was very sweet to us [but] he was *definitely* a ladies' man. No doubt about that.' All this sounds too much like Aldington to be true.

But of course in addition to Georgie Smithers, her parents and staff, there was one other resident at Holly Lodge, the fortuitous confirmation of which had been presented by the electoral register. In this hall of mirrors the fact that Aldington had been absolved from the need to create 'Coz' was almost beyond belief. From the first reading of *The Colonel's*

Daughter I had entirely discounted him from my search so fictional did he seem.

> *'Although Coz had been an athlete, and was indeed a pukka Sahib, he had somehow missed that physical beauty which belongs by divine right to both those summits of the human race. Perhaps, like a good many of them, he had merely gone flabby and whiskyish in maturity. His head looked like a small pink Brancusi egg balanced on a large tweed one. His arms and legs bulged with fat muscles. He had one of those unmistakably aristocratic faces which must be such a comfort to Nietzschean eugenists. His Nordic blue eyes overflowing with stupidity, had bulgy underlids, like a blood hound's, and his shaved red jowls imitated those of the nobler animal. A wispy yellow moustache, ominously stained – no philanthropist had ever insisted on his using a moustache mug – drooped hopelessly over a wobbly mouth which he held moistly half-open with astounding pertinacity.'*[33]

But 'Coz' was not as the author says, a relative of Alvina Smithers. Charles Stuart Mills was the general's brother; 'the bright one of the family' says Aldington satirically.[34] He would have been in his sixties during the 1920s and, Violet Roberts recalls, 'lived with them for years and years and years.' He was a 'nice old chap, similar build to his brother' was about all Mrs Hissey and Miss Vi-vi Mills cared to remember of him. General Mills' nephew, however, was more direct. Rather as Aldington did, he held his uncles dear, but could raise an objective smile at thoughts of them. 'A kind of parasite' was his description of 'Uncle Charlie', a view that coincides with Aldington's description of 'Coz.'

> *'At any rate he was pukka gentry, with a small inheritance which, by skilful mismanagement, he had reduced to £150 a year. He had led a life of exemplary uselessness, residing with one or other of the wealthier members of the family. Most of these having perished after helping to swell the statistics of longevity, Coz now resided permanently with the Smithers as a kind of under-paying guest. The Smithers were proud to have him, for his consanguinity increased the pukkaness of their Sahibdom.'*[35]

Recollections of the Mills elders brought that same smile of wonderment that Aldington experienced when the Roberts girls recalled 'Uncle Charlie's' amorous adventures. 'They were all at it!' they exclaimed. 'He had a girl in Reading... She was a librarian at Boots. He used to go and see her once a week, and he used to go off from Bridge House waving his walking stick. He was so excited.' His nephew, then in his teens, acquired a motorcycle and used to drive miles to come and see his uncles at Bridge House. He used to act as a go-between for 'Uncle Charles' and would relay messages from 'Uncle Charges himself to his lady friend, Nell, in "Boots the Chemist" in Reading. Always on early closing day.' He would push his motorbike to the top of the railway bridge and then, with Uncle Charles on the rear mudguard, would attempt to push start it down the slope on the other side. 'Imagine doing all that and then trying to get your leg over! If it didn't start by the time we got to the Bath Road, we were in trouble!'

In the spring of 1926 and only shortly before Lawrence met General Mills, Aldington had once more gone to Italy. He was only there for a short period and, as he says in *Life for Life's Sake*, he 'got back... in time to be involved in the general strike, which was conducted by both sides with a splendid inefficiency which led to the happiest result – an early peace.'[36] That Aldington did become involved is not so much for reasons that he particularly sided with the employers, he tells us that: 'For my part I warmly wished a plague on both their houses.'[37] It was the fact that a measurable portion of his own income depended on the regular production of *The Times* and *The Times Literary Supplement*. It was in his interest to try to restore the status quo as quickly as possible and get back to work. Besides which, the 'upheaval stopped dead the sales of my Voltaire, which had come out only three weeks before and was going very nicely... I was sufficiently disturbed by the prospect of civil confusion ahead not to be able to work with any enthusiasm; and when I got a telegram from The Times asking me to come and help the paper continue, I stuffed some underclothes and a book in my army pack and hitch-hiked to London, no regular transport being available.'[38]

Which of course meant that he was in London during the time when hundreds of Welsh miners passed along the Bath Road at Padworth on their way to the House of Commons. They had spent the previous night in the Corn Exchange at Newbury. According to the memories of one young boy 'they made an impressive sight carrying their pit helmets, lamps and picks, singing as they went. In attendance were ambulances and mobile kitchens to feed them on their travels.'[39]

That small boy may well have encountered Aldington and more probably, Hilda Brown, for Stan Bushell, too was a native of Hermitage.

At the time of this march, there were convoys of lorries travelling this same trade route to London and so susceptible were they to abuse or attack that volunteer guards were needed to ensure a safe passage. Who better for the job than General Mills and his brother? 'It would be unjust', Aldington asserts, 'to describe Smithers as a free thinker. As a disciplinarian he mistrusted freedom of any kind.'[40] which is presumably why, Violet Roberts tells us, General Mills 'and his brother used to go off in the mornings… and go with the lorries… from London and Bath… They picked them up on the Bath Road… [They would] go out with their truncheons in their belts in the mornings… We used to love [to watch] them going off in the mornings, with their truncheons hanging down! Oh, I think he [Aldington] would have loved it!' I have to agree.

On a number of occasions I have been told of Mrs Mills' love of the open air, inherited, we must suppose, from her uncle, the explorer Samuel Baker. It is easy from what we hear of her to imagine a free spirited woman. Mrs Mills would feel as chained to a life of domesticity as much as the general but whereas he still seemed to yearn for far horizons, Mrs Mills used to take refuge in their paddock at the back of the Malthouse where she took to keeping chickens. The Roberts girls remembered it well. 'She was quite active and used to spend the greater part of her time looking after her chickens.' From what I learned practically everyone in Padworth kept chickens during the 1920s, except Aldington. 'She was a great one for her chickens,' Violet Roberts continued. 'She kept them in the field and used to spend hours down there looking after the wretched chickens. She always expected you to boil up all sorts of stuff for the chickens.'

On one occasion, presumably at Mrs Mills' request, Aldington carted Mrs Todgers over the fence and into the chicken run where 'I had seen a young rat. She the exterminator of rodents, saw it at once, watched it running frantically about, and walked away.'[41] A small passage in *The Colonel's Daughter* suggests that it may well be based on careful observation of the author's neighbours. 'At one time Alvina noticed with displeasure that Coz's bantam cocks were making indecent assaults on her Rhode Island hens. This, thought Alvina indignantly, with true

Regular Army knowledge, will make the hens lay little eggs. After much hemming, she bashfully asked Fred to ask Coz to confine his feathered Lotharios; an embassy duly and gravely performed.'[42]

Aldington could equally capitalise on Alvina Smithers' instincts for self-sufficiency under duress. As when an unexpected guest arrived at very short notice. 'Then Alvina decided that they must have a chicken in addition to the unsucculent mutton chops supplied by a sullen and reluctant butcher. She therefore ordered Nelly to murder one of the youngest of the cockerels with a chopper. And when Nelly, flatly refusing, threatened to follow Lizzie in the "screamin' yesterics" line, Alvina most gallantly performed the deed – and a very tough young brute the victim turned out to be.'[43]

Equally high on Mrs Mills' list of priorities though was church going, in company with her fictional counterpart, Alvina Smithers. 'The Smithers ladies had a proper attitude towards Church-going – they considered it a duty *and* a pleasure. The elementary duty of divine worship, possibly in itself tedious at times (though the tedium was not to be advertised), was sweetened for them by the opportunity for observing fashion, for neighbourly greetings and invitations.'[44] But although they lived within the confines of Padworth parish, the Roberts girls told me that 'Mrs Mills and Helen used to go to Beenham Church.' That simple statement said so much. Suddenly I could picture people from different houses in the neighbourhood spick and span all going in entirely different directions and all for equally irrational reasons. The Draper Stranges had vacated Bridge House in favour of the Mills occupancy and, as neighbours therefore, may well have influenced Mrs Mills in her choice of church. Padworth church was rejected for Beenham. Miss Violet Mills (no relation) over at Beenham House remembers their Sunday morning journeys. 'The Draper Stranges used to go to Beenham church up through Shrub Wood.' So does Mrs Hissey. 'Mr and Mrs Draper Strange used to go to church in their... bath-chair-affair with a handle in the front, [converted into]... a shaft made for a pony. They'd have a little pony in there. I can see him going to church now up through Shrub Wood... of course the track was better then...' Chris Strange, himself no youngster, would join this pageant, quite likely collecting Mrs Mills and Miss Mills as they passed.

It is hardly worth mentioning but I knew, or at least I thought I knew, what General Mills' attitude towards church might be from what

Aldington suggests in *The Colonel's Daughter*. Smithers was not much of a one for church. He was: 'Less assiduous. No more parades for him, including Church parade… When he attended Church, it was, like Sir Horace, to give countenance to an institution which had its useful side.'[45] Violet Roberts once more confirmed my suspicions. 'Neither the general or Charles ever went to church. They'd take a walk with their dogs, Briar and Bramble – cocker spaniels. I always remember those dogs. They never went anywhere without them. They used to sleep in their rooms as well and always went for your ankles when you took their early morning tea in. I was scared stiff of them.' That may well be so but Briar and Bramble were to meet their match. Despite her previous apathy Mrs Todgers did excel herself on one occasion when she brought Aldington 'two monstrous great rats, each neatly killed with a nip in the neck. Nor did she ever turn tail from a hostile dog, however confident and fierce looking. My neighbours' cocker spaniels knew better than ever to enter the garden – you couldn't get them past the gate.'[46]

Sunday mornings would provide a wonderful opportunity no doubt, for a bit of man talk either up the lane or perhaps over the gate, although from the evidence of *The Colonel's Daughter*, Aldington's contribution to the conversation would be the author's stock in trade – undivided attention. No doubt the general would go on a bit, as he always did. Hunting, shooting or fishing, Aldington would take it all in. One of the general's distinct pleasures was racing. He never failed to tell the servants of his many and varied exploits. 'He was a *great* racing man. He was a great steeplechaser and broke nearly every bone in his body. Everything! Everything had been broken. He had lots of pictures of himself… He *loved* racing and steeplechasing especially. Oh! He was a real daredevil, you know, in his early days.' Maybe that was half of the problem.

Aldington would have a fairly shrewd idea where his eleven shillings a week rent was going. Alvina says as much in the novel. 'If there was any *real* consideration for Georgie she said, "half the income of this establishment wouldn't be spent on bookmakers and useless trips to London."'[47] One can judge that General Mills' life wouldn't have been worth living without these minor indulgences. Take away his military career and what was left? Padworth cannot have had the same appeal to the general as it did to his neighbour. 'Consequently, the evening-of-life as a hawkin, huntin, fishin English gentleman became a dull affair for

Smithers. He escaped the dullness by making minute but numerous telegraphic bets on certs with a bookie – and generally lost.'[48]

The Roberts girls would have almost as strategic a view of the world as the Aldingtons, for the kitchen at Bridge House faces sideways onto the lane and the canal. A huge elephant's tooth almost permanently held open the back door where the servants would pass the odd word with the Aldingtons. There was a certain charisma about the Aldingtons that attracted the Roberts girls. 'They were marvellous. They were always out walking together. We'd see them constantly. No one else had reason to go down that lane. It's lovely and quiet down there.' But it was more than a passing neighbourly acquaintance with Bridge House for Aldington would often pop in to see the general. As he says in a letter (16 April 1924) to Harold Monro from whom he regularly received *Country Life* magazine, he gained some 'slight applause by lending the thing to impoverished local gentry'.[49] On another occasion Miss Mills had taken to Aldington's little sister Patricia when she was staying at the cottage. Harold Monro had also come down on one of his fairly frequent visits and a good time was obviously had by all concerned for in another letter (14 July 1925) Aldington writes to Monro. 'You were angelic to Patty and Miss Mills. The latter thought you were very clever!'[50]

We can follow the natural progression from these meetings to the author's aspirations for his heroine in *The Colonel's Daughter*. 'Georgie wished she knew more young people, but nearly all her friends were rather old. It was rather beastly not really knowing any of the very smart people Margy Stuart knew – but then the Stuarts were rich – or even any of the awfully queer and annoying but interesting people who came to spend week-ends with Mr Purfleet, the local intellectual, during the summer.'[51] It is significant that whereas the servants speak of 'Miss Helen' Aldington talks of his neighbour more formally as 'Miss Mills.' One becomes aware that the perhaps paternalistic respect with which Aldington speaks of her to Harold Monro is a fair reflection of the sad sorrow that those who knew her felt towards the plight of the general's daughter. It is on Miss Mills' total subservience to her parents' wishes that *The Colonel's Daughter* is founded and that knowledge came not just from their neighbourly encounters. Aldington and Arabella had first-hand experience of the hierarchy of the household for as the Roberts girls told me: 'They frequently visited Bridge House and would come to dinner sometimes. They used to get on very well together.' The evidence of an empty cigarette packet of the period found here in the cottage shows that Aldington's virtue No. 2 as written to Harold Monro had been abandoned. The servants at Bridge House recall that the general was also not averse to the odd Gold Flake. 'He would smoke and smoke and smoke. He was never without a cigarette. He used to spend all his time shut up in his room – smoking.' From the writer's reports of the contents of Fred Smithers' study we must assume that Aldington was privileged to join the general on occasions. Knowing, as we now do, of the Mills family's frequent associations with the royal family there may even be some truth in the suggestion that in Smithers' desk 'was a large cigar. A piece of paper was tied to it with a ribbon, and on it was written "Given to me by his late majesty, King Edward VIII, then Prince of Wales, on the occasion of the Regimental Dinner, September 1895."'[52] Obviously General Mills was a hoarder for as Aldington says of Smithers in *The Colonel's Daughter*; his 'bedroom was a tumult of sporting implements and bizarre souvenirs, in some cases not even clear to the Colonel himself. If the stuffed, inconveniently large and slightly mouldy warthog recalled a jungle triumph, what was commemorated by the pimply-looking meteorite, the pair of fans painted with somewhat Europeanised geishas and the broken ivory back-scratcher. The colonel himself would have been flummoxed if sternly required to explain how he acquired them and why he kept them. Shelves and a large table were littered with papers hopelessly involved with such objects as collar-boxes, sharks' teeth, fishing tackle, dum-dum bullets, bills and County Court summonses.'[53]

It is interesting, in retrospect, to see how people's memories differ. What to one person may be considered unworthy of note may seem quite extraordinary to another. As I had learnt that Daisy's son John Hale had been born safely after the event – and indeed after the general had died and the ladies had moved to Bucklebury – it seemed obvious that if indeed he could add anything of any significance to my search it would be on the hearsay of his parents' recollections. But the fact that he was Miss Mills' godson was incentive enough to go and meet him for he, like his aunts, was totally unaware of the place in literature that they all occupied. John Hale told me that his parents had been retained by Mrs Mills after the general's death and that he had indeed been born at Oaklea, the Bucklebury home. But, more than that, Oaklea had acquired all the trappings of Bridge House. Despite the fact that he never met General Mills, John Hale nevertheless grew up in his presence. 'It was just like a museum. Inside the front door and all up the stairs was just all spears and African shields right up to the ceiling. I remember an elephant's head and a boar's head hanging on the wall!' This was presumably the one for which the general won the cup in 1897. Among one or two personal items – one of which is the bible presented to him by his godmother – John still has the elephant's tooth with which his mother propped open the back door at Bridge House. 'There was an elephant's foot as well. It was used as a waste paper basket. It caused us to wonder where the rest of the poor elephant went.'

It is obvious that Mrs Mills was not bothered about a gap-toothed elephant's head on the wall for, as Richard Hall tells us, her uncle Sam

'had shot more of the Ceylonese variety than any other man living. But when he studied the thick cranium of African elephants he doubted if they would be easy to bring down by the conventional forehead shot from an ordinary gun. With this in mind he had designed a massive muzzle-loader, firing a half-pound shell, which he nicknamed "The Baby". Unfortunately, it needed so much powder that even he could scarcely use it without being thrown on his back. There was going to be a time when Baker would confess his regret at having killed so many elephants. But that was in far later years and for the moment he rejoiced in what he called "whole hecatombs of slaughter". Hunting was the one activity in which he was incomparable and it answered a deep emotional want. (It is widely accepted by psychologists that stabbing has strong sexual connotations, so Baker's obsession with killing animals in this way may have reflected unfulfilled urges, canalized in displays of physical conquest.)… Baker's way of shooting elephants in Ceylon had been spectacularly bold, for he would creep as close as ten feet before firing. Once an angry bull had hurled him in the air, and frequently he narrowly escaped being trampled to death, but was nonetheless scornful of the hunting methods in Africa, where "according to all accounts, elephants are fired at [from] thirty, forty and even sixty yards."'[54]

It was as a result of mentioning this Baker connection that John Hale pointed out a side table that had originally belonged to Mrs Mills' mother

– the twin of Sir Samuel's first wife. I was surprised too, to hear that General Mills 'was a very good painter', and hope that I may be forgiven the slight smile when John described the general's masterpieces as 'still life' that portrayed 'ducks that had been shot and were hanging up. They covered the passages on the ground floor.' Over the years John has thrown away a lot of the general's sketchbooks that he was given when Miss Mills moved on to Crowthorne. 'They've all gone now,' he said to my horror. 'He was a photographer as well. There again, you see, I did at one time have all his glass plates. They were *all* photographs in India [but at the time] all his photographic stuff was put out to be collected by the council to be dumped. There was a builder – he was an undertaker as well. He was doing some decoration… and he carted a camera away and all his glass jars, scales and things. He also had a military collection of old helmets, caps and badges and uniforms – all gone!'

In fact, that is not quite true. Some of General Mills' possessions must still be around somewhere. In the eighteen months after I heard this fateful story and despite a relatively fruitless search I had not been idle. One can but hope that General Mills' photographic equipment might turn up and maybe the publication of these notes might one day flush it out. John Hale did tell me though that he thought some of the more treasured possessions had gone to one or other of the local museums. He is right. There are two index cards in Reading Museum that confirm donations from the family. The first records that Miss Mills gave to the museum two period dresses, one dated 1850 and the other more recent. The second card records that Charles Stuart Mills deposited with the museum 'one stuffed bird in glass case' and it is believed that the Army Museum may hold one or two items from General Mills. For such a remarkable man as General Mills it is a pity that all that remain are memories. In the strength of these memories though rests the charismatic nature of the man. Bill Austin has one particularly endearing story to tell about the fete on the lawns at Padworth House. 'We had a fete up at Darby Griffith's estate. We had a tug-o-war. Married versus single and I was single then and the ground was lopsided and whoever was pulling downhill always won. So I went to the general who was supposed to be in charge. I said, can't we have it on the level? There must be a level place here. "Wha! Wha! Wha! What do you want?" Army officer see! Couldn't even be thought that he was wrong … I wanted a level pull. You could keep on for half a day and you wouldn't be any better off. And of course the married men won and kept on winning. He wouldn't have it, so I packed it in. You couldn't argue with a general but an admiral would have listened to you.'

With the wisdom of maturity the general's nephew believes that he was the only one among his brothers and sisters (all of whom went on to gain notable achievements in their various careers) who was wholly accepted at Bridge House and that may well be due to the fact that he was the only one with a military career. The fact that he too, went on to become a brigadier tends to suggest that he was right. His brother who joined the RAF was never made to feel quite so much at home despite the fact that he ended up as air vice-marshal in later years. For those who are prepared to see it, an indication of the relationship between Aldington and General Mills is to be found in the general's unashamed listing of his interests in his *Who Was Who* entry. For even in the 1920s there were the forerunners of those of us who, today, find it totally unacceptable that anyone should list such sports as pleasures and to stick spears into pigs is as barbaric as bull fighting. It is not to be wondered that Aldington chose to satirise these assets of the General's nature and yet the apparently unconcerned exuberance with which the general not only enjoyed his sport but with which he recorded his success, brings to mind Squire Waterton again. The pleasure with which Aldington fictionalises the general's sporting activities is similar to the delight he registers on learning of Waterton's exploits in riding on the back of an alligator in the Amazonian jungle. No doubt the general thought Aldington was a weak-kneed-Bolshie in the same fashion that Mr Brown criticised Lawrence at times; indeed it would be to the General's eternal credit if he did. There was a bond of friendship between these two men. General Mills would keep their confidences within the bounds of the dining table. Aldington too, could be very discreet when it came to those in his own life – he would kiss but not tell – but when it came to his neighbours at Bridge House, he threw caution to the winds of fiction. But had Aldington not written *The Colonel's Daughter* what little we know of the Mills family may have remained hidden forever.

Chapter 11

The Village

Aldington's life is accessible through his writing. His novels, his poetry and his letters all give an insight to both the man and his surroundings. The fact that he was an established writer with the best of credentials is the reason, for example, why his correspondence with the literary men of his day is to be found in the libraries of the world's universities. But his contribution to the community of Padworth is equal to a few dozen people who lived alongside him. Every community produces its own eminent men and women but the relative achievements of, say, Aldington, General Mills, Anna Munro, Chris Strange, Major Strange or Darby Griffith in their individual fields are extremely difficult to evaluate. Were there the same degree of interest in brewing we could expect to find access to the life of Gerald Strange. As it is, the Army Museum may house some of General Mills' sketches and the Fawcett Library has an interest in the life of Anna Munro, but what of the ordinary folk who went to make up the rest of the village? What did they do with their lives and how did they all get on with each other? Well, of course, practically all of them appear as characters in Aldington's writing. *The Colonel's Daughter*, *Women Must Work* and *The Lads of the Village* build up a good picture of the neighbourhood, but what was life in Aldington's Padworth really like?

Three general elections in 1922, 1923 and 1924 saw a burst of enthusiasm for the Conservative party, a sharp decline in popularity for the Liberals and the rising popularity of the Labour party. It was a time of rapid social change that is as well reflected in *The Colonel's Daughter* as anywhere else, but Aldington's reaction was to shrink away from any form of authoritarianism from whatever quarter. It was all too expressive of an England with which he was to have less in common as time passed. 1926 was the year in which mains electricity was first brought to Padworth but it would be years before all the cottages would be connected. Aldington's water supply came courtesy of the brewery which had its own artesian well to obtain water for the beer and that 'privilege' remained in place until the 1980s.

The whole of January 1926 is recorded locally as having the worst weather of the decade. Snow fell like it had never fallen before. It was so bad that Mrs Plumer, the new headmistress, recorded in the school log book on 15 January 1926 that: 'Owing to the snow all the children from a distance were absent this morning, only seven being present.' Three days later 'deep snow again prevented the children from attending. Consequently the school closed today' and by 21 January: 'The attendance this week is lower than it has been for a considerable time owing to the bad state of the roads.' Indeed the entire situation at school had become so bad that when the time came for the annual school inspector's report in June he made reference to 'the exceptional difficulties during the past winter' and considered it 'an act of courage' on Mrs Plumer's part 'to accept an inspection'.

This was the time that Ron Bates' father started in business on his own account from the Mill House – 'haulage and one thing and another' – was to become Ron Bates' business until his retirement. Leslie Austin remembers the snow in Mill Lane. 'We had a terrible snowstorm and Mill Lane was about six foot deep all the way down from the White House to [the Mill House]. Six foot deep it was, you see, because there was a hedge each side and it just filled up.' Ron Bates remembered it too. 'We dug down from the White House to that field gate and then [drove] into the field and went down [that way].' Dorothy Adams remembers the village shop, 'a wooden building' by the roadside near the canal bridge. The old couple that ran it lived with a relative along the Bath Road but when things got bad they stayed put at the shop. It was too bad even for their short journey home. 'The back of the shop held a couple of old armchairs, absolutely full of old coats and blankets in which they wrapped themselves and spent the night.'

Life in the village and surrounding countryside was paralysed by the bad weather and it was to get worse. In those days there were not the sophisticated controls on the sluices of the River Kennet that we have nowadays and when the snow thawed, the river flooded. Over the intervening years the level of the road between the wharf and Aldermaston village has been built up by at least two feet. When the floods rose Aldermaston was cut off from the north to all but the most daring of pedestrians – like Mrs Adams. 'The thing was, they used to have a high platform along a great part of that road – a wooden platform like a pavement along the left-hand side… and you had to walk along there because the water flooded underneath.' Everywhere was affected, with the exception, it would seem, of Malthouse Cottage where, even allowing for the slight doubts raised in Aldington's letter to F.S. Flint, Aldington and Arabella remained:

> *'very cheerful and comfortable here, though as the country people say "the waters are out" very widely above and below us. For nearly a fortnight we were cut off from Aldermaston and Padworth; and Aldermaston road had two feet of water in it. The meadow by the Butt Inn became a small lake, but we were not menaced except that during the gale we expected the willows to go. They braved it out, however, with the loss of a few small branches… Padworth House was completely isolated for twelve hours as far as horse or motor traffic was concerned, for every road of approach had a huge tree in it.'[1]*

Curiously, and fortuitously for the Aldingtons, the cottage seemed to survive. With the canal only a few feet to the front and the river a few hundred yards to the rear it is surprising that they remained unaffected by the floods. Even Aldington, with his love of walking, would have been housebound for the duration. The contrast between the water meadows in summer time and their state after this period must have given food for thought on his sleepless nights when 'the immense sky, naked and stormy, circles with its illimitable round low white roof of our cottage.'[2] I like to imagine that his poem, 'A Winter Night' was written during this period of devastation. It certainly has that feel to it. The following extract is in direct contrast to 'The Berkshire Kennet'.

> 'Now the calm acres where I lay
> Through half a murmurous summer's day
> Nodding in these drowsy meads
> To the curtseying of the reeds,
> Are drenched and mournful, harsh and wild.
> Hostile to his late spoil'd child,
> The turbid river seems to sulk
> And hoarsely pours his swollen bulk;

Blind with swirling leaves, the year
Dreads the moist sheet drawing near,
Cowering hides his frosted head
And mourns his April Splendours fled.
The pattering rain falls loud and thick,
Quelling the old clock's gentle tick;
The tossing willows hiss and creak
As if long anguish forced them speak
And curse the loud tormenting gale;
And as their branches groan and wail,
The ivy taps the latticed pane;
The wind howls; and it taps again.'[3]

Around this time Aldington took a stroll along the board-walk towards Aldermaston. To his dismay he discovered that 'some fine old trees succumbed and those magnificent poplars near the river suffered heavily.' Even worse though was in store. 'Two gigantic elms on the Aldermaston road were snapped off like twigs and added to the confusion by blocking the road for all traffic.'[4] But Aldington wasn't alone on that cold January day. 'Mr Judd gazed at the ruin now revealed to his eyes. [The] stumps, each large enough to make a table, were rawly visible at ground level. The great trees had crashed to the earth, splintering twigs and branches with the force of their fall.' Mr Judd voiced Aldington's thoughts. He 'felt confusedly as if part of his life had been massacred.'[5]

After such an inauspicious start to 1926 a glance through the rest of that year's calendar helps to put things into perspective. February was obviously a time of recuperation and reassessment for all concerned, for nothing of any recorded merit happened in the village at all and Aldington caught up on his correspondence – one letter to Glenn Hughes, three to Harold Monro, two to Ezra Pound and five to Herbert Read. One, dated 18 February, from Herbert Read to Aldington suggested postponing his intended visit until Easter or beyond, which suited Aldington quite well for, as we have seen he went off to Italy this time to make a carefully planned tour of Tuscan and Umbrian Hill towns.[6]

On Monday 8 March the special meeting at which the war memorial was discussed took place at Padworth House. That month also, saw the publication of 'Bun' Salter's article 'The Prodigal Singer' in *Good Housekeeping*. The 23rd saw the open annual parish meeting at the school. The fate of the war memorial was obviously beyond question by now for the most the annual parish council could find to talk about on 12 April was the resolve to claim current expenses of £6 from the Parish overseers; the fact that that meeting again took place at Padworth House under the chairmanship of the Squire may well account for the lean meat of the agenda. At that meeting Chris Strange was appointed as one of the trustees to the Brightwell Charity. William Austin senior was one of the parish councillors at those meetings and the clerk was George Early, Mr Austin's senior at the brewery. Salter's article 'Marrying for Money' came out in April, and on the 16th of that month the annual school inspection took place. Mr Sargent, the benevolent inspector reported that the playground needed repairing. He really was trying to be helpful whereas on 29 April, Mr Windle the local sanitary inspector was at the school to investigate problems with the water supply in the company of Chris Strange in his role as school governor.

On 5 May, Richard's mother May Aldington turned up in Padworth. By the 18th Aldington had 'just returned' from three weeks' general strike duty with *The Times*. He says he hitch-hiked to London but circumstances might suggest that his mother gave him a lift and may well have been influential in his decision to go. The 6 June was the date of D.H. Lawrence's suggestion that the Aldingtons join him at Villa Mirenda later in the year for which they immediately started saving in order to do so. July was quiet except, no doubt, for a celebration of Aldington's birthday at the Butt Inn. Unusually for him, he had made no arrangements for a 'birthday treat' of visitors perhaps in the secure knowledge that Lawrence and Frieda were due down on 6 August. On 4 August he wrote to Herbert Read again informing him they were off to Italy on 25 August so perhaps he was planning to go straight back with Lawrence. From 6 to the 10 August the Reading Show was being held at which the Cappers may have been in attendance and so missing the chance to meet Lawrence. It would seem that Aldington and Arabella did set off on 25 August as planned. They arrived at Lawrence's Villa Mirenda on 6 September and stayed until 11 October. This is significant as Keith Sagar in *D.H. Lawrence: A Calendar of His Works* tells us that Lawrence only arrived two days beforehand and almost immediately began the first draft of *The First Lady Chatterley* perhaps even with Aldington in attendance. By 26 October Lawrence had reached page 41 and so had already committed to paper some of his circumstantial passages.

Reverend Lancaster had presumably had enough of being ignored in

Padworth and resigned; the vacancy was filled on 22 September by Rev William Pritchard Lord MA. H.D.'s name appears on the electoral register for the second consecutive year. On the 3 September, the Quaker journal *The Friend* tells us that at the 'Marlborough Nursing Home, 37 Bath Road, Reading, to Athol Harry and Jessie Capper, a son [was born] who was named John Brodie.' Aldington though was absent from home and would not have seen baby John until his return some time before 6 November. On 1 November yet another special meeting of the parish council was held. It gave them the excuse to fix the clerk's salary at £3 per annum but the main business was to discuss the future of the Kennet and Avon Canal that fronted Aldington's cottage. The council decided not to oppose the Great Western Railway's proposal to formally close the canal because a) it would not greatly affect the parish and b) by now it was of no practical use anyway.

Armistice day passed on 11 November with little of note in the village. No doubt Aldington would have paid his quiet respects but by now the ceremonies previously attached to the occasion were beginning to wane. On 6 December 1926 Aldington was in Newcastle to deliver a lecture on Remy de Gourmont 'A Modern Man of Letters' with whom he seemed to have an inordinate amount in common. The paper he delivered was published two years later by Glenn Hughes the editor of the *University of Washington Chapbooks*. The Reverend Lord officiated at the school on 23 December where the annual Christmas party was in full swing for both parents and pupils but by that time Aldington and Arabella had disappeared on their annual pilgrimage to the Withams at Devon. Even at surface level 1926 has a little more to offer than most years. It marks the watershed of Aldington's time in Padworth. Before 1926 his life was a period of settlement and adjustment after the war. Later circumstances suggest that this was the start of Aldington's latest seven-year-itch cycle towards both Arabella and Padworth.

But one thing happened that year which was to shed further light on the ordinary folk of Padworth in a quite delightful way. I was indeed lucky to come across it. On first meeting her, Jessie Capper's housekeeper at Arborfield told me in no uncertain terms that the Cappers had 'written books' on chicken farming. A letter to the British Library brought a disappointing response as there was nothing in their records to support this. Some weeks later I received a note from Jessie's aged housekeeper, she had found the book. But, bless her, it was not a book but a trade journal – *EGGS*. Among the ephemeral adverts for rat poisons and incubators and under the headline 'A Day on a Poultry Farm' by Mrs Athol Capper was a delightful vignette of the comings and goings at June Rose Bungalow. The periodical is dated 10 March 1926. The presumption that Jessie Capper was a regular contributor drove me to spend a frustrating day going through the entire *EGG* collection at the National Newspaper Library at Collingdale. But Jessie's piece was unique and the Capper name never appeared again, not even in the classified adverts at the back. It was immediately apparent though that Jessie's breezy chitchat showed just how wildly exciting life was on the opposite side of the canal with the first entry of the day.

'*6.30 the post arrives.*'[7]

Frank Downham was demobilised at the age of twenty-six. He had been a telegraph boy before he joined up and must have held out little hope of doing anything useful on his return to Padworth until Mr Albury the postmaster cum builder-undertaker, came round one night from the Wharf House and offered him a job at the post office. From there Frank went on to become a postman. He married Ellen Butler from Ufton in April 1920 and moved soon after to Beenham but continued delivering around his home territory for years afterwards.

He would have been one of the first people on the street each day rising at goodness knows what hour. With a chicken farm to administer the Cappers like most others who worked the land, would also be up early.

'*6.45 we look at [the post] while dressing. Observe that 'EGGS' contains lurid articles on BWB and coccidiosis. Reading details of the symptoms we feel like the man in 'Three Men in a Boat' who studied a book on diseases generally, and discovered that he had the lot with the exception of housemaid's knee*'

No doubt with little more than a quick cup of tea inside them the Cappers started their working day. 'Go out in a chastened mood to inspect the week old chicks, and feel convinced that all of the dread symptoms could probably be discovered among them if we had time to make a thorough investigation.' This particular day must have been after the bad weather had cleared; perhaps a crisp February morning. Obviously Frank

Fig. 31. Wedding photograph of Frank and Ellen Downham

Downham must have started his round on home territory and then worked his way to the village for at 7 a.m. Hilda Hearn recalls he was at Padworth House. 'When [Major Darby] was alone in the house, 6.30 a.m. was sufficiently early for the younger members of the staff to rise and get their early morning duties completed before the breakfast bell rang.' A cup of tea was evidently waiting on the kitchen table at 7 a.m. 'for the early risers'. No doubt Frank Downham arranged his timetable accordingly as Mr Adkins, the butler 'would take in the post, when the postman came to the side door at 7 o'clock'. The Butler's daughter would set off around this time to cycle the mile and a half to the station to catch the train to Reading. She was not encouraged to go into service; she worked as a typist. Down at the Mill House Mr Bates had strict limits as to the hours the turbine should be in operation – or not as the case may be. No lights after 10.30 'or before dusk' meant that the young Hilda had problems. 'The great inconvenience was in the early morning, before the turbine was started going, trying to clean the big rooms by candlelight, and even worse in the winter, when the turbine became blocked with leaves swept down on the current, for then we had to rely entirely on our candles.'

Mr Bates was as well aware as the rest of the village that Major Darby was the last of his line and that the day would shortly come when there would be no living to be made from the estate. Not only had he started up on his own but he had his small herd of cows to muck out and milk. The last thing he would have wanted to do would be to start clearing leaves from the generator. 'Old' Barney Wheeler would be up and on his way to work by about 6 a.m. as would all the brewery workers. Barney had to walk right from the top of the village down past the church across the Kennet meadows and down Mill Lane for a 7 a.m. start. Leslie Austin, who by now had earned a scholarship (the first boy from the village ever to do so) to Newbury Grammar school was getting ready to catch the train and would see Barney 'with a straw bag over his back with his stick. He lived with his brother Jimmy Wheeler.' As a parish councillor, William Austin senior would have been proud of his sons. William's first wife, the mother of the three boys who had fought in the war, had died leaving a fourth son and a daughter. William had remarried and had a further two sons and a daughter. By 1926 only the younger ones were still at home although William junior wasn't that far away.

Another 'old 'un,' Dave Wickens, would step out of his gate at No 3 Mill Lane and walk the few hundred yards to the malthouse where he would stoke up the furnace and open up the ventilators for another day's work. Very soon the pervasive bitter-sweet aroma of the malting barley next door would mark the start of another new day for Aldington. Dave Wickens was liked by everyone in the neighbourhood despite his personal failings. The children in particular looked forward to meeting him as he was known to carry peppermints and the fact that they were to disguise his bad breath would not have mattered to them. Mrs North who remembers him well and now lives in no. 3 proudly told me his initials are carved on the bricks just outside the back door. Of course, as old Dave worked right alongside Aldington they would have known each other well, but his family remains one of the few I have been unable to trace.

It was an accepted part of working life to start at 6.30 or 7 a.m. Without electricity 'early to bed, early to rise' was as much a way of saving on paraffin costs for the oil lamps as anything else. General Mills, no doubt, would continue in this, the best of traditions, and Aldington too, it would seem from *Life for Life's Sake,* was no exception. 'At that time I was working hard, and to get as much work in before breakfast I had formed the habit of shaving overnight.'[8] On the mornings that Mrs Bates was not helping out at Venture Fair, Mrs Adams remembers she would be helping her husband with the milking. Loading the milk churns cannot have been an easy task for despite the obvious strength needed they were 'both very thin and gaunt… round-shouldered. But they were so kind and used to bring the milk around. You were asked what you wanted and they took it out in a can.' Ron, their son, being that little bit older than Leslie Austin, was by now helping his parents with the milk round and used to deliver Aldington's milk. He would come down the lane before breakfast and would see Aldington sitting at his desk 'at his typewriter – a magical thing.' The Roberts girls, on the occasional walk down the canal from Bridge House remember seeing Aldington sat there, too. 'He would be working at the window. You'd see him sitting there. We used to see him from the canal walk.' Had Aldington's window faced north instead of west he would have caught a glimpse of the Cappers as they stopped for a break.

'8.00: *Breakfast. Look at the broadcasting programme, and are heartened to observe that a representative of the Ministry of Agriculture is going to talk this evening on "Useful Bacteria". Doubtless he will tell us of an antidote to the bacteria that are NOT useful to poultry farmers.*'

Everyone in Padworth seemed to have chickens. Even Major Strange kept up some semblance of a small Home Farmstead in the meadow alongside the Butt Inn that had so recently been flooded, but now it seemed every time a chicken sneezed it was whipped round to poor Jessie and Athol for advice. Hardly had they sat down to breakfast when at

'8.20: *A fumbling knock at the back door. (Every countryman is stricken with temporary blindness on encountering a bell, and resorts to his knuckles) "Please can Mr Capper lend Major… a broody hen?" This interruption (which is almost a daily occurrence) dealt with, we resume breakfast.*'

Aldington's breakfast time would be spent checking through his postbag. During this time, he was engaged in reviewing books and therefore his daily post would have included review copies, complimentary books and the like. So many new books poured in on him that he could only dip into them. Around this time he was concerned at the number of parcels and books that had been torn open on arrival. He was suspicious as to the apparently concerted nature of what he saw as an intrusion. It is known, for example, that the Stranges quietly considered him as *avant-garde*. Maude Albury, who ran the post office while her father saw to his other businesses, suggested that a formal complaint be lodged by the senders and Aldington wrote to Harold Monro accordingly. Nothing seems to have come of it but his suspicions alone show how Aldington believed he was susceptible to attack from whatever quarter.

The Albury's lived right opposite Malthouse Cottage and therefore as near next door to the Cappers as anyone. In fact, it was Mr Albury who built the bungalow for them. By a coincidence Ron Bates a year or so later went to work for Mr Albury and helped to build the extension at the back of the bungalow. Mrs Adams remembers Ron at that time. Mr Albury had been engaged to do some work on the outhouses at Venture Fair and Ron came along too. 'I hadn't noticed but [he] was sat up there astride the ridge pole with his back against the [main wall of the house] fast asleep in the sunshine.' Major Crook, ever keen to be seen to be doing something worthwhile, thought Ron would benefit from a career in the army and tried to persuade him to join up. But Ron wouldn't have any of that. 'I had enough sense to keep out of that then.'

Breakfast over, the village would once again settle down to work which for Aldington at this time was fairly hectic.

'This is what happened. I had expended a good deal of nervous and emotional energy in writing a long poem. Before it was finished I had undertaken to do a translation and a book on Voltaire, with rather short time limits. In addition I had my regular work for The Times and Nation. By working all day and every day for the four months allotted I could just do it. By some perversity of fate, a number of editors suddenly conceived the idea that they wanted articles from me. The London edition of Vogue wanted a series; the Spectator suggested I review regularly for them; Jack Squire wanted five thousand words on Napoleon Bonaparte; my old friend, Amy Lowell, wrote that the Saturday Review would like another article; Miss Cutting wrote from the North American Review… I mailed the last typescript – the book on Voltaire – the day before it was due. I then took a deep breath and a five-mile walk.'

Aldington collapsed from exhaustion by the roadside about a mile away from home and following a fretful two weeks overcame it in the only way he knew how. He sent off on a walking tour of Wales.

Despite his apparent isolation, Aldington was still totally dependent on his London editors for the continuing stream of what he characteristically calls hack work and one day a week was dedicated to their appeasement and to visiting the Bank at Reading on the way. He was more a man of routine than he would wish us believe for not only was one day a week set aside but it was always the same day. Wednesday broke the week conveniently into two manageable periods. If ever an appointment needed to be made he would suggest it be on a Wednesday, his appointed day in town. He saw T.S. Eliot one particular Wednesday. On others he met Virginia Woolf, F.S. Flint and all manner of business was carried out along with lunches and dinner engagements. 'I expect to be in town Weds 4th July 1923' he told Harold Monro, it was always a Wednesday. It is likely that it was one such Wednesday morning soon after breakfast that he met Major Darby at the station. 'I could not avoid travelling with him as he also had a third class ticket.'[10] This may even have been the date of Mrs Hearn's little windfall in the way of the pound note the major gave her. Of course there was always that chance that Anna Munro may have been on the same train but it is difficult to imagine that any of them would have had much to say to each other. While Aldington would indeed support her cause he may have been slow to approve of her as a person for he disliked forceful women as much as the more traditional macho male, the more so as she was ardently teetotal. We can only guess what Major Darby's attitude towards her would have been in this time of industrial strife.

Mrs Adams recalls with pride, the comings and goings at Venture Fair and how the locals would react to Mrs Ashman, as Mrs Adams preferred to call her. Mrs Adams soon found herself converted to the Mrs Ashman's cause and would go along herself on occasions to speak. Mrs Ashman was given a very rough reception at one particular meeting in Aldermaston and yet Mrs Adams spoke at length at a meeting outside the Round Oak without undue fear of reprisals. Perhaps the people of Padworth felt there was something to be gained. The thought of what the Cappers would make of the Ashman household still raises a slight smile on Mrs Adams' face. 'I think they didn't quite know what to make of us!' Rather than go next door where there would be a bountiful supply of eggs,

Mrs Adams remembers instead having to walk the length of Mill Lane to collect some from Mrs Bates. While they would, of course, be very well aware of each other, this sense of detachment from her neighbours is borne out by the failure to discover any contact between Anna Munro and Aldington.

'There was no question of any "servant" status though,' as Mrs Adams explained, 'I came and went as I liked.' That too is suggested by the potted biography prepared for me by Anna Munro's daughter. 'No domestic interest, normally had help in the house but coped if she had to, never at a loss. Unexpected guests, usually a tribe of my father's sisters and I have seen mother slipping down the garden path to dig potatoes.' That same positive spirit was to guide Munro on other occasions, such as when she learnt to drive. First time out 'she went to Basingstoke, second Newbury and third Reading. The only person who agreed to go with her was the housekeeper Miss Bransom, and it was only years later that it transpired she had put on clean underclothes for every trip.' Anna Munro learnt to drive 'rather late in life.' The militant suffragist, Lilian Lenton, had persuaded her to do so while she was visiting Venture Fair on one occasion. Lenton, one of the most respected suffragettes, was arrested, gaoled and force-fed several times.[11] Significantly, a Miss Lenton puts in a passing role as 'a strong-minded old maid of small but independent means' in *The Colonel's Daughter*. Aldington obviously knew about her, probably from the time spent teaching Anna Munro to drive. Mrs Ridgway confirmed that Lenton 'sat her in her Austin Seven and told her to go. Which she did – across the tennis court and through the tennis court the other side.' Fast heading towards the summerhouse, no doubt, where Sidney Ashman kept his forbidden alcohol. 'Father was quite shaken.'[12] So too would Jessie Capper have been, had she realised, for Anna Munro would be hard up against their boundary fence. But of course, Jessie would be otherwise occupied.

> *'9.10 – Then small maid, a recent importation, arrives breathlessly to announce that "a gentleman from London has come to see Mr Capper." Experience having shown me the wisdom of investigating such claims before seeking my husband, I interview the said gentleman, and find he wants to sell me a patent carpet sweeper and mop combined.'*

That 'recent importation' was Florence Downham from no. 7 Mill Lane. She had married Alfred Smith from Beenham only a month before Jessie's article was published and had settled down to married life in no 4. She was thirty-four at the time – the same age as Aldington – and had decided that a job a little nearer home would now be appropriate. 'I worked for them as a "daily" at the chicken farm. Athol was blind up to a point. He could see a certain amount but he could still manage. Nice feller he was. They started the chicken farm with the aid of St Dunston's, I think, wasn't it? They helped them start that chicken farm.' Presumably Mrs. Capper in her delicate state had decided she too needed a bit of help around the place. 'The Cappers were nice. I got on well with them… I used to do the housework cos they were always out with the poultry' exactly as Jessie suggests:

> '10.0 – Offer the chicks a feed of chopped sprout tops, and am distinctly reassured by their appearance. There can't be much wrong with chicks which fall upon their food like ladies at a bargain counter during Sale Week in Kensington High Street. My spirits rise only to fall again as I remember a sinister statement to the effect that chicks suffering from coccidiosis may, "when roused, eat and drink ravenously". They are doing that all right.'

Bill Austin was one of those who had also attempted to take up chicken farming. Major Darby, he told me, had been in South America in his younger days 'so we had something in common.' Anyway, Bill had successfully approached the major for the use of a couple of acres 'down Mill Lane and open the first gate on the right hand side – that paddock there that had otherwise been grazed by a couple of cows. There was a tiled shed that I'd put the broodys in. I used to sell a lot of eggs in Reading. My wife used to cycle [in] with a basket of eggs on the handlebars. I [also] used to sell some settings; a setting is one cockerel to ten hens.' Disaster struck on one occasion. 'My father had a collie bitch and one morning – she was having pups – and I took her in with the chickens (the biggest mistake I ever made) because when they flew down off their perches the dog got excited and went for the birds and killed a lot – about fifty. So I gave them away to all the people in the village. Whether in this instance it was Bill Austin or not, even he cannot remember but he did used to go round to the Cappers.

'10.30 – A fellow poultry farmer arrives, to find me in the middle of making a pudding. I divest myself of an apron and surplus flour, and prepare to hunt for my husband over six acres of poultry farm. It is far worse than searching for the proverbial needle in the haystack, but we track him to earth at last in the incubator room, supplying a customer with day-old chicks. The customer is a maiden lady who is just starting fowls. I don't think she can have been from Padworth and apparently has never seen chicks fresh from the egg, for she is terribly worried at their tired appearance. "They must be weak" she says anxiously. The poultry farmer friend has blown up his incubator and wants to know if we can incubate 200 eggs for him. To the best of my knowledge all our drawers are full, but I leave my husband to struggle with the situation, and return to my pudding.'

Certainly Bill Austin was round there the day after his disastrous experience. 'Every one of those was worth a guinea a time. Mr Capper suggested they were all at point of lay and worth a guinea each.' Around this time of the morning 'Young George Hale' the hoop maker – and, born about 1865, *he* was actually fairly old by then – would be setting his bundles of hazel spars in the canal outside his shed opposite Bridge House. George Hale was the father of Bill Hale whom Daisy Roberts, housemaid at Bridge House, married and is therefore the grandfather of John Hale, Miss Mills' godson. 'Young George' himself was the son of 'Old George Hale' (born about 1840) who founded the family business in the late 1880s. Young George had been making hazel hoops for wooden sugar barrels for as long as anyone can remember. He was one of the very last of his trade. *Country Life* magazine evidently wrote an article on Mr Hale some time during the 1940s just before he died. In his day 'Young George Hale was the wharfinger and as such kept a tally of the traffic passing up and down the canal, but, that's all gone now and so too have the osier beds that Aldington's cottage overlooked. Florence Downham believed that Young George Hale's business came to an end when fire broke out in his work sheds but, as she says, 'that was a good many years ago'.

General Mills' compact acreage adjoined the eastern and southern boundary of Aldington's garden. Downstream to the east of this paddock, canal-wise, were the osier beds and inland to the south of the field, stood the allotments at the back of the two blocks of cottages in Mill Lane. Ron

Bates' father had four of these allotments and Leslie Austin's father had three ('two too many!') There were other osier beds at one time, near the Mill House as they are shown on the old maps of the district. Living at opposite ends of the Mill Lane, Messrs Austin and Bates had the rutted lane staked out as their territory in those boyhood days. Ron Bates had to dash off to the Butt Inn to get the beer in for his father. Leslie Austin didn't need to as a barrel under the kitchen table was one of the perks of working at the brewery. On the mornings when he was not at school, Leslie's appointed task was to pop across to Chris Strange at 'Red Cott' and borrow his copy of *The Times* for his father, that is if Chris Strange was there. For, as often as not, weather permitting, he was out in the fields sketching or, failing that, in his studio on the other side of the Bath Road, painting.

Mid-morning would see everyone hard at work. On a cold spring day, safe in the knowledge that the smell of the sprouting barley would overpower the bad breath of the maltster, the brewery workers would surely have been attracted to the heat of the malthouse in the way that Gabriel Oak was drawn to Hardy's malthouse in *Far from The Madding Crowd*. Aldington would watch them all come and go from his window alongside while only a stone's throw away – over the canal – Jessie Capper's consternation would be further roused by the continued healthy behaviour of her brood.

'11.0 – The week old chicks are still eating ravenously.'

What follows next in Jessie's diary shows, not only that she was soon to be distracted from the worst fears of coccidiosis, but that Frank Downham's second visit confirms the superior postal service that was enjoyed in the 1920s.

'12.0 – The midday post brings a sheaf of bills, a small cheque, and a letter from a lady who wants three dozen Light Sussex pullets at four weeks old – they must be pullets, she says'.

One such morning, next door at Venture Fair, Mrs Adams was to witness a most astonishing sight. The actress, Kate Evans, who was 'secretary and general dogsbody' to Madame Novello Davies, the mother of Ivor Novello, was one of those who often used the place as a 'retreat' or 'resting place.' She was often to be seen 'with three pairs of stockings, each one to cover the other's holes. Anyway, on this occasion Kate turned up, bringing with her a large trunk. The day she arrived Mr Ashman asked me when he came home what Kate wanted two gallons of petrol for. I confessed I didn't know, but was enlightened the next morning when she asked me if we had an old fashioned bath, the type people used for their weekly washing. We found one in the granary and she promptly emptied the petrol into it – outside, of course, by the granary steps – and started washing a pile of evening dresses in the petrol, hanging them up on the clothes line to dry. When the trunk was empty and the line full, I spent the rest of the day absolutely petrified lest the sparks from passing and shunting engines would ignite the lot.'

By tradition the tradesmen of the times called in the morning. Heelas, the Reading department store, had for years been delivering 'needlework materials, calico and zephyr' to Padworth school. Dunlops and W Cook similarly were the local coal merchants and Messrs Basins from the Falmouth Arms at nearby Woolhampton, the local charabanc proprietors, were well known for their bright red open tourer, known locally as 'Basins' scarlet runner'. Later, when the Hughes were at the cottage in Aldington's absence, Aldington was most concerned that his American friends should not be rooked over their purchases. He writes on 22 September 1928:

'We are delighted to know that you and Babette and Mary Anne are "pretty comfortable" in that poor old English cottage. You seem from what you say and from what Mrs Capper tells to have made very good arrangements, and we hope you will enjoy yourselves thoroughly… I hope you find the tradesmen bring you decent food? I have never found that English tradesmen try to cheat in the abominable Italian manner – i.e. sticking up a price to a foreigner and giving short change. But the English tradesman may think you don't know quality, especially in meat. If you pay for English beef or mutton, show it to Mrs Stacey and see that you have it. Tom Hann's fellow is quite honest, I think. Mr Ford at the post office or the butcher will cash cheques for you, if you say you are a friend of mine.'[13]

The thatched barn that stood alongside Mr Albury's cottage – right opposite Malthouse Cottage – was where Mr Albury undertook the bulk of his business.[14] And this is where Ron Bates was taken on as apprentice carpenter, joiner and undertaker. When they weren't overly busy Ron would deliver the occasional telegram for the ladies' side of the business, the post office. But most of the time Ron was amply employed holding the candle while Mr Albury got on with the business of making coffins. There was no light in the workshop. On one morning such as this the traveller from the timber firm arrived as Mr Albury had complained about some particularly knotty timber. The matter was settled over a pint at The Butt Inn for which Mr Albury never expected to pay.

Aldington was known to have popped along to the Butt around lunchtime in an effort ostensibly to make arrangements for rooms to be made available for the likes of Frank and Ruth Flint.

'I went to see old Mrs Spencer at the Butt this morning. Berkshire people are very funny; they simply hate answering a straight question and like all peasants want to examine any proposition from the "gentry" in case there should be a catch in it. I feel pretty sure she will say you can come and I think you will find the terms very reasonable. She is a rare type – the undercharging kind and I sometimes have to prove to her that she's cheating herself. She is to let me know midday Weds, and I will write off to you at once – or if you prefer, will wire – her terms and what she says. Perhaps I had better only wire if she can't bring herself to arrange it or if the terms seem exorbitant. But from my knowledge of her I should say it is o.k. in all respects.'[15]

How wrong he was. My guess is that 'old Mrs Spencer' wasn't as daft as Aldington thought. Anyone else yes, but not a poet – even if he did work for *The Times* which she probably wouldn't have believed anyway. 'I'm afraid the trip is torpedoed for the time being. The old innkeeper is booked up until June 24th.'[16]

'1.45 – Lunch. This is not the normal time for this meal, which was ready at one, but it was the time when my husband arrived for it. He explains that during the past three hours the ordinary routine of the farm was interrupted by:- An ex-soldier endeavouring to sell a map of Berkshire; A representative of an insurance company wanting to insure the farm and bungalow; A

Fig. 32. Mrs Spencer at the door of The Butt Inn

> *neighbour who wants him to choose a breeding pen for her this evening, as, in spite of years of keeping fowls, she cannot tell a layer from a "boiler"; A professional rat-catcher who was prepared to play the Pied Piper for the sum of £3; A boy sent to borrow the ladder, which, having previously been borrowed by someone else, was nowhere to be found; and the baker's boy who let seven hens into the kitchen garden.'*

Poor Athol; it seems everyone was dashing round there for no end of inconsequential things. It could well be that Mrs Mills was in need of that broody pen. No one else in the vicinity fits the bill quite so well. Within hours of arriving in England for their protracted stay in 1928, Glen and Babette Hughes had met Mrs Stacey in order to get the key to the cottage. Then they were on their way round to the Cappers at June Rose Bungalow. Aldington tells them in his letter of 31 August 1928 to 'ask Mrs Stacey to show you where the Bungalow is here. Go there and tell Mr and Mrs Capper who you are, and they will give you any assistance.'[17] Poor Jessie would still be busy.

> *'2.15 – A knock at the front door. A labourer wants to buy four hens for 3/- each. It is pointed out to him that the lowest price at*

which we could with honour sell him a hen would be 10/-. This seems to stagger him. 'I don't want one of your fancy "pedigree birds," he says; "all I want is a hen to lay eggs." We remark that that is precisely what the pedigree implies – that the hen is bred to lay. The suggestion that any hen could lay as many as 200 eggs in a year leaves him frankly sceptical. "Must be forced," he says. "Anyways I could buy a hen in Reading Market for half-a-crown." We agree that this would doubtless be his best course, and return to finish our lunch.'

There is nothing much of significance to report of the afternoon's activities. Nurse Banner, from 'Lyndale' in Mill Lane might have been on her afternoon rounds; Chris Strange on his way to or from his studio; Major Crook would have cast the occasional rod into the Kennet. Sidney Ashman may have been out fishing, too, as he leased a beat from the Aldermaston estate. Had Aldington not been in town on a Wednesday he might well have witnessed the departure for Reading of 'Uncle Charlie' on the back of his namesake's motorcycle. There are times, though, when as we all know, the truth is stranger than fiction. Most afternoons you would have seen a 'tiny little woman' traipsing across the neighbourhood. According to the Roberts girls, Emily 'Wiggy' Wickens 'was a very quaint little person – but very clean. She always referred to her husband as 'man' …never called him by his Christian name. All the neighbours would hear her step out of the back door if he was down the garden 'Dinner's ready Man,' Eccentric couple really. She used to spend a lot of time with an old pram, collecting wood. She'd go through the woods and across the fields – day after day.'

On one such sunny afternoon young Master Austin, in the company of the station master's son had been out in the marshes near the Lower Lodge. They had their jumpers stuffed with moorhen's eggs and were completely oblivious the existence of Major Darby fast bearing down on them from Padworth House. Major Darby, they knew, was chairman of the magistrates and would as soon birch them as anything else if he'd caught them. But they got away. 'Bloody old fool! If he hadn't shouted, we'd never have seen him.' There was a time when young Leslie had got himself in an awful tangle with a fishing line the result of which was that he had the hook firmly bedded in his finger. No sooner had he got him than his mother packed him off to Miss Mills as she knew they could cope with wounded warriors over there.

Around the middle of April 1926 an event occurred that was to prove to be a watershed in Aldington's life. 'I was sitting as usual at my work table [when] to my astonishment – for no visitors were expected that day – I saw a large car coming along [the lane]… I was still more astonished when it stopped and slowly disgorged Jack Squire and a well-dressed, urbane-looking gentleman who was totally unknown to me.'[18] Aldington had every reason to be astonished. John C. Squire – later Sir John – was at that time the editor of the *London Mercury* the quality literary magazine for which Aldington and his friends would write occasionally. The gentleman accompanying Mr Squire

> 'turned out to be Mr Crosby Gaige of New York, who had acquired the costly but laudable hobby of producing unpublished works by his favourite authors in books designed by that great printer, Mr Bruce Rogers. I was one of the authors honoured by Mr Gaige's notice. I realised at once that Mr Gaige must be a man of iron will and energy if he could persuade Jack Squire to bring him to me on such an errand, and I listened favourably to his proposals. Unluckily, owing partly to the fact that I had recently published a volume of essays and another of poems, and partly because of my absurd obsession with honest work, I had nothing original to offer him. But there was one long-cherished "literary" project of mine, so apparently uneconomical that I had never even dared mention it to a publisher – namely, a collection of Romance lyric texts with translations and comments. I mentioned this unhopefully to Mr Gaige, and to my surprise and delight he accepted it. But for Mr Gaige this book would never have been done, and it happens to be the one I like best of all the products of my misguided "literary" energy. I am told that when Mr Rogers saw the script, he refused at first to tackle such a complicated typographical problem. He had to deal with texts in Provençal, mediaeval and Renaissance French mediaeval and Renaissance Italian; an English prose translation en regard; and introductory comments ranging from a few lines to a couple of pages. He solved the problem so admirably that when the book was later set up in England by Chatto and Windus (who prided themselves on their typography) they admitted there was nothing to do but to follow exactly what Mr Rogers had done.'[19]

Art for art's sake. Obviously Aldington was pleased, elated and flattered. As far as I am able to ascertain, his first subsequent letter to Mr Gaige is dated 20 April 1926 but it wasn't until 6 November, when the work for the book was progressing well that he dared even hint, in a letter to Ezra Pound, that he had been associating with Jack Squire. The book, *50 Romance Lyric Poems*, exactly as Aldington describes it, was published in 1928 in an edition limited to 900 copies and nine extra specials for immediate distribution to friends. In the meantime though, a strong bond of friendship developed in their letters between Gaige and Aldington. Aldington helped Gaige to assemble a collection of his own work to date and the two met in London whenever Gaige was over here. For the first time in his life it was as if Aldington had found a true patron and a trip to America was planned for the autumn of 1927 when Aldington planned to check over the proofs of his new project.

Gaige was promised an early copy 'of his DHL pamphlet'. Aldington had his photo taken for press purposes and for the first time ever he had been given the confidence to be able to look forward to a release from his hack work and get back to poetry. But in part, through his own persecuted misunderstanding of the motives on the part of Doran, the publisher to whom he had been introduced by Gaige, a silly state was reached whereby Doran withdrew his offer – made on Gaige's recommendation – to underwrite the trip to America. This didn't stop Aldington from continuing to believe that he could make the trip without Doran's help but the adventure finally had to be abandoned due to the ever deepening crisis in his personal life.

He really was his own worst enemy. In a letter of 18 July 1927, Aldington tells Glenn Hughes that 'A nice American recently delighted us by presenting us with an original chalk and wash picture by Maurice Utrillo, quite an excellent thing… so it now hangs on the wall in the front room along with the reproductions of Van Gogh.'[20] The nice American had to be Crosby Gaige and the identity and whereabouts of that Utrillo will haunt this cottage forever. Late afternoon and Jessie Capper was still at work.

'4.0 – Take another look at the chicks. A Rugby football match appears to be in progress, between the Bresse and the Rhode Islands, an unfortunate worm acting as football. The Rhodes may score in solid scrummaging, but the Bresse are certainly much faster, and among them are certain excellent "wingers". Some of

their "spoiling" and "breakaways" could give points to our International team ...'

The mere thought of sport would bring out the best of Aldington's satire: 'From prep school to middle age, life becomes an orgy of balls for both sexes. For the males there are pre-eminently footballs, where one is round and vulgar, and the other oblong and aristocratic.'[21] By late afternoon though those that did so would be taking tea but Jessie was checking the journal.

'4.30 – Tea. Consult 'Eggs' once more, and discover that it is only when roused that the chick affected with coccidiosis eats and drinks ravenously. That is all right then. Ours require no rousing.'

The day's work at the brewery came to an end at 6 pm and the whole of the neighbourhood began to unwind. Miss Mills would be setting out for a meeting of the guides at Beenham but the Cappers though would have been jolted by their earlier promise.

'7.30 – Select a breeding pen for our neighbour.'
'8.30 – We sit down to supper. One of Major.....'s retainers selects this moment to return the broody hen, which is alleged to be unwilling to sit. He enquires where he shall put her? As the creature is held in the speaker's arms, we can hardly tell him to put her down anywhere until we have finished our meal, and supper is therefore postponed until the hen has been restored to her home.'

No doubt supper at Malthouse Cottage would have been a fairly modest affair except on those occasions when guests were in residence. One weekend with the Georgian poet Harold Monro is particularly well documented by Aldington in *Life for Life's Sake*.

'Harold and I were old friends and I knew he was one of those afflicted people who for their own sakes ought to be rigid teetotallers. He was not intemperate; indeed I have known many men who drank a good deal more with no evil results. The trouble with Harold was this; up to a certain point wine seemed to have no effect on him at all, and then at a quite indeterminate moment another half-glass or even a sip would make him hopelessly drunk. Knowing this I carefully provided one small flask of Chianti for

each meal, thinking that shared among three it could do him no possible harm. Unfortunately, Harold also knew me, and knew that when I am working I usually go on the water wagon. Anticipating a drinkless evening he must have tanked up nicely before leaving London, and probably brought a brandy flask with him. He seemed perfectly sober when he came down to dinner. Now, those small Chianti flasks hold exactly six glasses. Harold sipped his first glass in the normal civilised way, and just at the end of dinner I refilled the glasses. To my consternation he seized his and drank it off with horrid avidity as if it had been water; and in a second my old friend had become a feckless and rather unpleasant lunatic.

'I promptly called for coffee; but before it was ready, Harold insisted on going for a walk, and became violent when I tried to persuade him out of it. So for a walk we went, and I took him by the nearest way to the squire's park, hoping the cool evening air would sober him. Not a bit of it. He kept embracing and kissing tree trunks, and telling me how much he loved trees. Of course, I knew all Georgian poets love trees, but I thought he should not have been so ostentatious about it. Then, unfortunately while it was still light, he insisted on returning, appearing to get more instead of less drunk at every step. He stumbled about so alarmingly that I took his arm, and together we lurched back, Harold talking very loudly and incoherently, past all the cottagers sitting at their front doors in the cool of the evening.

'Finally I got Harold back to the cottage intact, and made him drink strong coffee. It seemed to have the same effect on him as brandy on other men. He kept insisting that he must go into the garden and "laugh at the stars", which I recognised as another disquieting Georgian symptom. While laughing at the stars he tripped over backwards, and knocked his head on the flints bordering the path. For a moment I thought he'd killed himself, and wondered how I should explain his corpse to the police. But no, he was totally unharmed; and after a lot more silly pranks eventually agreed to go to bed.'[22]

Obviously Aldington recalls this with some relish, particularly – as with the issue *of Country Life* magazines – there was some local capital to be gained: 'From this arose a pleasing local legend that I regularly indulged in "filthy orgies" ('g' hard as in classical Greek) with deboshed Londoners.'[23] All good-humoured banter; but with whom? Quite fortuitously Aldington reveals the remainder of the story. Glenn Hughes must have talked at length in one of his letters to Aldington about the enjoyment to be had in the temporary incumbency of the cottage. He had presumably made good use of 'the gramophone records, good and bad... including several negro songs and jazz' to which Aldington had given him access and in addition he had obviously visited the local hostelries for Aldington writes on 22 September 1928: 'Your purchases of drink (wish we could share with you) sound like what Mrs Hood, down at the Hare and Hounds calls "an orghie".'[24]

> '9.10 – The Ministry of Agriculture's speaker over the wireless is not very helpful. His main interest is crops. ...
> 10.0 – Oil the incubator, and take a last look at the brooder lamps.
> 10.30–11 – Do accounts and enter up trap-nest records.'

By which time all the locals would be getting tipped out of the local pubs; the Round Oak, the Hare and Hounds and, of course Aldington's more accessible local. The Butt Inn was entirely owned by Strange's and, as it was next door to the brewery, would be one of the prime outlets for their beer. Most of the customers would be those whose daily grind was actually producing the stuff. Aldington was a self-acknowledged frequent visitor. Ten years after his spirit left Padworth, Aldington includes in his novel *Very Heaven* a quite accessible memory of The Butt Inn. 'At this point in his mental ravings, Chris found himself not four hundred yards from home opposite the village pub which was just opening for evening service. After some hesitation he went in to buy a pint of beer, in the vague and uncertain hope that it might cause him to write another Shropshire Lad, that being the approved recipe.'[25]

According to Aldington's sister, Margery, The Butt was 'the only link with the outside world. We went up there occasionally; probably for an extra celebration he had another half pint and perhaps even another ten Woodbines – I don't know.' Certainly Aldington took his friends there. Glenn Hughes' first visit in 1925 was made the more memorable by staying at the Butt. He recalled it in May 1927 when sending a cheque to Aldington: 'I enclose a money order for twenty five dollars which I trust you will not spend entirely at the pub. Wasn't it Mrs Spencer's?'[26] Later that year when Hughes was making plans to return to England Aldington makes reference (in a letter of 1 June 1928) to a mixture of gin and beer that 'amused' Hughes. 'As soon as you get to England we can talk everything over a glass of the dog's nose and try to arrange a good year for you.'[27] All this confirms that Aldington was a regular at The Butt Inn.

Certainly his fictitious friends were to be found there. Coz saw Purfleet in there one evening. 'He's a confounded cad. Why, by Jove, he was in the pub the other night when I passed drinkin' with Judd and a lot of other workin' people. Found his own level for once, I suppose.'[28] Colonel Smithers popped in on one occasion, quietly he hoped. But, as if to keep a literary eye on him, Purfleet was sat in the corner. 'The Colonel slipped out judiciously, and returned from the pub with a bottle of whisky and a bottle of alleged port. Unluckily, he had to pay cash for them – otherwise he would have bought a great deal more. As he sneaked along – awful disgrace if someone like old Ma Eastcourt saw him carrying a brace of bottles – he deplored his own lack of economy and regretted the London excursions and the too numerous bets on "certs", which had proved so expensive.'[29] Mr Judd, though, saw the medicinal qualities of a little drink as more important than quaffed quantities of the stuff. The local in *The Colonel's Daughter* is only very thinly disguised from its true counterpart, The Butt Inn: on one occasion 'Mr Judd conspiratorially drew a small bottle from his pocket. "I slipped into the Buck afore I come along".'[30]

Unless this happened to be one of those evenings when house guests were staying when time was called at the Butt, the lights would long have been out at Padworth House and Hilda Hobbs would have made her mad dash to the far end of the servants' quarters. By virtue of its elevation the whole of Cleeve would have watched as the lights went out. Only now were the Cappers finally able to abandon their obligations.

> *'11.0 – The end of a perfect – well, the end of a typical day, anyhow. At least the fowls have been fed and watered – the latter was done at 12.30, all earlier attempts having failed. According to schedule, this is the day for cleaning out the fowl houses, but, curiously enough, there has been no time for this. Let us hope it will snow tomorrow. Nothing less will keep interrupters away.'*

Under different circumstances, admittedly, Aldington himself confirmed:

> *'There is a novel in that, if one could work it out.'[31]*

Chapter 12

The Watershed

1926 was a watershed year in Aldington's life in many ways. Quite whether Mrs Todgers survived to meet Lawrence in August of that year is in doubt. 'Her death after six or seven years living with us, was a sad affair.'[1] I hope she did though for the head-strong cat and Lawrence possessed the common ability to live their lives on their own terms. Aldington's entire future life can be seen, from *Life for Life's Sake*, to pivot around Lawrence's visit. 'In the intervals between working hours I thought of him a good deal.' But it was not Lawrence's writing that was to affect Aldington as much as: 'His talk and his personality, the many glimpses of his life, gave point and concentration to the vague rebellious tendencies I have described in myself.'[2] 'Within myself' would more accurately describe these tendencies for it was against his own nature that Aldington was beginning to rebel, not against the world: 'It seemed to me that I was being rather cowardly and foolish in allowing so much of life to slip by in mere labour and by allowing my energies to be diverted from writing about what I myself felt and thought to other subjects.'[3]

He had already abandoned at least one attempt to write what would become his first novel, *Death of a Hero,* and he could well have been contemplating his second. But he would have known that *The Colonel's Daughter* could never be published while he remained in Padworth. It was indeed when he reflected on life in the village that he realised that there was something drastically wrong with his England. Anna Munro would probably agree. She would look forward to a more egalitarian society. Aldington didn't. He looked backwards, back to the days before Queen Victoria and the authoritarianism of the nineteenth century, back to a time when life was lived for life's sake, art for art's sake, a time when Europe was the world and all was seemingly well in it. Back to a time when he naively imagined he would escape reality. 'Can it be possible, I asked myself, that a great nation which has been so opulent should be housed so meanly, should live in such inaesthetic squalor?'[47]

Aldington was beginning to feel the need to escape. To be in any way answerable to anyone at all was more than he could cope with even, it would seem, his own family: 'How ghastly families are declared Purfleet. Each member preventing the other from doing what they want.'

Somehow he wanted to free himself but until Lawrence came there was no way that Aldington could see a way out. Perhaps significantly in 1926 he had reached the age of thirty-four, a time when middle age would be on the horizon, a time when he too was experiencing a growing dissatisfaction with his own life. By now he had started to achieve some measure of self respect which would give him the confidence to consider moving on. Aldington was an authority on classic French literature and felt lured to Paris. Unless he took himself in hand he would probably rot away in Padworth forever. Confidence, incentive and money were needed and he was acquiring each as time passed. Although he would never be totally at ease, he had largely recovered from the 'shake-over' of the war.

He and Arabella took time out in Paris in March 1927 before heading down to Italy where they joined up with Lawrence and Frieda in the autumn. Lawrence was drafting *The First Lady Chatterley*. Aldington then had a 'hunch' that he and Arabella may take a small apartment back in Paris. For Arabella this was a return visit to the city which they had both, although separately, fallen in love before the war; Aldington's 'hunch' though, may have had more significance.

At the end of June 1982 Sotheby's held an auction of literary letters among which were those Aldington wrote to The Society of Authors. I knew that they were vital to this period of his life and felt I had to bring them back home with his books. It is significant to what follows to note that the first one was written from the cottage on 2 April 1927 shortly after his spring visit to Paris. It is simply an application for membership but the particular motive behind it may have a lot to do with his hunch. Already Aldington was talking of his intentions with Bruce Richmond, the editor of *The Times Literary Supplement* who was happy to receive the continuing reviews from Aldington wherever he may be based. That would be encouragement enough for him to proceed. He writes to Glenn Hughes again on 18 July. 'Possibly we are going to Paris for a few weeks to shake off the hayseed of Padworth and see some modern paintings.' Hughes had applied for a Guggenheim Scholarship to come over from the USA and was hoping to meet the Aldingtons again. There was even a suggestion from Aldington that the Hughes join them in Paris. 'We'd be able to put you up there as well as Padworth.'[6]

The 'we' by this time did not necessarily include Arabella and his hunch had now become a hope for the future. In the event Hughes failed to get his scholarship and his European visit was postponed. But Aldington's future plans seem not to have worked out quite as he would have wished. In the autumn of 1927 he and Arabella returned for another winter in the cottage. *The Colonel's Daughter* holds the clues to what happened next. One day – in early September it must be assumed – the narrator had called at the fictitious Holly Lodge to visit the colonel. The 'door opened and revealed Alvina astoundingly garbed in the full dress uniform of a hospital matron... "Fred's very ill. The doctor has just left, and says he must be kept quiet... "Double pneumonia."'[7]

Brigadier General George Arthur Mills C.D., on whom Aldington based Lieutenant Colonel Frederick Smithers, died on Sunday, 19 September 1927. 'The nurse took the shaded lamp and held it over the Colonel's face. Then she turned to Georgie. "I think you'd better go and call your mother, my dear."'[8]

On the Thursday of that week Aldington wrote to Glenn Hughes. 'The old General my landlord, died on Monday [Aldington was a day out] and we've got to go to the funeral. Dorothy has had a lovely time buying a wreath and getting black to wear, and she is as excited as if she were going to the play, because she has never seen an English funeral. I am not so gay about it; first because I have seen English funerals, and then I am wondering whether this demise will upset my tenancy of this cottage.'[9] Obviously Aldington was thrown by the general's death in a way that at first is not obvious. 'I never intended to stay here forever, but it doesn't suit me to move at present.'[10]

The funeral of General Mills took place at the other side of the Bath Road at Beenham church in accordance with the wishes of his wife. This time though the journey to church was by road rather than the well trodden footpath up through Shrub Wood. The cortège carrying the general, his family and friends was made up entirely of Rolls Royces. Nothing was left to chance – except one small thing. The Roberts girls, Daisy, Violet, and Florence, as mere servant girls, travelled in the last Rolls and had hardly got onto the Bath Road when disaster struck. Their car 'ran out of petrol just past the Halfway House. We were in the last car and it stopped! It ran out of petrol! The driver just managed to get into the side road where you turn up to Beenham and had to walk back to the Halfway House to get some petrol. And he got a can of petrol, filled up and away we went! And they were all waiting for us at the church. They wouldn't go on until we arrived. It was quite a thing; it really was.'

We don't know quite what Mrs Mills' reaction was to the passing of her husband. Aldington's sympathies lay with her daughter as he describes in the novel:

> 'At the funeral everyone noticed how ill and miserable Georgie looked.' Mr Judd spoke Aldington's words for him. '"Poor lass!" whispered Mr Judd to his wife, thinking of the undutiful Lizzie – "There's one that cares about her Dad going"'... Mr Judd's enjoyment of the funeral, which was enlivened by a Union Jack and a great many cheerful valedictory flowers from Sir Horace (not present), was utterly marred by the fact that the victim was the Colonel. Even so, its splendour fell far short of Mr Judd's anticipation. He did not realise that since the Colonel was merely a half-pay officer without money and connections, the Garrison at Cricton couldn't possibly afford to send a Bearer and Firing Party and a bugler. So they didn't even sound the Last Post over the Colonel's grave.'[11]

The Roberts household at Lyndale, Mill Lane were also a little confused over their future. Mrs Roberts had been given the tenancy of the cottage by the general following her husband's death a year or two earlier and her family had moved in with her. Her daughter Violet remembered the general's promise to her mother that she should inherit the cottage on his passing. She was not to know that he was not strictly speaking the owner of the estate and was therefore sadly disillusioned when the will came to be read, but, of course, she may have been mistaken in her expectations. In a way though, the general's death would have eased the financial burden of his trustees but only after a respectful period of adjustment for Mrs and Miss Mills had been arranged. Aldington too was to benefit from their kindness for on Armistice day, he wrote to inform Glenn Hughes: 'Apparently we have at least another years certain tenancy here' – which was also the case for Miss Mills and her mother – 'the rest is in the lap of the Gods.'[12]

This gave Aldington another year in which to sort out his intentions towards Arabella. He had been appointed editor of Routledge's series *The Broadway Library of Eighteenth Century French Literature* and by the end of 1928 had overseen twelve volumes of translation, with a further eight in preparation. Around the time of Lawrence's visit in 1926 Aldington got back in touch with Brigit Patmore and invited her to undertake one of those in the pipeline. Patmore accepted. 'I wrote back agreeing to translate any book that he wanted me to do and soon a contract arrived for me to translate *The Memoirs of Marmontel* by a famous writer in France during the eighteenth century. This offer came at a particularly fortunate time as I was rather apprehensive about the future' especially as Derek [her son] was away.[13]

The feeling that sooner or later he would have to move as a direct result of the general's death was becoming more and more obvious to Aldington. His letter of 10 March 1928 informed Hughes that Mrs Mills 'is trying to sell the place. I don't feel like buying the cottage; first because I haven't got the money; second, neither Dorothy nor I want to own property; third, it is in a damnable state of repair' and, 'fourth, he might have added, he was hoping that he could persuade Brigit to up sticks and go with him to Paris or wherever. But at the time he wrote to Hughes he still didn't know whether she would so it didn't yet suit his purpose to move. He continues: 'we shall hang on as long as possible, and they certainly can't get us out this year.'[14] It would appear that an agreement for a further year's tenancy until 1 March 1929 had already been signed. Mrs Mills had reached a decision. General Mills' estate was being sold to Sidney Baker from whose son I was eventually to buy the cottage.

Aldington therefore had another year in which to entice Brigit to Paris. Within a week of the new tenancy agreement he was again writing to the Society of Authors. 'Can you give me your information and assistance in the following small matter. I am thinking of taking a flat in Paris and spending part of the year there. I understand authors enjoy some privileges in the matter of obtaining permis de sejours... I should be much obliged if you could tell me how one goes about getting the requisite permission.'[15] In his introduction to his mother's memoir Derek Patmore tells us that he 'noticed from her letters that there seemed to be a change in their relationship.'[16] If Derek had noticed that change from a distance of 3,000 miles, imagine how Arabella must have reacted here at the cottage to what Aldington refers in *Life for Life's Sake* as his 'exuberant mood… It was like a second youth – second childhood; if you prefer – at thirty five.'[17] Had either Aldington or Brigit made known the true extent of their feelings towards the other in the course of the next three weeks or so, Aldington's dreams would have been fulfilled and Arabella would have been deprived of a return visit to the city she loved but Aldington's correspondence shows that he and Arabella went off to Paris on 27 March.

On 14 April Miss Mills and her mother moved to Bucklebury. The Baker's occupancy of Bridge House was delayed pending builder's work to bring the place to order for it too, we must assume, was in as damnable a state of repair as the cottage. By 23 April at the latest, Aldington and Arabella were settled at 17 rue Vauquelin, Paris 5, where they stayed until late June. Springtime in Paris; you would never know from his letters that Aldington's mind was elsewhere. Despite the fact that he and Arabella were obviously enjoying the art galleries and theatres his thoughts were with Brigit. His long poem, *A Dream in The Luxembourg*, was written in Paris but nevertheless has its roots firmly based at his writing desk in the cottage in Padworth to which 'for a series of reasons too complicated to explain' Aldington temporarily returned for the summer months. Arabella cannot have been insensible to Aldington's feelings particularly during the time it would take to write this poem. Back in the cottage the manuscript was well within Arabella's reach. In his subsequent letter of 10 December 1928 Aldington asked Glenn Hughes to fish it out for him. 'Finally, in the same bookcase upstairs, on a half empty shelf about midway under the Roman classics, you should find the mss [manuscript] of a long typescript poem of mine called A Dream in The Luxembourg. Could you send this along too, if you find it?'[18]

Except in severely expurgated editions, Lawrence's *Lady Chatterley's Lover* was considered obscene before its famous trial in 1960. But the unexpurgated first edition was published in Florence as early as the summer of 1928. Copies were being smuggled into the country by Lawrence's friends and in a letter to Arabella, Lawrence asked if Aldington would rescue thirty of them from their friend S.S. Kotelionsky. Aldington takes up the story in *Life for Life's Sake*. 'That summer Lawrence published *Lady Chatterley's Lover*, a grave error from the point of view of his reputation, as the Huxleys, I believe, tried to tell him. But once the book was out, there was nothing to do but support it, especially as those infallible critics, the policemen of England and America, were trying to destroy it. For a series of reasons too complicated to explain I was temporarily back in my English cottage; and naturally undertook to help distribute the book to subscribers.' Aldington goes on to make a very subjective judgment, probably informed by his time in the trenches. 'One trouble with Lady Chatterley is that it isn't a very good novel. And Lorenzo showed a strange lack of artistic tact in trying to revive in their primitive Anglo-Saxon sense certain words which have unhappily acquired associations of vulgarity and vice.'[19] Even though during these weeks, Aldington's mind was elsewhere, he nevertheless did what he could to help and Lawrence made the most of it. 'Still, I saw clearly what Lawrence was trying to do and approved his intention; so I had no difficulty in writing him favourably about Lady Chatterley. Apparently all but five of his other friends took the opposite view, and said so with that wounding frankness one seldom experiences from one's worst enemies.'[20]

By the middle of August though and no doubt feeling as exhausted as Aldington, Lawrence suggests to Arabella that all four of them go off together somewhere for the autumn.[21] With time running out on his lease, Aldington was enthusiastic. He doesn't say so but it is obvious that Aldington wrote immediately to Jean Paulham the editor of the *Nouvelle Revue Française*. To travel with Lawrence was an opportunity not to be passed by but that left the problem of Glenn Hughes. Hughes had successfully reapplied to the Guggenheim Institute and was being funded to come over to write about the imagists. Ezra Pound had seen the movement as little more that a distraction to his own agenda. H.D. was a mere woman, of course, and this left Aldington in the driving seat. In 1930, obviously inspired by Hughes' interest, Aldington rounded up the old gang and produced a new *Imagist Anthology*. For Hughes to be able to stay with Aldington would be a significant feather in his academic cap. Hence Aldington's suggestion that he bring his wife Babette and their baby daughter and use the cottage as their base. By late July Aldington was well and truly committed to being their host whatever may be the situation between him and Arabella. On 28 July he wrote a very considerate letter suggesting routes to the cottage and outlining the facilities available locally for the care of the Hughes' daughter who had fallen ill. Obviously Aldington would introduce Hughes to his friends and let him use his books.

Aldington tells us in *Life for Life's Sake* that he received an offer of a lifetime from Jean Paulham. Paulham had a lease with the French government for the vigie of Port Cros, a small look-out fort with a signal station of which there are several on the French Riviera. Aldington could take the place in October and November of 1928. 'Port Cros is the middle one of the three islands of Hyeres and from M. Paulham's description sounded both remote and beautiful… From the very accurate plan of accommodation… I saw there was plenty of room.'[22] And that caused him to embark on a plan about which Arabella must have had mixed feelings. A letter to the Lawrences outlining his plans immediately appealed to Frieda and Aldington very rapidly suggested to the Lawrences that they be joined 'by another old friend in London.'[23] No imagination is needed to see who that old friend was and to judge how readily Aldington set about making plans to leave Padworth. During the next few weeks he set about selling some of the books from the cottage, and yet, all the time, he knew the Hughes would be arriving from America expecting him to receive them at the cottage. Aldington must have been squirming as he penned a letter to them on 31 August as they were about to sail for England.

'A most difficult and curious situation has arisen which makes it impossible for us to be here on your arrival. Briefly, my old friend, Alec Randall, is very ill in Italy, and he and his wife have begged us to go to them and help them through a difficult time. It was impossible for us to refuse, and we are leaving by the night boat and travelling day and night to Italy to help them.'[24] It rather seems that Aldington had cornered himself and that Alec Randall's ill-health proved a convenient scapegoat.[25] Nevertheless, Aldington does his best to make amends. The cottage was to be entirely at Hughes' disposal, everything would be left ready for occupation. The same letter is interesting on two counts: first, we get another glimpse inside the cottage and second we learn that Brigit would still be in London when Mr and Mrs Hughes arrived here on the fourteenth. Aldington left letters of introduction to Eliot, Flint and Mrs Patmore on his writing desk and told them that Mrs Patmore would give them the address of someone who would find a suitable place for the child and that Eliot and Flint would also introduce them to some of the poets.[26]

Brigit cannot have remained in London long, for by early October Aldington was writing letters from 'la Vigie' and as he says in *Life for Life's Sake* 'we duly picked up our friend at Marseille' on the way.[27] In his biography of *D.H. Lawrence: The Priest of Love,* Harry T. Moore tells us Lawrence waited until the middle of October before Frieda arrived and they went on to the island. It was here that Aldington felt sufficiently free to settle down in earnest to work on his first novel, *Death of a Hero*. In 'Conversations with D.H. Lawrence' that Brigit published in *The London Magazine* in June 1957 she says that Lawrence found it hard to endure disharmony between his friends when discord developed on the island, and yet when parts of that same article appear in her later memoir, *My Friends When Young*, the whole episode of la Vigie is omitted.[28] Harry Moore believes that Lawrence had heard Aldington stealing into Brigit's bedroom during the nights.

Fig. 33. Brigit Patmore

There can be no doubt that there was 'disharmony'. When they left this island paradise they all went their separate ways. Lawrence and Frieda passed the rest of that winter in the Hotel Beau-Rivage at Var in France, Brigit returned home, Aldington went off to Paris and Arabella headed back to Padworth. It was the last time that they would all be together. Lawrence died a year later. Aldington wrote to Hughes on 30 November while they were in the cottage; he told him that: 'We are going to be so much on the continent that I have decided to give up the cottage on 1st March.' In the best Aldington tradition of 'kiss-and-not-tell' he leaves Arabella to tell them precisely what has transpired in the previous hectic weeks.[29] 'I expect Dorothy will be down before long and will tell you all about it. Please stay on until we move or sell the furniture, of which we will give you due notice – certainly it won't be until after Christmas at the very earliest.'[30] The following day, 1 December, Aldington wrote to Crosby Gaige to whom he must have felt the need to explain quite why he wouldn't be making the trip to the States. He says that he and Arabella had agreed to separate and that they were leaving the cottage and three days later, he finally tells Hughes, but only in the knowledge that Arabella had probably by now told them herself. He was anxious, of course, that no one at Padworth should know anything about it. One person in the village might be particularly affected by the news – Jessie Capper, to whom he dedicated a copy of his long poem, *A Dream in The Luxembourg*, signed and dated: 'J. Capper. June 1930'.

That Aldington told Gaige that he was living alone in Paris beggars belief. There were far more complications than anyone might imagine. A letter dated '27th' that Aldington sent to Ezra Pound poses a lot of questions.[31] It was written from the Hotel Select, Place de la Sorbonne, Paris. The distraught writer opens his heart to his friend in Rapallo, the one person who would know all the participants in the drama being played, bar one, that is. For the last few years in Padworth Aldington was having an affair with Jessie Capper and poor Jessie had made her way to Paris to be with her disingenuous man only to find not just that he had rejected her dear friend Arabella but that he was making plans to be with Brigit. Jessie had left her three-year old son with Athol and invested her all in Aldington but had to return to the village without him. In later years, under the by-line Jennifer Courtenay, Jessie wrote a splenetic novel, *Several Faces*, in which she lays down the exact chronology of who was doing what with whom and in some instances, exactly how and where. Jessie would have realised that *A Dream in The Luxembourg* was not written for her as she may otherwise have imagined. When the long poem was published its dedication read 'For Brigit'.

Brigit too, was being subjected to a form of emotional blackmail by a man she identified only by an initial. It would take some time before she was able to make the final break but Brigit did go back to be with Aldington in Paris for Christmas as she suggests in her own memoir[32]. Once they had finally broken all their ties, Aldington and Brigit were planning to join Pound in Rapallo. Aldington came back to London to tidy up his affairs. It would have been more than his life was worth to return to Padworth where poor Arabella and Jessie were left to rake over the carnage of their lives. Arabella arrived back at the beginning of December. Later evidence shows that Jessie and H.D. came into contact and there remains the possibility that Jessie and Arabella talked about their experiences, but we cannot be sure. Whether war-wounded Athol ever knew about the affair is not known.

No doubt Babette would have had every sympathy with Arabella when she came home but Glenn was here for the specific purpose of gathering material for his book on the imagists and needed to follow Aldington to Paris and beyond. His book *Imagism and The Imagists: A Study in Modern Poetry* was published by Stanford University Press in 1931. The cottage presumably lay empty until the lease finally expired on 1 March 1929. During the early part of 1929 Mrs Stacey continued to keep an eye on the cottage and collected and sorted Aldington's incoming mail including the ever increasing pile of press cuttings, for which task Glenn Hughes was instructed to pay her five shillings which he would subsequently claim back from Aldington when they actually met in Paris.

Miss Mills and her mother by that time would be getting straight at their new house. It is obvious that they were well catered for by the Bakers. Oaklea had been built fairly recently and indeed had quite substantial grounds. It also had modest staff quarters. Along with the Mills went the faithful Daisy and her husband, Bill Hale, where they continued as housekeeper and gardener. In 1929 their son John was born and it was only natural that Miss Mills became his godmother. John's childhood memories of the two ladies remain firm to this day. 'They were both slightly eccentric,' he recalls, but Mrs Mills perhaps more so. Ever the outdoor type, at Oaklea she used to pitch a tent on the front lawn and would spend the night out there. John's aunt Violet married John Sambells, a butler from Newbury on 6 December 1928 at a time when Aldington's telegrams were beginning to fly between London and Paris. Indeed the day their wedding photograph was taken in Mill Lane may be the very day on which Arabella returned to the cottage.

Mr and Mrs Sambells left to live in Portsmouth. Florence, the youngest of the Roberts girls, had only stayed with the Mills family a short while during the national strike and by 1929 was working in Reading. Their father, Albert George Roberts, had died a week after General Mills. Presumably Mrs Mills was sympathetic; Mrs Roberts, while not inheriting the cottage, had at least been allowed to stay on in Lyndale as a tenant where she remained when the other Bakers bought Bridge House. Her son became under-gardener to the Bakers, the senior position having been taken by John William Street who moved into Aldington's cottage with his wife. Presumably Mrs Street would have taken over at Bridge House where Daisy had left off.

It was a while before the Bakers were to have the benefits of their new home. While the alterations were under way, and only a matter of weeks after the expiry date of Aldington's formal tenancy, Sidney Baker died leaving his wife, two sons and a daughter. It was as if history was about to repeat itself rather quickly as Mrs Baker tried to sell Bridge House. However, the state of the market following the Wall Street Crash was such

Fig. 34. Wedding photograph of Violet Roberts and John Sambells, Mill Lane, 6 December 1928

that no one came forward and, following the confusion that would inevitably have arisen, Mrs Baker and her family moved in during September 1929.

Aldington's writing was informed by life in Padworth and by reading between his lines we can reflect on reality. Miss Mills' uncle, Charles Stuart Mills, had probably left shortly after his brother's death in 1927 for in the novel Aldington would have us accept that: 'Grumblingly Coz packed his bags and left.'[33] Presumably, therefore, for the first time in their lives, matriarchy truly ruled in their new home and Miss Mills was able once again to throw herself back into the church and her girl guides. But not for long. Mrs Gardner tells me that suddenly, right out of the blue, 'Uncle Charles' appeared again, this time with Nell – 'this ghastly female [he] called "Pussy".' He married her in the end and went to live in Budleigh Salterton where Ron Bates bumped into him years later. But in the meantime, as Mrs Gardner reminds us: 'Poor Miss Mills was stuck with "Uncle" again – and this "Pussy" – for years. [Pussy] used to stay in

231

bed in the morning and Miss Mills used to have to take her breakfast up to her.' Aldington, too, would sympathise. 'Poor Georgie.'[34]

It was with those two words that Aldington ended the story of the colonel's daughter. The implication throughout the novel was that no matter what sympathy the village felt towards her plight, no matter what opportunities were placed before her, 'poor Georgie' was the product of her upbringing and would never break free. It would seem that the satire was proven in this respect at least. Miss Mills never married. Further judgment on the value of Aldington's satire comes even closer to home than he can ever have imagined even in his most bitter moments. Even before the Second World War, he makes continued references to what he termed 'the long armistice' refusing even to consider that the 11 November 1918 marked the end of European hostilities. In fact, he was criticised during the Second World War for abandoning ship. But he so firmly foresaw that a second war was inevitable that by the time it came he had gone to America and left his 'beloved Padworth' and cottage to his memories. He talks of his departure in *Life for Life's Sake*. 'I threw the papers contemptuously aside, and looked through the train window at that cold grey landscape. The forty miles to Reading were entirely familiar – I had passed up and down that line hundreds of times... I thought of my cottage under the tall willows by the canal, and wondered who now lived in it.'[35]

The irony of what did happen to his cottage would not have pleased him. In the Second World War a German aeroplane returning from a fruitless bombing raid, decided to offload the remainder of his cargo just as he was passing over this small corner of the world. Three bombs were dropped, one of which landed in the centre of General Mills' paddock at the rear of the cottage. The effect was cataclysmic. I am told there used to be a walnut tree right in the middle of the paddock with a seat under it. The bomb hit the walnut tree and killed a cow, demolished the 'ancient' wing of the malthouse and practically destroyed Malthouse Cottage. The entire gable wall was blown in and had to be rebuilt. What had been the Albury's cottage on the opposite side of the canal had the tiles blown off the roof and the blackout blinds were sucked up the chimneys with the blast. The chances are that it was Mr Street who was pulled from the wreckage of Aldington's cottage. He was physically well enough but in the shock he suffered he was more concerned about the loss of his pipe than of his cottage. This was the only time that the Second World War came anywhere near the cottage. No doubt Aldington would understand the tragedy. Aldington's autobiography, *Life for Life's Sake,* was first published in the United States in 1941: 'They say I am bitter. The trouble is I am not bitter enough. Tragedy upon tragedy, destruction upon destruction, another generation lost and in my "bitterness" I dimly foresaw it.'[36] He would take no pleasure in being proved right.

Bridge House had been requisitioned for the duration of World War Two as a government office, and part of Strange's Brewery had been taken over as the headquarters of the Great Western Railway, precisely in order that it should be safe and secure against attack from the air. 'Bunny' Strange, the only son of Major Frederick Gerald Strange and his wife and heir to the brewery business, was killed over Berlin. It was a tragedy with which the family never came to terms. As a result, in 1952 Major Strange sold the brewery, literally lock, stock and every last pub and barrel and moved with his wife and daughter to Jay's Wood, a house he had built in Beenham a mile or so away. Brewery House, the home they left behind was demolished in 1980/1 to make way for the sight lines on the approach to the newly built bridge over the canal. It was around this time the death of a Major Crook was announced in the *Daily Telegraph.*

The Colonel's Daughter was known in the village but what the people of the village thought about their fictional reflections remains largely unknown. The last of Major Darby's school visits is recorded on 7 June 1932 although no one was to know that that would be the case. He remained as chairman and often hosted the parish council, the local Conservative Association and the magistrates until early in the morning of the Friday of Armistice Day in 1932. Major Christopher William Darby Griffith was found dead on the floor of his bedroom at Padworth House. He was found by Kate, his remaining housekeeper, when she took him up his early morning cup of tea. He had shot himself. He had been lonely and depressed for some time and had been going blind as a result of a cataract, which would now be easily treatable. The whole village went into mourning. Major Darby's funeral broke church doctrine that prevented suicides from being buried within the church boundaries. The Darby Griffith family vault was opened up for the occasion and the major was buried in Padworth churchyard and his dog sat at the top of the steps as he was carried down. The funeral was a very grand affair. For someone who was suffering loneliness a surprising number of people turned up for the service.

Fig. 35. Major Darby's funeral procession setting out from Padworth House

To this day the estate workers remember him with pride and gratitude as a friend, but where all the other, more honourable guests got to in his later years is to be wondered at. The cortège was led by Mr Bath, one of the major's 'old comrades' who had become a policeman in Reading. The remainder of the comrades formed a guard of honour for the very short journey from Padworth House to the north-east gate of the churchyard, Major Darby's own personal gate as it were, just inside which lay the remains of his closest friend, Sir George Holmes. Two days after his death the congregation would gather for the annual Armistice day service in the church but this time mourning the additional loss of the squire.

Across the valley at Beenham church a very similar service was being held. It was reported in the *Newbury Weekly News* on the Thursday that a 'memorial service was held on Sunday afternoon, the rector, the Rev J.D. Marshall officiating. Ex-servicemen paraded near the 'Six Bells' and marched to the church headed by the Beenham Brass Band. The Girl Guides under Miss Mills and the Brownies under Miss M Giles also attended.' Miss Mills would have been full of thoughts for her father as

234

it was just over five years since he had died. Aldington would also have mourned the passing of an era. In his autobiography he tells us so. He also knew what happened afterwards: 'The squire was unmarried and the last of his long line. On his death – he eventually committed suicide I am told – everything went to a distant cousin, a peer in the Guards.'[37] True. His cousin, Lord Roundway, of Roundway Park, Devizes, inherited the entire estate that included most of Padworth village.

In the knowledge that the one thing his cousin didn't need was another country seat, Major Darby had willed Padworth House to Lord Roundway's daughter but she died before him in tragic circumstances and, it has been suggested, Major Darby 'forgot to change his will.' As a result Lord Roundway promptly put the whole lot up for sale. The contents were sold on 26 September 1933, the house and estate came up very soon after. A significant dent appears on the map produced for the sale: the land and buildings of Aldermaston Brewery. Another significant but small parcel of land: 'This highly desirable freehold residence, comprising etcetera, with 1 ac. 2 ro, 1 p of land' on which stood Holly Lodge did not, as in *The Colonel's Daughter* 'cut a monstrous cantle in the estate of Sir Horace Simms.'[38] It formed part of Major Darby's estate. But the auction did allow a number of Major Darby's tenants to buy their own homes. One small cottage was even reputed to have been given to its then tenant, Barney Wheeler. What was then a very primitive affair on the common, Barney's Cottage has now been altered beyond recognition.

Padworth House itself was bought by the Carmichael family and remained a family home for some years, but in truth as well as in fiction its stately days were limited even in the reduced acreage that remained with the house. Aldington would be pleased that it never fell into the hands of a profiteer. Now known as Padworth College, the house is an independent college. But Major Darby's land did not fare quite so well. It was parcelled up into lots and auctioned off separately. In the 1980s Padworth's most valuable asset was the gravel that lies below its surface that was extracted at the permitted rate of nine acres a year. A mile to the west, Aldermaston Court became the head office of one of the largest cement manufacturers in the world. Aldermaston Park was similarly sold off when the government bought a massive acreage for an airfield. Gradually that evolved into the Atomic Weapons Research Establishment, the focal point of the Aldermaston peace marches, a place so secret that it doesn't exist. A glance at any map in the 1980s shows Aldermaston

Park exactly as Aldington would have known it. Enemy spies are hoaxed into believing that the deer park with its woodland rides and decoy pond still exist. Padworth Common is now exactly midway between the Royal Ordnance Factory at Burghfield to the east and Greenham Common on the outskirts of Newbury to the west and was the venue, much to the disgust of some members of the village's Commons Advisory Committee, of the speeches made during the momentous chain of hands that linked the two bases over the Easter weekend of 1983. The Round Oak pub did a roaring trade that day. Under the squire's park at Padworth now lies one of the most massive aircraft fuel reservoirs in the country with direct pipelines from all the refineries in the south of England and leading in turn to Greenham Common and every other military air base for miles around.

Another sad loss during the Second World War – this time at Hermitage – was the passing of William Brown. He was not that old. He suffered a stroke a short while beforehand and was unable to work towards the end. Goodness only knows how much he worried about the garden during his illness. He died on 25 January 1943. Mrs Brown, his unsung wife and mother of Hilda who had been quietly 'doing' for the Radfords and the Aldingtons, later died peacefully at her daughter's home. Mr and Mrs Brown are buried in unmarked graves in Hermitage churchyard. I believe all the Radfords are buried in Hampstead churchyard, with the exception of Dr Muriel that is. She now rests where she passed the last years of her life – on the edge of glorious Exmoor.

Only a few years had elapsed since the Russian Revolution. John Cournos, Aldington's close friend, to whom Arabella had been engaged, had gone out to Russia to report on the uprising so Aldington would be well informed of the new social order blowing in from the East. Socialism was taking a hold while he was in Padworth. The first Labour government was very nearly elected in 1929 and the early 1920s saw political parties yo-yoing for position. The suffragist activity had already become history and by 1928 the franchise was extended to all women over the age of twenty-one. Anna Munro was a founder member of the Newbury Labour Party. She too visited Russia, in 1929. She stood for and was elected to Padworth parish council, later becoming the first woman to hold the chair. Socialism by that time, for a great many at least, was worth striving for. Her husband's business continued to flourish. By a curious coincidence, for that is all I can imagine it to have been, the Mills and the Munro

Ashmans were to 'meet' again. In 1948 Mrs Helen Henrietta Mills died. She was buried with her husband in Beenham churchyard. Miss Mills put the house up for sale and moved to Crowthorne. Oaklea, thereafter, became the home of Anna Munro's son Donald.

The 'infamous' cottages in Mill Lane that in Aldington's day 'housed twenty-five people in half the space of Craigie's house' are still there, some of them still occupied by descendants of Aldington's neighbours. The cottages were sold along with the brewery to the new factory owners – the heirs of Craigie's factory. A lot of what Aldington had to say about them is still as valid today as it was then. And yet still there remains a considerable number of the older folk particularly at the top of the village who remember Major Darby and who still feel that his death took away something from their lives. They may now own their own houses with deeds going back no further than 11 November 1932. They may go about their business in their own way but Major Darby's death took away that cohesion that held them together even under the occasionally adverse conditions of his squirearchy. The squire and his tenants were totally interdependent. As long as one needed the other all went well and a curious security existed on both parts. After his mother's death in the 1920s, Chris Strange eventually went off to lead a chequered career in a flat in far away Reading. I am told that he rather went to the dogs and spent all his money. My heart goes out to him. I would have liked to have known more about him.

Arabella though must remain high on that list too. She disappears from my records after returning to pick up her belongings from the cottage. In the 1960s she took up correspondence once more with John Cournos who she had left all those years before. There is a sparkle to that correspondence that is not born of nostalgia. It is due to the generosity of John Cournos' stepson that I am able to include the photo of Arabella that his stepfather had kept for so long. It is easy to see why he didn't let it go. Arabella eventually found her way back to the States where she died in 1962. She ended up making that longed-for return visit to Paris in the company of the proprietor of the rest home where she spent her last days. She never married.

H.D.'s *Bid Me To Live* is a *roman à clef*. So, too, is Cournos' *Miranda Masters*, in which to those who can read between the lines, all the characters are as thinly disguised as those in *The Colonel's Daughter*. Each one would immediately recognise the other as indeed they would if

Aldington and Arabella had read H.D.'s *Palimpsest* when it was first published in 1926, the year that Aldington included H.D.'s name on Malthouse Cottage's electoral register. We find them all in Lawrence's *Aaron's Rod* too; Aldington, H.D., Lawrence, Frieda, Arabella, Cournos and Brigit Patmore. By the time H.D. published *Bid Me To Live* she was in her seventies and she and Aldington had kept in touch almost constantly. He visited her on a number of occasions. Towards the end of *Life for Life's Sake* Aldington tells us that on two occasions the complications of life took him back to Europe. But this simple statement hides a multitude of transgressions. After seven years with Brigit, Aldington was about to become a father. But Brigit was not the expectant mother. Aldington had been having an affair with Netta McCulloch, some twenty years his junior and who only three years before had married Brigit's son Michael Patmore. Aldington and Netta needed to marry for the sake of the child, but Aldington needed a divorce as he was still married to H.D. They needed a dispassionate witness to confirm Aldington's adultery. Brigit was too close to all concerned to be considered. Aldington was never married to Arabella and, in any event, she had returned to the States. There was only one person to whom H.D.'s lawyers could turn, Jessie Capper put her conscience on the line when she stood as a key witness to Aldington's earlier infidelity with Arabella. The divorce went through and Aldington married Netta, who gave birth to Aldington's only child. Catherine Aldington was born in Marylebone on 6 July 1938.

Perhaps precipitated by Jessie's torment, the Cappers upped sticks around this time and moved to Arborfield. They extended their business to include a nursery garden as well as the chicken farm, partly with the help of grants from St Dunstans for Athol was now completely blind. Jessie became a prominent member of the housing committee as a councillor on Wokingham District Council and here again came a tragedy that no one could have predicted. We are left to ponder the reason why, but in 1958 Jessie Capper became depressed and committed suicide. She was sixty-three. Her sixty-five-year-old husband Athol Harry Capper died later that year. I have been unable to trace their son John.[39]

At the approach of war Aldington took his new family to the States and on to Hollywood only returned to Europe at the end of hostilities when they settled in France. Netta left Aldington shortly afterwards and returned to England. Catherine stayed with her father in France where they settled in Montpellier. Catha, as she was known, went on to university in Paris and became a clinical psychologist. For the first time in his life, Aldington lived alone. Since her separation from Aldington, H.D. had been in a relationship with Winnifred 'Bryher' Ellerman but she and Aldington remained close. Towards the end, Aldington took Catha to meet H.D. in a nursing home in Switzerland and as a result H.D. and Catha became close. H.D. died in Switzerland in 1961 and Catha and Aldington both mourned her death.

Fig. 36. Richard Aldington in Moscow, June 1962

Aldington was effectively blackballed by the publishing world after publication of his book *T.E. Lawrence: A Biographical Enquiry* in 1955. He exposed aspects of Lawrence's life that the establishment was not prepared to tolerate. As a result, Aldington suffered ill health and a serious financial downturn. He was effectively rescued by a devoted, young Australian writer, Alister Kershaw, who while working at UNESCO bought a small bungalow among the vineyards in the Loire Valley as a weekend retreat. This became Aldington's final resting place and Kershaw became his literary executor. Aldington, accompanied by Catha, was received as a guest of honour by the Russian Writers' Union and celebrated his seventieth birthday in Moscow in June 1962.

A fortnight after their return Aldington collapsed and died on the steps outside the front door, where he was found by his very dear friend, the neighbouring vintner. The population of Sury-en-Vaux numbers no more than that of Padworth and his neighbours mourned their loss. Had he survived a few months longer he would have felt vindicated. On 10 December 1962 David Lean's film 'Lawrence of Arabia' – largely informed by Aldington's book – premièred in London. What had been so unpalatable in 1955 was being celebrated only seven years later.

Chapter 13

The Colonel's Daughter

When I flippantly promised Norman Gates these notes on *The Colonel's Daughter* in 1978, I had no idea where this search would lead me. Two years were to pass before we had the faintest clue to the identity of the inspiration for the fictional colonel. It was after all 125 years since his birth and more than fifty years since his untimely death. The colonel's daughter seemed no more than the anonymous 'one d' attributed to her father in *Who Was Who*. I had no idea what her name might be. It has only been by asking around that I was directed towards Bucklebury three miles away up on the hills 'beyond Beenham.' It was there that, in the same fashion that Norman Gates had found this cottage – by enquiring at the local post office – that I found myself knocking at the door of Oaklea, a not inconsiderable detached house in the Tudorbethan style of the 1930s, that gives lie to the idea that Aldington creates of the little cottage to which the colonel's widow and daughter were forced to retire to. It was here that my hopes were dashed. The present owner had no idea what had happened to Mrs Mills and her daughter. It was from the postmaster that I learned of the Ashman family's later connection with the house towards which I directed my equally fruitless search.

Another letter to the *Newbury Weekly News* was called for this was the one to which Leslie Austin responded. He was certain he couldn't help me (how wrong he was), but rang specifically to suggest the name of someone who perhaps could. My first letter to Mrs Gardner, therefore, was very brief with no mention at all of why I was enquiring after them. I only hope I have since been forgiven for my stunned response to a phone call the following day. Mrs Gardner phoned quite unperturbed at the enquiry. 'Oh yes,' she said, 'I visited Helen last week.' Never was there such pleasure as that with which I subsequently added that Christian name to my cardex. Miss Helen Mills – the colonel's daughter! It was only as I explained how far and wide I had searched and the reasons for doing so that I became aware that what I was saying was not unknown to Mrs

Gardner. She knew that the novel was based on Helen Mills and so, evidently, did Miss Mills herself. Nevertheless Mrs Gardner offered me a letter of introduction to Miss Mills on one very strict condition: that I made no mention *whatsoever* of *The Colonel's Daughter*. So it was that Miss Mills learned of my interest in her father for a projected social history of Padworth which, curious as it may seem, was no more nor less than my intention at the time. At the beginning of November 1980 I received a significant letter from a remarkable lady.

'Dear Mr Wilkinson,
Many thanks for your kind letter. Mrs Pam Gardner who is a friend of mine has told me that you would like to visit me, and tell me about the career of my Father, Brigadier George Arthur Mills. I mean, that I wish to tell you about him! He was born in India during the days of the Indian Mutiny. He and two brothers were born there, and their father was very brutally murdered by some of the wicked mutineers. My Grandmother, a Scottish lady, was left a widow of about 37 years old, Mrs George Longley Mills. She brought her sons down to the sea-coast, with a lot of other folk escaping, and guarded by some soldiers. When they arrived at the sea, the officer in charge of them, went to Mrs Mills' little tent, saluted her, and said "Madam, I salute you. On that long journey down to the coast, you never kept us waiting for a single moment." Their ship brought them all the way to the south of France and landed them at Marseilles. From there they travelled to Calais, and were met by a relative who took them to Bristol. I forgot to tell you that I lived in Ceylon with my Granny, as much later on, when my father was a soldier he was coming home from Ceylon with my mother Miss Helen Henrietta Baker, who he had married in Ceylon, and I was on the way. At Cairo, the ship they were in was met by an uncle of my Mother's, Sir Samuel Baker, who was in Egypt trying to stop the slave trade. He asked my Father if he would like to command a section of the Sudanese Mounted Infantry. My Dad said "Would I not?" So the river Nile was near and Sir Samuel asked them if they preferred a Nile boat to a tent. Oh, a tent, certainly they said. And that was where I was born in the yr. 1886!

'When the first World War broke out my Dad was in it. He came safely through the Boer War, which was before the first one. In the first one, he was wounded in the battle of Alleman's Nek, while he stood watching for the large army to attack them. Suddenly while he carried a carbine under his left arm he felt a blow, which twisted him round but did not knock him down. He wondered where the blood was coming from. His Sergeant-Major ran to him and said "Come out of that, Sir, or you'll be hit again" and led him away. The bullet had hit him between his thumb and first finger, and had run up and come above his wrist. That hand never got really well, but my mother made him a special glove, to keep his finger and thumb together. If you can visit me I shall be very glad to meet you. Please tell me the day and hour when you can come. Not in the morning, but fairly early in the afternoon, and not on a Sunday when Brigadier Charles Mills and his wife visit me. We can have a nice chat without annoying any of the other patients in this home, because I am a bedridden cripple. I want to get this letter into our post-box tonight, when the night-nurse comes, which she may do very soon. Today being Sunday a post can get away tomorrow, November 3rd. My kind regards to you Mr Wilkinson, and hoping that you will have a safe and nice journey, I remain, yours very sincerely
Miss Helen M. Mills'.[1]

A postscript sought my forgiveness for mistakes and blots, a diligent search for which fails to find any of significance. This was a warm, proud, positive letter from a lady aged ninety-four who was stepping straight from the pages of one book and into this one. It was the mention of his name by Miss Mills that later caused me to dwell on such people as Sir Samuel Baker. There was an irony in the fact that the heroine of Aldington's novel had outlived the author. In fact she had outlived them all – the squire; the businessman; the rectors and, of course, her father. Her mother, Miss Mills told me when we met, had died in 1946 and was buried with her father in Beenham churchyard. This was the first clue I'd received that their spiritual loyalties lay in that direction rather than within Padworth. It was after her mother's death that Miss Mills had moved on to Crowthorne. From there a further two or three changes of address had finally brought her to the rest home near Winchester where I was very warmly welcomed on a surprisingly cheery, hospitable November day.

Fig. 37. Brigadier General George Arthur Mills with his daughter and her grandmother

Twice on that fateful journey to Winchester, the thought in the forefront of my mind was that I was doing something wrong, once when I set out and then again as I knocked on Miss Mills' door. Despite my promise to Mrs Gardner, I sensed that Miss Mills would know why I was there and react accordingly. I carried with me the guilt that lay elsewhere – or did it? Perhaps I was equally as guilty for resurrecting the whole episode. In the course of my quest I must have recorded well over sixty hours of conversation with all those I had come across but on this occasion the tape recorder failed me and I had to make do with my own personal shorthand. At times though, well aware of what I was doing, Miss Mills deliberately repeated herself, so well was I received.

When, in 1918, she and her mother came in advance of the menfolk to Bridge House, Helen Mills was just thirty-two years old. Aldington, when he arrived here two years later, was twenty-eight. At the time of the novel, Georgie Smithers was twenty-six. There are distinct parallels between the circumstances of Georgie in *The Colonel's Daughter* and Rosamund Norris in Aldington's 1939 novel *Rejected Guest* who 'belonged to that most deplorable of all classes, that of people who have seen better days'[2] and that too, following the collapse of his own father's business, may be seen to fit the author's circumstances with a telling poignancy.

Bridge House at Padworth was Miss Mills' first family home, as the general did not finally retire from military service until 1920. His daughter was born, as we have seen, on the banks of the Nile in Egypt in 1886 at a time when her father was aspiring to higher ranks in the army. As a result, Helen Mills was separated from her parents and lived with her grandmother during her formative years. Here, and in Warwickshire she was to receive her education, or what education was deemed proper for the daughter of Victorian parents. 'I went to school at Leamington, Warwickshire. I couldn't play piano, or sing. I always wanted to draw and used to write asking my father to draw pictures so that I could copy them.' From John Hale's descriptions of the subject matter of her father's drawings we are left to ponder on those the general may have sent his daughter. From a reservoir of memories going back to her childhood at Brewery House, Mrs Gardner recalls that Helen Mills was more than the merest of amateurs in the field. 'She had a talent as an artist,' she recalls. Indeed, it would be precisely in the field of the minor and domestic arts that a young Victorian lady of substance would receive her education. Miss Mills showed me with justifiable pride two very competent watercolours which she had painted in her younger years; one of the steps to Canterbury Cathedral which brought back memories of her childhood days with her grandmother.

During her years at Padworth too Miss Mills was often seen around the village, painting. To my knowledge she painted at least one portrait of Bridge House, now believed to be in the possession of Lady Mollie Mills. Lady Mollie's husband, the late air vice marshall Sir George Holroyd Mills, Miss Mills' cousin, takes his place, as do most of the family, in history, for in his later role as Black Rod he would demand the attendance of House of Commons in the House of Lords for the State Opening of Parliament. Another of Miss Mills' paintings used to hang in Brewery House. Miss Mills gave it to the major and Mrs Strange. Miss Mills was good with a needle, too, I'm told, which was as to be expected from the picture Aldington portrays. While Georgie Smithers was inspired by Miss Mills, she was though - in the author's eye – representative of a whole generation of Georgies who were bound, even at the age of twenty-six, to their allotted role in life. Their gratuitous education 'gave them no escape from their duty to the home and to their parents. But when you're doing something important such as hemming a new petticoat or reading a serial, it was rather bothersome to be looked out to go to Cricton. Besides, Georgie hated biking… It is up to Georgie to bicycle the seven miles into Cricton and back to fetch the missing matters.'[3]

In the certain knowledge that I was scribbling down her every word, Miss Mills very slowly and deliberately recited a little verse she had penned after a fall in later life. She was highly amused to think that anyone could be so foolish as to be interested. I gave Mrs Sambells a copy of *The Colonel's Daughter* to read and very soon back came her verdict. 'He's got the general. Absolutely. But not Miss Mills. *Definitely* not Miss Mills.' Without wishing in any way to be unkind to Mrs Sambells, there was, though, something in Miss Mills' smile that was recognisable when I went back to the book on my return, for Aldington draws attention to 'those robustious, already slightly pendulous'[4] cheeks that to me were so characteristic of the lady I met. But even without asking the obvious questions, Miss Mills herself gave me every reason to agree with Mrs Sambells' conclusions. Aldington makes great derogatory play of Mrs Mills' involvement with the Red Cross and there are occasional references to Georgie's similar interests. For Miss Mills though, it was a different matter. For more years than she cared to remember, her left leg, the cause of her fall, had given he trouble. She told me with an un-Georgie like smile, how it came about. She used to drive 'an ambulance during the First World War. It was allocated to "GB" from Canada but it was not needed so we used it for convoy purposes. That's where I got this leg from! Pressing the pedals down! Driving those big lorries made you feel like a currant on a bun!'

Perhaps recalling something of the horrors that stimulated Aldington to write of her mother, Miss Mills was vehement in her response to my asking whether she ever took to nursing. 'Oh, no! I could never nurse anyone.' For all the same reasons I was even more surprised to find that she disliked hunting. After all, as Aldington suggests, the fictional colonel 'contrived to love horses and dogs with a tender passion while waging ruthless war on all wild things, from grouse to trout.'[5] As a very young girl Miss Mills had a rocking horse that she rocked towards the window and frightened her parents to such an extent that they removed the rocker. 'I *hated* hunting,' she expostulated. Nevertheless though, she presumably obeyed the call of duty. Mrs Sambells was to recall what she remembers as the general's 'old horse. They kept him till he died.' Miss Mills was better able to recall the precise circumstances. 'Father had chestnuts [in the past]. I mostly rode Polly, a mare. Uncle Charlie was farming in the north and bred a large black mare that was brought down to Padworth. This was Polly. A boy used to come over to ride Polly. He asked my father, "Can you trust her with me?" He answered, "Can we trust you with her?"'

If we are to believe Aldington and in this his veracity has yet to be truly doubted, then Mrs Mills' heart was far from her own hearth at times. It seemed that the colonel's daughter, like the author himself, was more susceptible to the whims of mother than father. 'Never in all her hunting years had Alvina forgotten the place, time and hour of the meet, but rare indeed were the weeks when she remembered everything for the house.'[6] Similar to the 'amazonian' attributes of Alvina are Miss Mills' memories of her mother on horseback. If I am not mistaken they too were recalled rather in the spirit of Aldington. 'Mother was funny about riding. She wouldn't ride side-saddle. On one occasion Mother had a fall. The horse went wild and we were twelve miles from home. Goodness knows how we got back.'

There was something almost intangible about the feelings I had as I came away from this meeting with the brigadier's daughter, something that seemed to suggest that perhaps Aldington was at least right about the circumstances of Georgie's life. But while the colonel was a product of his time and status, it seemed that it was Alvina who was most frustrated by her expected position as the Victorian wife. Certainly, given half a chance, my guess is that Mrs Mills could well have achieved on her own as much, if not more, than her husband, although quite in which field of activity will probably never be known. Perhaps she would have continued in the tradition of her own branch of the family – the Bakers – had she ever considered renouncing the expected virtues of a lady of her position. Had Alvina been the archetypal Victorian housewife, maybe *The Colonel's Daughter* would never have been written. While I am sure that there were innumerable, inconvenient crosses to bear, Miss Mills would never have said so, and it is that aspect of her life that Aldington fictionalises. Miss Helen Mills was *very* proud to be her father's daughter, and pride, an ambivalent virtue, contributed as much to the life of General Mills as it did to that of his fictional counterpart. Mrs Gardner, who knew the family better than anyone else I've met, sides with Aldington on the underlying principle of the novel. Miss Mills, she recalls, 'really suffered the most terrible life of anyone I know. She led a very miserable life as a result of her father… He was a real martinet.'

Poverty is always relative to expectations. The general's nephew underlined what was hidden away in the jargon of the deeds to Malthouse Cottage. 'As a family they were poor,' he told me. The employment of servants in the household reflects again the expectancy of their wage rather than the wealth of the employer. We have seen an indication of how little Aldington himself had to pay Mrs Stacey for her occasional help around the cottage. Purfleet, in *The Colonel's Daughter* 'lived twice as well as the Smithers on a relatively smaller expenditure.' It's no wonder therefore that Miss Mills had to undertake the tasks allotted her, not so much by her father, but by circumstances. Her cousin remembers 'one occasion when the general was cleaning out the gutters along the canal frontage. The general was up the ladder scraping out the leaves and Helen, down below, got covered.' Among the various and oh, so logical activities that Miss Mills undertook was that of captain of girl guides at Beenham. Despite the fact that, sat alongside Major Darby in the old comrades photo, we see Mrs Rayner the local area commander, there was no guide troupe at Padworth as it had combined with Beenham. There were times, however, when their summer camp took place among the washing lines on the 'drying ground' at Padworth House. Aldington was obviously well aware of this for amid the tedium of Georgie's days at Holly Lodge: 'Something exciting might happen at any minute, though Georgie admitted with a slight shock of surprise at her own rebelliousness, it very seldom did; but perhaps the new Vicar from Cleeve might call – she wanted to see him – or Kitty Colburne-Hosford to arrange a Girl Guide rally.'[788]

Mrs Warwick – young Mary Fidler as she was then – remembers Miss Mills with affection and often went to guide camp. Miss Mills, to the surprise of the recipient, even presented Mary with a tea set on the occasion of her subsequent wedding. Margaret Ashman, Anna Munro's daughter, always 'felt very intimidated' by Miss Mills, her guide mistress, but remembers that 'she was always kind and just.' But, hand in hand with guiding went Miss Mills' church activities. The friendship between

Miss Mills and Mrs Gardner stems from those days when, as the young Pam Strange, the latter attended Miss Mills' Sunday school. Mrs Hissey would see Miss Mills set off. 'She used to go up to Beenham church. She would walk up through the wood. They had no carriage. They always walked.'

A major theme running throughout *The Colonel's Daughter* was that of the compounding effects of the old order as they infringed on the circumstances of Georgie Smithers and it is all too easy in retrospect to see that both the fictional Georgie and Miss Mills herself were totally deprived of the company of male peers. Aldington drummed away at this point in practically every book he wrote. 'Where were the Hunt Balls, the country-house parties, the brilliant gatherings of which Georgie had dreamed? Where were the skating parties, the hunting, the race-going, the County events, the golf, the bridge, the motoring? Six hundred a year is the answer. And where were the young men who should have come a-wooing the Colonel's lovely daughter, for she is grown so fair, so fair? Georgie wasn't pretty, Georgie wasn't rich, and thousands and thousands of the young men lay dead in rows... Apart from Saturday afternoon football or cricket on Sir Horace's valuable field and from a rare "village concert" of depressing sentimentality and more depressing humour, there was nothing to do in leisure hours.' There would be no socially acceptable alternative except perhaps in church activities and it is precisely in the person of the new curate that Aldington offers fictional salvation to Georgie. 'And why not?' Aldington might say.

Mrs Gardner gave me the first clues that there was perhaps more to this than novelist's licence. Aldington's first novel *Death of a Hero* was an overnight bestseller in 1929, and when it came out in 1931 *The Colonel's Daughter* was required reading for anyone who knew him. Mrs Gardner knew only too well the devastating effect the novel had on Miss Mills. 'Helen *did* have an affair with a curate from Beenham.' The Roberts girls knew of it too. 'The Reverend Kingill had a mild flirtation with Miss Mills. He was a... tall, grey haired man – and handsome! Miss Mills helped him to run the Sunday school.' The mere mention of a head of grey hair suggests a maturity that Aldington was quick to correct. 'Mr Carrington elderly! Despite his good grey head, he couldn't have been more than forty-five.'[8] Everyone, it seemed, knew of Miss Mills' circumstances and yet hardly dared voice their thoughts until fifty years after the event. Speculation was rife below stairs at Bridge House. Violet

Roberts was very taken with Kingmill, so much so that in 1928 when she was to marry John Sambells she considered having the ceremony at Beenham. 'He used to come to Bridge House quite often' her sister Florence remembers with awe. Violet is a little more objective. 'He was a tall, stately man. He was charming and said, "If you want to be married at Beenham you must come and stay at the vicarage" in order to comply with the residential qualification. There was most definitely something in the air between him and Miss Mills. I remember Miss Helen was very fond of him,' Florence mused 'and she had a mild flirtation with him.' Mrs Hissey echoed the thoughts of those over at Brewery House. 'We always thought there would be a romance,' she told me.

Aldington concurred. 'The whole village had a sort of Christmas card feeling about Miss Georgie and wished her about as much luck as if she had been the robin in the snow under ye olde English churche.'[9] It was fairly obvious to anyone who knew Miss Mills: the novelist again: 'She scarcely remembered the listless Georgie who biked so reluctantly and wearily to and from Cricton; now busy with thoughts, plans, emotions and almost happy confusion, she simply flew the ground. Things, she felt, were happening. She neglected the Guides.'[10] For Miss Mills, it was not to be. There were too many pressures on her to allow her to contemplate anything other than to obey the social code and remain as a dutiful companion to her parents. As Mrs Hissey commented: 'I don't think she was the marrying sort, more of an old maid' which is precisely how Miss Mills ended her days. In the course of conversation with her, Helen Mills constantly drew my attention to her cousin who was looking after her affairs and I set about making a tentative approach with a view to meeting him. I say tentative because even though I didn't know half of what I have now been able to write, I knew far more than the family might wish and of course I had now met Miss Mills.

General Mills' nephew, the namesake of the real 'coz' Charles Stuart Mills, and himself a brigadier, invited me down to meet him and his wife where I was very warmly received in a fashion that my guilt initially would not entirely allow me to enjoy. Like Lawrence's visit to Aldington in 1926 this meeting 'began a little inauspiciously' as the coincidence of my address had been immediately recognised by the brigadier. Surprised as I was though, the reason for my visit was quickly dispatched and entirely accepted by the brigadier. Very soon though, he had told me the various stories I have already attributed to the general's nephew. He well recalls the visits to Bridge House for a 'spot of fishing' where as Aldington reminds us, 'the fish existed by kind permission of Sir Horace'. As a result therefore, the brigadier tells me, 'the nearest I got was casting on the lawn!'

Indeed, the brigadier had a great deal of sympathy with the general tenor of Aldington's stance against profiteers. It was a common feeling among soldiers, even those like the brigadier who saw service in World War Two. Perhaps seeing him around but not knowing Charles to be General Mills' nephew, Aldington introduces a friend of the family, another eligible bachelor, as a guest of the fictitious household. 'The old man was not a little excited, and half lost in his own drear; that this might have been the home coming of the son he had never had… And then Alvina arrived, rather hot and bad tempered and hoity-toity; but the hyacinthine locks and the wide shoulders succeeded with her too (though not with the coup de foudre which had smitten Georgie into silence) and she too forgot her prepared speech.'[11]

The garden holds vivid memories for the brigadier. 'The house used to have a pond in the garden with a bridge over it and I particularly remember a well-formed chestnut tree in the paddock at the rear as it had been chewed to a well-defined line by the cattle.' That tree was important to Aldington too, for Georgie received a particularly apocryphal letter at one stage and took it to the one spot in the grounds where she knew she would have the privacy to read it. 'She took the letter into the garden and read it again, sitting on a "rustic" bench underneath the large walnut tree'.[12] Trees seem to have a particular significance in this narrative. There are the 'unpolled willows' guarding the cottage from the canal to which Aldington refers in *Life for Life's Sake*. We have seen the destruction of Mr Judd's emblematic elm trees and now this singular tree overlooked by Aldington's garden. It matters not whether it is remembered as a chestnut or a walnut. It is the self same tree that was hit by the bomb during the Second World War and which has now been supplanted by quite a substantial lime tree in the shallow remains of the crater.

Miss Mills did read *The Colonel's Daughter* where there is almost enough in the opening sentence for her to realise the truth of what she was about to find. Page after page would confirm the horrifying fact. Mrs Gardner underlined this. 'Miss Mills realised she was the heroine of the book.' The damage was done. Miss Mills *knew*. And not only that, she would know that others knew too. For it cannot have taken long before everyone knew and Helen Mills would be conscious of that. Mrs Gardner remembers her parents talking about it at Strange's brewery over the road. They too would be likely to realise their fictional roles and a similar reaction can be imagined. The whole village would have reason for seeing themselves or their neighbours in it but to Miss Mills the effect would be cataclysmic. Her cousin, in talking about it, told me that the story caused her 'great distress' and that understandably, the family considered the book 'a stab in the back'.

One of the brigadiers' earliest questions when I met him was to enquire whether I had mentioned the book to Miss Mills. As I explained to him, in obedience to my promise to Mrs Gardner I made no reference at all to *The Colonel's Daughter*. Miss Mills and I must have talked for a good two hours during which time we ranged freely over practically everything from the royal family to the robin's nest in her 'Baby Austin runabout' which she later acquired and which Aldington so generously suggested Georgie ought to have. However, I did admit to the brigadier that at the end of the afternoon as I was collecting my things I could not leave without asking Miss Mills one peripheral question. 'Do you remember a neighbour of yours, Richard Aldington, who lived in my cottage?' Despite a very immediate and fluid memory on everything else we had talked of, her answer was very firm and absolutely certain.

'*No!*'

I suspect that Miss Helen Mary Mills had known all along. Aldington had a fairly shrewd idea of what the colonel's daughter would inevitably think of him. He allows Georgie to speculate on Purfleet. 'Hitherto she had always rather resented his perpetual chatter and bookishness. His avowed dislike for killing things, the fact that he obviously preferred sitting still and talking to running about after balls, had prejudiced her judgement of him. Such a man, Georgie felt, must be spineless and inefficient, if not a degenerate.'[13] In the final paragraphs of the story, Purfleet makes a return visit to Cleeve and sees Georgie coming towards him.

'Hullo, Georgie! How are you?'
Georgie *'made no answer to his greeting but gave him a curt little peck of a nod, and rode on.'*[14]

251

As Aldington says: 'There are some fancy and caricature in that book, but on the whole I am prepared to go before a commissioner for oaths and have him say to me of it: "This is your name and handwriting you swear that the contents are true so help you God amen eighteen pence please you must get change I haven't got it", which according to Dickens is the true formula for swearing an affidavit in the United Kingdom.'[15]

Miss Helen Mary Mills died aged ninety-five on 9th September 1981, less than a year after we met. It is as if she was determined to stay alive long enough to be able to make her point.

Notes and References

Chapter 1: The Quest
1. Aldington R (1968) *Life For Life's Sake,* Cassell & Company Ltd, London: 222.
2. Ibid. 230.
3. Fifteen and a kick was slang for fifteen shillings and sixpence (equal to 75p) which was an officer's wage in the First World War. The other ranks (OR) earned the one shilling [5p] or two tanners [2 x 2.5p] that Aldington mentions.
4. Aldington R (1931) *The Colonel's Daughter* Chatto & Windus, London: 55.
5. Ibid. 56–7.
6. Proverbs chapter 15, verse 1.
7. Aldington R (1954) *Pinorman: Personal Recollections of Norman Douglas, Pino Orioli and Charles Prentice.* William Heinemann, London.
8. Moore HT (1970) Preface. In: Kershaw A [Ed] (1970) *Richard Aldington: Selected Critical Writings 1928–1960.* Southern Illinois University Press, Carbondale.
9. Ibid.
10. Ibid.
11. Knightly P (1973) Aldington's enquiry concerning T.E. Lawrence. *Texas Quarterly* winter edition.
12. Aldington R (1968) *Life For Life's Sake,* Cassell & Company Ltd, London: 29.
13. Ibid. 226.
14. Ibid. 228.
15. Aldington R (1931) *The Colonel's Daughter* Chatto & Windus, London
16. Ibid. 74.
17. Ibid. 99.

Chapter 2: The Lads of the Village
1. Aldington R (1992) 'The Lads of The Village' in *Roads to Glory* Imperial War Museum, London: 189.
2. Ibid. 191.
3. Ibid. 189.
4. Ibid. 191.
5. Ibid. 191.
6. Ibid. 191.
7. Ibid. 191.
8. Ibid. 192.
9. Ibid. 197.
10. Ibid. 198.
11. Ibid. 199.
12. Aldington R (1929) *Death of a Hero: A Novel.* Chatto & Windus, London: 297.
13. Ibid. 297.
14. Ibid. 296.
15. Aldington R (1992) 'The Lads of The Village' in *Roads to Glory* Imperial War

Museum, London: 196.
16. *Newbury Weekly News*. 15 April 1982.
17. Aldington R (1931) *The Colonel's Daughter* Chatto & Windus, London: 71.
18. Harrington F (1973) *Richard Aldington 1892–1962: A Catalogue of the Frank G Harrington Collection of Richard Aldington and Hilda "H.D." Doolittle comprising Books, Manuscripts and Miscellanea.* Temple University Libraries, Philadelphia.
19. Aldington R (1929) *Death of a Hero: A Novel* Chatto & Windus, London: 128.
20. Ibid. 253.
21. Aldington R (1992) 'The Lads of The Village' in *Roads to Glory* Imperial War Museum, London: 196.
22. Aldington R (1929) *Death of a Hero: A Novel* Chatto & Windus, London: 259.
23. Ibid. 376–7.
24. An oft-repeated memory of Aldington.
25. Aldington R (1929) *Death of a Hero: A Novel* Chatto & Windus, London:
26. *Newbury Weekly News*. 10 February 1921.
27. The Parish Council Minute Book for 8th March 1926.
28. Aldington R (1992) 'The Lads of The Village' in *Roads to Glory* Imperial War Museum, London: 198.

Chapter 3: The Berkshire Kennet
1. Gates NT (1977) *A Checklist of the Letters of Richard Aldington.* Southern Illinois University Press, Illinois.
2. Two biographies of Aldington have subsequently been published. Charles Doyle's *Richard Aldington: A Biography.* Macmillan Basingstoke and Vivien Whelpton's (2013) *Richard Aldington: Poet, Soldier and Lover 1911-1929* The Lutterworth Press, Cambridge.
3. Aldington R (1968) *Life For Life's Sake.* Cassell & Company Ltd, London.
4. Ibid. 208.
5. *Eumenides*, poem by Richard Aldington.
6. *Retreat*, poem by Richard Aldington.
7. *Eumenides*, poem by Richard Aldington.
8. Ibid.
9. Ibid.
10. Aldington R (1923) 'To Those who Played for Safety in Life' In: *Exile and Other Poems* George Allen & Unwin, London.
11. Aldington R (1968) *Life For Life's Sake,* Cassell & Company Ltd, London: 224.
12. Aldington R (1955) *The Berkshire Kennet*, poem The Peacocks Press, Hurst.
13. Aldington R (1968) *Life For Life's Sake,* Cassell & Company Ltd, London: 236.
14. Aldington R (1933) *All Men are Enemies.* Chatto Windus, London.
15. *A Winter Night*, poem by Richard Aldington.
16. By 2011 that signpost had gone and the cricket field had long since become an amenity area for an estate of houses alongside.
17. Aldington R (1931) *The Colonel's Daughter*. Chatto & Windus, London: 57.
18. Mr and Mrs Leslie Austin in conversation with the author. August 1981.
19. Aldington R (1931) *The Colonel's Daughter*. Chatto & Windus, London: 187.
20. Ibid. 75.

21. Ibid. 124.
22. Ibid. 3–4.
23. Ibid. 37.
24. The log books of Padworth School.
25. Aldington R (1931) *The Colonel's Daughter*. Chatto & Windus, London: 62–3.
26. Aldington R (1934) *Women Must Work*. Chatto & Windus, London.
27. Aldington R (1931) *The Colonel's Daughter*. Chatto & Windus, London: 66.
28. On my last pilgrimage I found that this building had been demolished.
29. Aldington R (1931) *The Colonel's Daughter*. Chatto & Windus, London: 66.
30. Aldington R (1968) *Life For Life's Sake,* Cassell & Company Ltd, London: 224.
31. Aldington R (1934) *Women Must Work*. Chatto & Windus, London: 171–2.
32. Ibid. 176.
33. Ibid. 375.
34. Ibid. 378.
35. Aldington R (1931) *The Colonel's Daughter*. Chatto & Windus, London: 67–8.
36. At a Gate by the Way, poem by Richard Aldington. 1923.
37. Aldington R (1968) *Life For Life's Sake,* Cassell & Company Ltd, London: 226.
38. Ibid. 226.
39. Ibid. 224.
40. Ibid. 226.
41. Ibid. 228.
42. T.S. Eliot's tribute to Richard Aldington In: Kershaw A, Temple FJ (1965) *Richard Aldington: An Intimate Portrait*. Southern Illinois University Press, Carbondale
43. Ibid.
44. Access to that side gate has since been blocked by the adjoining landowner.
45. Aldington R (1968) *Life For Life's Sake,* Cassell & Company Ltd, London: 27.
46. Ibid. 237.
47. Ibid. 238.
48. 'Having Seen Men Killed', poem by Richard Aldington.
49. The Berkshire Kennet, poem by Richard Aldington, first published by Holbrook Jackson at the Curwen Press, 1923. Courtesy: Alister Kershaw, Aldington's literary executor, 1986.

Chapter 4: Malthouse Cottage
1. Aldington R (1968) *Life For Life's Sake,* Cassell & Company Ltd, London: 222.
2. Selwyn Kittredge. *The Literary Career of Richard Aldington.* University Microfilms International. Authorized facsimile of Kittredge's Dissertation. Undated, unpainted
3. Copp M (ed) (2009) *Imagist Dialogues: Letters between Aldington, Flint and Others* The Lutterworth Press, Cambridge: 327.
4. Ibid. 322.
5. Ibid. 323.
6. Aldington R (1968) *Life For Life's Sake,* Cassell & Company Ltd, London: 369.
7. Copp M (ed) (2009) *Imagist Dialogues: Letters between Aldington, Flint and Others* The Lutterworth Press, Cambridge: 342.
8. Ibid. 348.

9. Ibid. 377.
10. Aldington R (1968) *Life For Life's Sake,* Cassell & Company Ltd, London: 274.
11. Ibid. 274.
12. Moore HT [Ed] (1962) *The Collected Letters of D. H. Lawrence*: *Volume Two.* William Heinemann, London: 901.
13. Aldington R (1968) *Life For Life's Sake,* Cassell & Company Ltd, London: 275.
14. Ibid. 276.
15. Aldington R (1968) *Life For Life's Sake,* Cassell & Company Ltd, London: 279. The pamphlet to which Aldington refers is *D.H. Lawrence: An Indiscretion,* first published in USA the following year and in England as *D.H. Lawrence* in 1930. He sent a copy to Lawrence some time in May 1927.
16. Moore HT [Ed] (1962) *The Collected Letters of D. H. Lawrence*: *Volume Two.* William Heinemann, London: 978.

Chapter 5. The Search for Mr Brown

1. Aldington R (1931) *The Colonel's Daughter*. Chatto & Windus, London: 62.
2. Aldington R (1968) *Life For Life's Sake*. Cassell & Company Ltd, London: 215.
3. Ibid. 215.
4. Aldington R (1934) *Women Must Work*. Chatto & Windus, London: 314/5
5. Aldington, R (1968) *Life For Life's Sake*. Cassell & Company Ltd, London: 216.
6. MacGreevy T (1931) *Richard Aldington: An Englishman.* Chatto & Windus, London: 71.
7. Aldington R (1931) *The Colonel's Daughter*. Chatto & Windus, London: 62–3.
8. Aldington, R (1968) *Life For Life's Sake*. Cassell & Company Ltd, London: 222.
9. Ibid. 214.
10. As its present name suggests it used to be known as The Plough and was served by Simonds the brewers from Reading, who are now part of the Courage conglomerate.
11. Kapp Y (1979) *Eleanor Marx.* Virago 1979, London.
12. Radford M (1945) *Poems by Maitland Radford with a Memoir by some of his friends*. George Allen & Unwin Ltd, London.
13. Delaney P (1979) *D.H. Lawrence's Nightmare.* Harvester Press, Sussex.
14. Aldington R (1931) *The Colonel's Daughter*. Chatto & Windus, London: 61.
15. Another of the Meynell daughters, Madeline, was married to Percy Lucas, the brother of E.V. Lucas, the writer, who lived nearby. Inevitably the Meynells and the Radfords would have spent time in each other's company and, perhaps on some such occasion, Dollie and Ernest – or perhaps Dollie, as Ernest suffered a stroke and died in 1919 – would have been introduced to E.V Lucas's cook Mrs Pocock.
16. The Radford home in Hampstead.
17. Aldington R (1968) *Life For Life's Sake,* Cassell & Company Ltd, London: 217.
18. Aldington R (1934) *Women Must Work*. Chatto & Windus, London: 286.
19. Ibid. 291.
20. Aldington R (1968) *Life For Life's Sake,* Cassell & Company Ltd, London: 214.
21. Lawrence D.H (1974) 'The Princess' from *The Collected Short Stories* of D H Lawrence. William Heinemann, London.
22. Ibid.
23. Ibid.

24. Aldington R (1968) *Life For Life's Sake,* Cassell & Company Ltd, London: 214.
25. Lawrence D.H (1974) 'The Princess' from *The Collected Short Stories* of D H Lawrence. William Heinemann, London.
26. Sagar K (1980) *The Life of D H Lawrence.* Eyre & Methuen, London.
27. Aldington R (1934) *Women Must Work.* Chatto & Windus, London: 286.
28. Ibid. 287.
29. Aldington R (1968) *Life For Life's Sake,* Cassell & Company Ltd, London: 222.
30. Aldington R (1934) *Women Must Work.* Chatto & Windus, London: 316.
31. Ibid. 310.
32. Ibid. 311.
33. Ibid. 285.
34. Ibid. 289.
35. Aldington R (1968) *Life For Life's Sake,* Cassell & Company Ltd, London 215.
36. Ibid. 217.
37. Aldington R (1934) *Women Must Work.* Chatto & Windus, London: 291.
38. Ibid. 291.
39. Aldington R (1968) *Life For Life's Sake,* Cassell & Company Ltd, London: 215–6.
40. Lawrence D.H 'Monkey Nuts' from (1974) *The Collected Short Stories* of D.H. Lawrence. William Heinemann, London.
41. Aldington R (1968) *Life For Life's Sake,* Cassell & Company Ltd, London: 214
42. Ibid. 214–5.
43. Ibid. 216.
44. Aldington R (1933) *All Men are Enemies.* Chatto & Windus, London: 132.
45. Aldington R (1931) *The Colonel's Daughter.* Chatto & Windus, London: 61.
46. Ibid. 61.
47. Aldington R (1968) *Life For Life's Sake,* Cassell & Company Ltd, London: 215.
48. Aldington R (1933) *All Men are Enemies.* Chatto & Windus, London: 203.
49. Aldington R (1931) *The Colonel's Daughter.* Chatto & Windus, London: 188.
50. Aldington R (1938) *Seven Against Reeves.* William Heinemann, London: 34.
51. Aldington R (1931) *The Colonel's Daughter.* Chatto & Windus, London: 63.
52. Ibid. 65.
53. Hermitage Horticultural Society Minute Book.
54. Correspondence from Frieda Lawrence to Hilda Brown, 6 January 1920. Simon Hewett Collection.
55. Ibid.
56. Boulton JT, Andrew Robertson A (1984) The Cambridge Edition: *The Letters of D.H. Lawrence: Volume III. 1916-1921* Cambridge University Press, Cambridge: 548.
57. Correspondence from Frieda Lawrence to Hilda Brown, 10 November 1936, Kiowa Ranch, New Mexico. Simon Hewett Collection.
58. Nehls E (1958) *D.H. Lawrence: A Composite Biography gathered, arranged and edited by Edward Nehls. Volume Two, 1919–1925.* The University of Wisconsin Press, Madison: 46.

Chapter 6: Women Must Work
1. Aldington R (1931) *The Colonel's Daughter.* Chatto & Windus, London: 300.
2. A biography of Anna Gillies MacDonald Munro (1881–1962) appears in the 2004 edition of the *Oxford Dictionary of National Biography.*

3. Communication from Mrs Margaret Ridgway to the author.
4. Ibid.
5. Letter from Aldington to F.S. Flint. 17 December 1922, Malthouse Cottage, Padworth. In: Copp M [Ed] (2009) *Imagist Dialogues: Letters between Aldington, Flint and Others* The Lutterworth Press, Cambridge: 344.
6. Letter from Aldington to F. S. Flint. 19 January 1925, Malthouse Cottage, Padworth. In: Copp M [Ed] (2009) *Imagist Dialogues: Letters between Aldington, Flint and Others* The Lutterworth Press, Cambridge: 344.
7. 90 he social life at the time. e about Alice Munor Aldington R (1923) 'At a Gate by The Way' In: *Exile and Other Poems.* George Allen & Unwin, London.
8. Aldington R (1934) *Women Must Work*. Chatto & Windus, London: 15.
9. Ibid. 26.
10. Ibid. 38.
11. Ibid. 44–5
12. Ibid. 21
13. Aldington R (1933) *All Men are Enemies*. Chatto & Windus, London: 82.
14. Aldington R (1934) *Women Must Work*. Chatto & Windus, London: 74.
15. Ibid. 39.
16. Ibid. 298.
17. Ibid. 63.
18. Ibid. 286.
19. Ibid. 291.
20. Ibid. 310.
21. Ibid. 318.
22. Salter OM (1926) A Prodigal Singer. *Good Housekeeping*, March.
23. Salter OM (1927) Running a Country Hotel. *Good Housekeeping*, February.
24. Aldington R (1934) *Women Must Work*. Chatto & Windus, London: 201.
25. Aldington R (1929) *Death of a Hero: A Novel.* Chatto & Windus, London: 252.
26. Salter OM (1925) Stocks and Shares in Adversity. *Good Housekeeping.* February.
27. Salter OM (1925) Out of Touch. *Good Housekeeping.* August.
28. Salter OM (1925) The Human Equation. *Good Housekeeping.* September
29. Salter OM (1926) Marrying for Money. *Good Housekeeping.* April.
30. Salter OM (1926) A Prodigal Singer. *Good Housekeeping.* March.
31. Ibid.
32. Ibid.
33. Aldington R (1934) *Women Must Work*. Chatto & Windus, London: 255.
34. Salter OM (1926) A Prodigal Singer. *Good Housekeeping.* March.
35. Aldington R (1934) *Women Must Work*. Chatto & Windus, London: 318.

Chapter 7: The Squire
1. Snow CP (1938) *Richard Aldington: An Appreciation with a List of The Works.*
2. Both published by Evans Brothers, London.
3. Aldington R (1968) *Life For Life's Sake,* Cassell & Company Ltd, London: 227.
4. Aldington R (1931) *The Colonel's Daughter*. Chatto & Windus, London: 14.
5. Thomas MacGreevy T (1931) *Richard Aldington: An Englishman* Chatto & Windus, London.

6. Aldington R (1968) *Life For Life's Sake,* Cassell & Company Ltd, London: 227.
7. Aldington R (1949) *The Strange Life of Charles Waterton 1782–1865.* Evans Brothers, London.
8. Aldington R (1968) *Life For Life's Sake,* Cassell & Company Ltd, London: 187.
9. Ibid. 228.
10. Ibid. 236.
11. *Life For Life's Sake* was first published in America, in 1941, hence the use of the word gasoline.
12. Aldington R (1968) *Life For Life's Sake,* Cassell & Company Ltd, London: 228–9.
13. Ibid. 229.
14. Aldington R (1931) *The Colonel's Daughter.* Chatto & Windus, London: 289.
15. Ibid. 289.
16. Ibid. 63.
17. Aldington R (1968) *Life For Life's Sake,* Cassell & Company Ltd, London: 228.
18. Aldington R (1931) *The Colonel's Daughter.* Chatto & Windus, London: 357.
19. Ibid. 353.
20. Aldington R (1968) *Life For Life's Sake,* Cassell & Company Ltd, London: 227.
21. Ibid. 229.
22. Ibid. 230.
23. Aldington R (1931) *The Colonel's Daughter.* Chatto & Windus, London: 15.
24. Ibid. 15.

Chapter 8: The Businessman
1. Aldington R (1931) *The Colonel's Daughter.* Chatto & Windus, London: 61.
2. Ibid. 62
3. Ibid. 62
4. Ibid. 123–4
5. Ibid. 62
6. Soon after writing this, the cricket field was left to grow wild again and in the years since I left, it has become an amenity area for an estate of houses constructed nearby.
7. Aldington R (1931) *The Colonel's Daughter.* Chatto & Windus, London: 351.
8. Personal communication rom Mrs Margaret Ridgway to the author.
9. *Newbury Weekly News.* 24 February 1921.
10. Aldington R (1931) *The Colonel's Daughter.* Chatto & Windus, London: 354.
11. Aldington R (1933) *All Men are Enemies* Chatto Windus, London: 153.
12. Aldington R (1931) *The Colonel's Daughter.* Chatto & Windus, London: 355.
13. Aldington R (1923) 'To Those who Played for Safety in Life'. In: *Exile and Other Poems* George Allen & Unwin, London.

Chapter 9: The Church
1. The adjoining cottage was extended to encompass the rectory room shortly after I wrote this.
2. Padworth School log book.
3. Aldington R (1931) *The Colonel's Daughter.* Chatto & Windus, London: 29.
4. Ibid. 29.
5. Ibid. 29.
6. Ibid. 29

7. Ibid. 29–30
8. Ibid. 30.
9. Ibid. 30.
10. Ibid. 30.
11. Ibid. 30.
12. Ibid. 30.

Chapter 10:
1. Brigadier-General George Arthur Mills died at Dunedin [clinic], Bath Road, Reading on 19th September 1927. Probate was granted to Charles Stuart Mills and to his brothers William Burton Saville Mills leaving effects in the sum of £2,896 1s 7d.
2. Aldington R (1931) *The Colonel's Daughter*. Chatto & Windus, London: 11.
3. Ibid. 10.
4. Ibid. 11.
5. Ibid. 11.
6. Ibid. 11–12.
7. Ibid. 12.
8. *Who Was Who*. Adam and Charles Black, London.
9. Aldington R (1931) *The Colonel's Daughter*. Chatto & Windus, London: 12–13.
10. *Who Was Who*. Adam and Charles Black, London.
11. Aldington R (1931) *The Colonel's Daughter*. Chatto & Windus, London: 13.
12. *Who Was Who*. Adam and Charles Black, London.
13. Aldington R (1931) *The Colonel's Daughter*. Chatto & Windus, London: 14.
14. *Who Was Who*. Adam and Charles Black, London.
15. Aldington R (1931) *The Colonel's Daughter*. Chatto & Windus, London: 12
16. Ibid. 3.
17. Hall R (1980) *Lovers on The Nile: An Idyll of African Exploration* Collins, London: blurb.
18. Ibid.
19. Aldington R (1931) *The Colonel's Daughter*. Chatto & Windus, London: 4.
20. Ibid. 7
21. Ibid. 11.
22. Ibid. 10.
23. *Who Was Who*. Adam and Charles Black, London.
24. Aldington R (1931) *The Colonel's Daughter*. Chatto & Windus, London: 12.
25. Ibid. 7.
26. Aldington R (1968) *Life For Life's Sake,* Cassell & Company Ltd, London: 276.
27. Ibid. 275.
28. Ibid. 276
29. Aldington R (1931) *The Colonel's Daughter*. Chatto & Windus, London: 14.
30. Lawrence D.H. (1977) *The First Lady Chatterley*. Penguin Books, London: 233.
31. Aldington R (1931) *The Colonel's Daughter*. Chatto & Windus, London: 3.
32. Ibid. 17.
33. Aldington R (1949) 'A Gentleman of England' in *Soft Answers* Penguin Books, London: 171.
34. Aldington R (1931) *The Colonel's Daughter*. Chatto & Windus, London: 100.
35. Ibid. 7

36. Ibid. 101.
37. Aldington R (1968) *Life For Life's Sake,* Cassell & Company Ltd, London: 272.
38. Ibid. 273.
39. Newbury Weekly News 12 April 1984.
40. Aldington R (1931) *The Colonel's Daughter*. Chatto & Windus, London: 19.
41. Aldington R (1935) Mrs Todgers In: *Artifex: Sketches and Ideas,* Chatto & Windus, London.
42. Aldington R (1931) *The Colonel's Daughter*. Chatto & Windus, London: 34.
43. Ibid. 241–2.
44. Ibid. 18–9.
45. Ibid. 19.
46. Aldington R (1935) Mrs Todgers In: *Artifex: Sketches and Ideas,* Chatto & Windus, London.
47. Aldington R (1931) *The Colonel's Daughter*. Chatto & Windus, London: 10
48. Ibid. 17.
49. Letter to Harold Monro, 16 April 1924. Humanities Research Centre, Austin, Texas.
50. Ibid.
51. Aldington R (1931) *The Colonel's Daughter*. Chatto & Windus, London: 8.
52. Ibid. 339.
53. Ibid. 131.
54. Hall R (1980) *Lovers on The Nile: An Idyll of African Exploration*. Collins, London.

Chapter 11: The Village
1. Letter from Aldington to F.S. Flint. 16 January 1925, Malthouse Cottage, Padworth In: Copp M [Ed] (2009) *Imagist Dialogues: Letters between Aldington, Flint and Others* (Cambridge: The Lutterworth Press, 2009), 374.
2. Aldington R (1923) Meditation. In: *Exile and Other Poems.* George Allen & Unwin, London.
3. Aldington R (1948) A Winter Night. In: *The Complete Poems of Richard Aldington* Alan Wingate, London.
4. Letter from Aldington to F.S. Flint. 16 January 1925, Malthouse Cottage, Padworth In: Copp M [Ed] (2009) *Imagist Dialogues: Letters between Aldington, Flint and Others* (Cambridge: The Lutterworth Press, 2009), 374.
5. Aldington R (1931) *The Colonel's Daughter*. Chatto & Windus, London: 68.
6. Aldington R (1968) *Life For Life's Sake,* Cassell & Company Ltd, London: 270.
7. This and the following quotes are from the article by Jessie 'Mrs Athol' Capper, 'A Day on a Poultry Farm'. *Eggs*, 10 March 1926.
8. Aldington R (1968) *Life For Life's Sake,* Cassell & Company Ltd, London: 239.
9. Ibid. 266.
10. Ibid. 228–9.
11. Film of Lillian Lenton features on *Pathé News* footage that can now be seen on YouTube. https://www.youtube.com/watch?v=fyImzmaypJ8
12. Personal communication from Mrs Margaret Ridgway to the author.
13. Letter to Glenn Hughes. Humanities Research Centre, Austin, Texas.
14. All that remains of this thatched barn are a few timbers alongside what was the Albury Cottage.

15. Letter from Aldington to F.S. Flint, May 1923. Malthouse Cottage, Padworth Humanities Research Centre, Austin, Texas.
16. Letter from Aldington to F.S. Flint, 5 May 1923. Malthouse Cottage, Padworth. Copp M [Ed] (2009) *Imagist Dialogues: Letters between Aldington, Flint and Others* (Cambridge: The Lutterworth Press, 2009).
17. Letter to Glenn Hughes. Humanities Research Centre, Austin, Texas
18. Aldington R (1968) *Life For Life's Sake,* Cassell & Company Ltd, London: 281.
19. Ibid. 282.
20. Letter to Glenn Hughes. Humanities Research Centre, Austin, Texas.
21. Lahr E (1931) *Balls and Another Book for Suppression.* Blue Moon Booklet No. 7, London.
22. Aldington R (1968) *Life For Life's Sake,* Cassell & Company Ltd, London: 239.
23. Ibid. 239.
24. Letter to Glenn Hughes. Humanities Research Centre, Austin, Texas.
25. Aldington R (1937) *Very Heaven: A Novel.* William Heinemann, London.
26. Letter from Glenn Hughes, May 1927. Humanities Research Centre, Austin, Texas.
27. Ibid.
28. Aldington R (1931) *The Colonel's Daughter.* Chatto & Windus, London: 128.
29. Ibid. 241.
30. Ibid. 257
31. Aldington R (1968) *Life For Life's Sake,* Cassell & Company Ltd, London: 69.

Chapter 12. The Watershed
1. Aldington R (1935) Mrs Todgers. In: *Artifex: Sketches and Ideas.* Chatto & Windus, London.
2. Aldington R (1968) *Life For Life's Sake,* Cassell & Company Ltd, London: 279.
3. Ibid. 279.
4. Aldington R (1935) Sea Travel. In: *Artifex: Sketches and Ideas.* Chatto & Windus, London.
5. Aldington R (1931) *The Colonel's Daughter.* Chatto & Windus, London: 118.
6. Letter to Glenn Hughes, 10 April 1927. Humanities Research Centre, Austin, Texas.
7. Aldington R (1931) *The Colonel's Daughter.* Chatto & Windus, London: 324.
8. Ibid. 330.
9. Letter to Glenn Hughes, Humanities Research Centre, Austin, Texas.
10. Ibid.
11. Aldington R (1931) *The Colonel's Daughter.* Chatto & Windus, London: 333.
12. Letter to Glenn Hughes, Humanities Research Centre, Austin, Texas.
13. Patmore B (1968) *My Friends when Young.* William Heinemann, London.
14. Letter to Glenn Hughes, 10 March 1928. Humanities Research Centre, Austin, Texas.
15. Letter to Society of Authors. Simon Hewett Collection.
16. Patmore B (1968) *My Friends when Young.* William Heinemann, London.
17. Aldington R (1968) *Life For Life's Sake,* Cassell & Company Ltd, London: 291.
18. Letter of 10 December 1928 to Glenn Hughes. Humanities Research Centre, Austin, Texas.
19. Aldington R (1968) *Life For Life's Sake,* Cassell & Company Ltd, London: 293.

20. Ibid. 293.
21. Letter dated 17 August 1928. In: Moore HT [Ed] (1962) *The Collected Letters of D.H. Lawrence.* William Heinemann, London.1962), 1077.
22. Aldington R (1968) *Life For Life's Sake,* Cassell & Company Ltd, London: 296.
23. Ibid. 296
24. Letter to Glenn Hughes. Humanities Research Centre, Austin, Texas.
25. Alec Randall had indeed been desperately ill back in April when Aldington was in Paris and from where Aldington had written a very understanding letter to his 'old friend'. Alec Randall's correspondence from his friends was subsequently placed in the Huntingdon Library, San Marino, USA from where we learn that the nearest we get to this date is a letter of 29th September from Aldington - written on returning to Paris in readiness for the trip southwards again to the vigie.
26. Letter to Glenn Hughes. Humanities Research Centre, Austin, Texas.
27. Aldington R (1968) *Life For Life's Sake,* Cassell & Company Ltd, London: 297.
28. Patmore B (1968) *My Friends when Young.* William Heinemann, London.
29. Arabella was known formally to Glenn Hughes as Dorothy.
30. Letter to Glenn Hughes. Humanities Research Centre, Austin, Texas.
31. The contents of the letter suggest its exact date to be 27th November 1928.
32. Patmore B (1968) My Friends When Young. William Heinemann, London
33. Aldington R (1931) *The Colonel's Daughter.* Chatto & Windus, London: 327.
34. Ibid. 347
35. Aldington R (1968) *Life For Life's Sake,* Cassell & Company Ltd, London: 369.
36. Ibid. 173.
37. Aldington R (1968) *Life For Life's Sake,* Cassell & Company Ltd, London: 228.
38. Aldington R (1931) *The Colonel's Daughter.* Chatto & Windus, London: 14.
39. Subsequent research (by others) suggests that HD made contact via Jessie's sister, Emily Allingham. HD was taking analysis with Freud and Emily was acquainted with Freud's associate, Havelock Ellis, who was an Aldington family friend.

Chapter 13 The Colonel's Daughter
1. Personal communication from Miss Helen Mills to the author, November 1980.
2. Aldington R (1939) *Rejected Guest* William Heinemann, London.
3. Aldington R (1931) *The Colonel's Daughter.* Chatto & Windus, London: 4.
4. Ibid. 6.
5. Ibid. 11.
6. Ibid. 3.
7. Ibid. 4.
8. Ibid. 25.
9. Ibid. 268.
10. Ibid. 162.
11. Ibid. 238.
12. Ibid. 199.
13. Ibid. 119.
14. Ibid. 347.
15. Aldington R (1968) *Life For Life's Sake* Cassell & Company Ltd, London: 230.

Bibliography

Richard Aldington titles consulted (in chronological sequence).

Exile and Other Poems (1923) George Allen & Unwin, London.
Fifty Romance Lyric Poems (1928) Crosby Gage, New York.
Death of a Hero: A Novel (1929) Chatto & Windus, London.
A Dream in The Luxembourg (1930) Chatto & Windus, London.
The Colonel's Daughter (1931) Chatto & Windus, London.
Balls and Another Book for Suppression (1931) E. Lahr, Blue Moon Booklet No.7, London.
Stepping Heavenward (1931) G. Orioli, Florence.
Soft Answers (1932) Chatto & Windus, London.
All Men are Enemies (1933) Chatto & Windus, London.
Women Must Work (1934) Chatto & Windus, London.
Artifex: Sketches and Ideas (1935) Chatto & Windus, London.
Very Heaven: A Novel (1937) William Heinemann, London.
Seven Against Reeves (1938) William Heinemann, London.
Rejected Guest (1939) William Heinemann, London.
The Complete Poems of Richard Aldington (1948) Alan Wingate, London.
The Strange Life of Charles Waterton 1782-1865 (1949) Evans Brothers, London.
Portrait of a Genius, But… (The Life of D.H. Lawrence) (1950) William Heinemann, London.
Pinorman: Personal Recollections of Norman Douglas, Pino Orioli and Charles Prentice (1954) William Heinemann, London.
Lawrence of Arabia: A Biographical Enquiry (1955) Collins, London.
The Berkshire Kennet, poem (1955) The Peacocks Press, Hurst.
Life For Life's Sake (1968) Cassell & Company Ltd, London.
'The Lads of The Village' in *Roads to Glory* (1992) Imperial War Museum limited edition, London.

OTHER BOOKS CONSULTED
In alphabetical order according to author/editor.
Beaumont CW (1920) *'The Art of Lydia Lopokova'* with an appreciation by Beaumont and illustrations by Dorothy 'Arabella' Yorke. Beaumont, London.
Boulton JT, Robertson A (1984) *The Cambridge Edition: The Letters of D.H. Lawrence: Volume III. 1916-1921.* Cambridge University Press, Cambridge.
Capper, Mrs Athol (Jessie): 'A Day on a Poultry Farm' in *Eggs*, 10 March 1926.
Clinton Rev WO (1911) *A Record of the Parish of Padworth and Its Inhabitants.* Privately published, Padworth.
Copp M (ed) (2009) *Imagist Dialogues: Letters between Aldington, Flint and Others.* The Lutterworth Press, Cambridge.
Cournos J (1926) *Miranda Masters* Alfred Knopf, New York.

BIBLIOGRAPHY

Courtenay J (pseudonym of Jessie Capper) (1930) *Several Faces* Gollancz, London.

Delaney P (1979) *D.H. Lawrence's Nightmare* Harvester Press, Herts.

Doolittle, Hilda 'H.D.' (1960) *Bid Me to Live*. Grove Press, New York.

Gates, Norman Timmins (1977) *A Checklist of the Letters of Richard Aldington*. Southern Illinois University Press, Illinois.

Hall R (1980) *Lovers on The Nile: An Idyll of African Exploratio*n. Collins, London.

Harrington F (1973) *Richard Aldington 1892-1962: A Catalogue of the Frank G Harrington Collection of Richard Aldington and Hilda "H.D." Doolittle comprising Books, Manuscripts and Miscellane*a. Temple University Libraries, Philadelphia.

Hughes G (1931) *Imagism and The Imagists: A Study in Modern Poetry*. Stanford University Press, California.

Kapp Y (1979) *Eleanor Marx* 2 vols. Virago, London.

Kershaw A (ed.) (1970) *Richard Aldington: Selected Critical Writings 1928-1960*. Preface by Harry T. Moore Southern Illinois University Press, Illinois.

Kershaw A, Temple, F.J. (1965) *Richard Aldington: An Intimate Portrait*. Southern Illinois University Press, Carbondale.

Kittredge SB *The Literary Career of Richard Aldington*. New York University, University Microfilms International. U.M.I. Authorized facsimile of Kittredge's Dissertation.

Knightley P, Simpson C (1969) *The Secret Lives of Lawrence of Arabi*a. Thomas Nelson, London.

Knightley P (1973) Aldington's Enquiry concerning T.E. Lawrence. In: *Texas Quarterly*. Winter 1973.

Lawrence D.H. (1974) *The Collected Short Stories of D H Lawrence*. William Heinemann, London.

Lawrence D.H. (1923) *The Fox*. Martin Secker, London.

Lawrence D.H. (1944) *The First Lady Chatterley*. Dial Press, New York.

Mehl D, Jansohn C (2001) *The First and Second Lady Chatterley Novels, The Cambridge Edition of the Works of D.H. Lawrence*. University of Cambridge Press, Cambridge.

MacGreevy T (1931) *Richard Aldington: An Englishman*. Chatto & Windus, London.

McNiven I, Moore HT (eds) (1981) *Literary Lifelines: The Richard Aldington – Lawrence Durrell Correspondence*. The Viking Press, New York.

Moore HT (1962) *The Collected Letters of D.H. Lawrence*: *Volume Two.* William Heinemann, London.

Nehls E (1958) *D.H. Lawrence: A Composite Biography gathered, arranged and edited by Edward Nehls. Volume Two, 1919-1925.* The University of Wisconsin Press, Madison.

Patmore B (1957) 'Conversations with D. H. Lawrence'. *London Magazine*, June.

Patmore B (1968) *My Friends when Young*. William Heinemann, London.

Radford M (1945) *Poems by Maitland Radford with a Memoir by some of his friends*. George Allen & Unwin Ltd, London.

Risk RT (ed) (1978) *The Dearest Friend: A Selection from the Letters from Richard Aldington to John Cournos*. Typographeum Press, New Hampshire.

Sagar K (1980) *The Life of D.H. Lawrence*. Eyre & Methuen, London.

Salter OM (1925–7) Short stories and articles. *Good Housekeeping.*
Snow CP (1938) *Richard Aldington: An Appreciation with a List of The Works.* William Heinemann, London.
Who Was Who. Adam and Charles Black, London.

Newspapers and Magazines
Eggs
Good Housekeeping
Newbury Weekly News
Reading Mercury
Slough Observer
Times Literary Supplement

Padworth Parish Records
Padworth School log books
Padworth Parish council minutes
Padworth Electoral register
Padworth Parochial church records

Recommended Reading
Doyle C (1989) *Richard Aldington: A Biography.* Macmillan, Basingstoke.
Whelpton V (2013) *Richard Aldington: Poet, Soldier and Lover 1911-1929.* The Lutterworth Press, Cambridge.

Index

INDEX

INDEX